TWAYNE'S WORLD AUTHORS SERIES
A Survey of the World's Literature

Sylvia E. Bowman, Indiana University

GENERAL EDITOR

DENMARK

Leif Sjöberg
State University of New York at Stony Brook

EDITOR

Georg Brandes

TWAS 390

Georg Brandes

GEORG BRANDES

By BERTIL NOLIN

University of Gothenburg

TWAYNE PUBLISHERS
A DIVISION OF G. K. HALL & CO., BOSTON

Library of Congress Cataloging in Publication Data

Nolin, Bertil.
    Georg Brandes.

    (Twayne's world authors series) TWAS 390
    Bibliography: p. 199–202.
    Includes index.
    1. Brandes, George Morris Cohen, 1842–1927.
PT8125.B8Z837   809   76–2718
ISBN 0–8057–6232–9

"Poor is the power of lead that became bullets as compared to the power of lead that became print."

Georg Brandes

Contents

About the Author

Bertil Nolin was born in Sweden in 1926. He attended the University of Uppsala and received his M.A. there in 1954 and his Ph.D. from the University of Stockholm in 1966. His thesis was a comparative study of Georg Brandes as a European critic and was published under the title *Den gode europén. Studier i Georg Brandes' idéutveckling 1871–1893.*

As a Fulbright scholar, Bertil Nolin was visiting professor at the University of Chicago 1968–1970 in modern Scandinavian literature, and since then he has been affiliated with the University of Gothenburg. Dr. Nolin has also published studies within the field of theater and drama.

Preface

This book on Brandes is an attempt to present a comprehensive picture of his life's work, which, because of its many aspects, is difficult to survey. The source material is practically overwhelming and I have been able to deal with certain works only in passing. Most of the previous researchers have chosen to portray Brandes by taking up certain idea complexes or by following certain lines of thought in his writings. Here I have chosen to attempt a more chronological line of approach, presenting one work after the other, as much as space permits, as they were published. It was not possible to effectuate this method completely.

A great deal of Brandes' extensive correspondence has now been published, though certain complementary additions were necessary, and I was permitted to make these in the Brandes archive at the Royal Library in Copenhagen. I was also able to study some of Brandes' still unpublished diaries there thanks to the obligingness of Georg Brandes' daughter, the late Edith Philipp. I have had valuable help from Kåre Olsen, head of the Department of Manuscripts of the Royal Library, and from Dr. Tue Gad. Lector Jørgen Gjedsted has read through the book in manuscript form and made several valuable suggestions, as did my colleague from the University of Gothenburg, Dr. Gunnar Hallingberg.

And finally I am deeply thankful to Mrs. Elly Nolin for all the criticism, encouragement, and help I have been fortunate enough to receive from her.

I began this book in Chicago in 1970. The major part was written here in Gothenburg, where the English version was composed in very stimulating cooperation with Mrs. Katy Lissbrant. I warmly thank her for her help.

BERTIL NOLIN

University of Gothenburg

Chronology

1842   Born in Copenhagen, February 4.

1849–
1859   Studies at the von Westenske Institut in Copenhagen.

1857   Bar mitzvah.

1859   Enters the University of Copenhagen to study law but soon shifts to aesthetics and literature.

1864   M.A. received.

1866   *The Dualism in Our Newest Philosophy.*

1866–
1867   First stay in Paris. Makes the acquaintance of Hippolyte Taine, leading critic in France.

1868   *Aesthetic Studies.* Trip to Germany and Switzerland.

1869   Translates John Stuart Mill's *The Subjection of Women* into Danish.

1870   Ph.D. from the University of Copenhagen. His dissertation deals with Taine and French criticism: *Contemporary French Aesthetics.* In addition to that, *Critical Studies and Portraits* appears. Long trip abroad. Meets with Hippolyte Taine, Ernest Renan, and John Stuart Mill in Paris. Also visits Mill in London. Travels in Switzerland and Italy. Is taken ill in Rome.

1871   November 3, begins his series of lectures "Main Currents in Nineteenth Century Literature."

1872   *Main Currents*, I: *Emigrant Literature. Explanation and Defense.* Trip to Germany. Visits Ibsen in Dresden.

1873   *Main Currents*, II: *Romantic School in Germany.* New trip to Germany.

1874   *Main Currents*, III: *The Reaction in France.* Visits Germany again. Editor of the magazine *Det nittende Aarhundrede (The Nineteenth Century)* together with his brother Edvard.

1898   Trip to Italy. *Julius Lange, Henrik Ibsen,* and *Poetry from my Youth*. Takes sides for Dreyfus together with Zola and Anatole France. Trip to Poland.
1899   Visit in France.
1899–   *Collected Works,* I–XII.
1902
1901   In Paris.
1902   Becomes titular professor.
1903–   *Collected Works,* XIII–XVII.
1906
1905–   *My Life,* I–III.
1908
1906   Lectures in Stockholm.
1908   Lectures in Finland.
1910   *Collected Works,* XVIII.
1911   Trip to France. *Armand Carrel. Then and Now: Two Tragic Fates.*
1913   *A Bird's-Eye View.* Visits Italy. Lectures in Naples and Rome.
1914   Lecture tour in the United States.
1915   *Wolfgang Goethe,* I–II. Break with Clemenceau. Public dialogue with William Archer.
1916   *World at War.*
1916–   *Francois de Voltaire,* I–II.
1917
1917   *Napoleon and Garibaldi.*
1918   *Cajus Julius Caesar,* I–II.
1919   *The World Tragedy.*
1920   *Speeches.*
1921   Trip to Italy. *Michelangelo Buonarroti,* I–II. Lectures on Homer in Copenhagen.
1922   Visits Italy and Greece.
1923   *The Duchess of Dino and the Prince of Talleyrand.* Trip to Germany, Switzerland, and France.
1924   *The Irresistibles.*
1925   *Jesus: A Myth* and *Hellas.* Lecture tour to Berlin and Vienna.
1926   *Petrus.*
1927   *Original Christianity.* Dies February 19.

CHAPTER 1

The Making of a Critic

GEORG Brandes was one of the leading critics in Europe at the beginning of this century. His name is especially associated with Ibsen, Strindberg, and Nietzsche. Through his activity, Brandes altered the cultural climate in Scandinavia and in so doing prepared the way for the modern breakthrough in Scandinavian literature. But Brandes' influence was not limited only to Scandinavia. He lived in Berlin for five years and also wrote books and articles in German. He lectured in the great European cities: Moscow, Saint Petersburg, Prague, Vienna, Warsaw, London, Paris. His books were even translated into such exotic languages as Japanese, especially his best-known work, *Hovedstrømninger i det nittende Aarhundredes Litteratur (Main Currents in Nineteenth Century Literature)*. Very few critics before or after him have had such a broad international approach to literature. Brandes was interested, not only in the literature of the major countries outside Scandinavia, but also in what was written in, for example, Polish, Czech, and Flemish. He looked for good writers wherever they could be found. He also contributed to magazines and newspapers outside Scandinavia, especially in Germany, Austria, Poland, and Russia. An article or essay from his hand could give a writer a worldwide reputation, and writers from almost all of Europe, such as Friedrich Nietzsche, the German philosopher, and the young André Gide, sent him books for reviewing. And while it is true that his fame had already begun to fade before his death in 1927, still, no one wishing to understand the realistic and naturalistic movement in Europe can ignore him.

I *The Sociocultural Setting*

Denmark in the middle of the 1800s, when Brandes was growing up, was a society with definite social classes. Agriculture was to a rather great extent dominated by large estates, and landowners had a strong influence on the political life. They formed a special party in the Parliament, and from 1875 until 1894 Denmark was governed by a conservative landowner by the name of Estrup, who set aside the principle of parliamentarianism. The majority in Parliament was held by a liberal left party that basically consisted of farmers. In his autobiography Brandes described one of his classmates, the son of a noble landowner, who rode to school every day on his horse followed by a mounted servant. He always came late to school, was treated with special politeness by the teacher, and was allowed to place the high silk hat he wore in the teacher's closet. This noble boy was of only average intelligence and lazy in his studies, but he nevertheless became a minister in the government later on. This memory gives a fairly clear picture of the class differences that existed at the time.

Another influential group were the academically educated public servants who set their mark on the National Liberal party and whose core consisted of an upper class intelligentsia that controlled the influential newspapers. This relatively small group in Danish society was nonetheless the bearer of an aesthetically advanced culture, which is referred to as the golden age in Danish history. It had originated in Danish romanticism with Oehlenschläger as the leading figure, and had reached full bloom in the middle of the century with men like Hans Christian Andersen, Søren Kierkegaard, and Johan Ludvig Heiberg in literature, Bertel Thorwaldsen in art, and Hans Christian Ørsted, the discoverer of electromagnetism, in the natural sciences. When Thorwaldsen returned to Copenhagen as an internationally renowned sculptor in 1838, he was given a battleship for the journey home and was received as a prince in the world of art. The city of Copenhagen built a special museum to house his works.

Brandes grew up in this cultural environment where art, literature, and philosophy were highly valued. Copenhagen was the natural center for this upper-class culture, the largest city in Scandinavia with its 180,000 inhabitants in 1870, and referred to as the Athens of the north. Copenhagen had a relatively large number of theaters, with the Royal Theater the most important, and there young Brandes could still see the celebrated prima donna of the golden age, Louise Heiberg, whose position in the art of acting was equal to that of Hans Christian Andersen in literature. While

Brandes was still a boy, the Socrates of this Athens of the north, Kierkegaard, wandered its streets. The critic would later write about him in his biography:

Another day you could see him in the crowd on Østergade in the afternoon between two and four and follow the lean and spindly figure with his hanging head, his umbrella tucked underneath his arm. It was almost impossible not to find him here on his "route" along the "Corso" in Copenhagen. He greeted people every five minutes, spoke sometimes with one and sometimes with another, once heard a little street urchin call out "Either-Or" after him, spoke with Tom, Dick, and Harry, as accessible to everyone on the street as he was inaccessible in his home, here just as generous with himself as he was otherwise stingy, here seemingly wasting his time in repayment of the fact that he stubbornly refused to receive people at home.[1]

But the cultural environment described here naturally had its negative aspects, which revealed themselves in a farm-worker's proletariat in the countryside and in a growing group of underpaid industrial workers in Copenhagen. This proletariat made its first attempt at organizing itself and forming the basis of a socialistic movement in Denmark at about the same time that Brandes made his first appearance with his lecture series in 1871. Louis Pio, the leader of this movement, and some of his closest associates were, however, arrested and sentenced to several years in prison, and thus the Danish worker's movement was effectively suppressed for a long time.

II *Boyhood and Youth*

Georg Brandes was born in Copenhagen on February 4, 1842. His parents were Jewish but the family had lived in Denmark for several generations. He grew up before the big wave of anti-Semitism, which culminated during World War Two, had begun, but it was nevertheless an unpleasant experience to be a Jewish child in Copenhagen during the middle of the last century. In his autobiography he described how he discovered that he was a Jew:

But one day when I heard the shout again I wanted to know, and when I came home I asked Mother, "What does it mean—Jew?" Mother said, "Jews are human beings." "Ugly people?" "Yes," Mother replied smiling, "sometimes rather ugly people, though not always." "May I see a Jew?"

"Sure you can," said Mother and promptly lifted me up before the mirror that hung over the sofa. I screamed so she quickly put me down on the floor, and I appeared so frightened that she regretted that she had not prepared me. She sometimes spoke of it later on.[2]

Brandes was a gifted child. At the age of two he knew the English, French, and German words for the most common things around him.[3] He learned to read before he was four years old, and at five he had a private tutor. In school and later at the university his intelligence drew the attention of his teachers. At the university he began to study law but very soon was captivated by the study of literature and philosophy. He planned to be a poet and wrote poetry as a student. Heinrich Heine was his admired master. Brandes did not, however, publish his verse until he was a well-known critic, and it is evident that he was not a born poet.

The most remarkable thing about Georg Brandes as a young man was his appetite for books. Between the ages of seventeen and twenty-three, 1859–1865, he kept a record of his reading, and the list contained 1,217 titles. Every month he added up the number of books he had read and when he was most industrious he could read as many as forty-five, that is, more than one book a day. The list gives us a good idea of the breadth of his literary and philosophical orientation. During this period of his life he absorbed the great European literary tradition: the classic Greek playwrights, the Spanish writers of the sixteenth century, Shakespeare, the French classicists, the German romanticists, and, of course, the most important Scandinavian writers. Goethe was the central figure in Brandes' reading for a long time. He read Goethe's autobiography *Aus meinem Leben (From my Life)* when he was about eighteen years old and was fascinated by the comprehensiveness of Goethe's personality. He made up his mind to read all the books Goethe himself had studied as a young man, and although he could not fulfill this intention, Goethe played an important role for him throughout his life.

Together with Goethe, Shakespeare was the great name in the postromantic atmosphere in which Brandes grew up. He read Shakespeare in Danish and German translations first, but later on also in English. One of his most important essays, "The Infinitely Small and the Infinitely Great in Poetry," was devoted to his favorite play, Shakespeare's *Henry IV*. There he demonstrated the importance of the small, apparently irrelevant detail in conveying a feeling of reality to the reader. It was Shakespeare's realism that interested him.

Georg Brandes' parents were far from Orthodox, but he went through with the bar mitzvah in a synagogue although he did not believe in the ceremony. Many of his friends at the university were non-Jewish and one of them especially, the gifted art student Julius Lange, tried to persuade him to become a Christian. Influenced by his Christian friends, Brandes began to read the Bible and Søren Kierkegaard. Since he kept a diary during practically all his lifetime, it is possible to follow the different steps of his development. From this we can see that he went through a religious crisis when he was about twenty years old.[4] Søren Kierkegaard's special view of Christianity primarily appealed to him. He tried honestly and seriously to accept the Christian faith but failed in the end.

Along with Kierkegaard and the Bible, Brandes studied the German philosopher Friedrich Hegel. A note from his diary from 1861 is rather significant: "Reading plan: Biblia. Hegel Logic, Phaenomenologie des Geistes, Encyclopaedie, AEsthetics. Greek Accidence and Syntax and New Testament in Greek." Hegel's philosophy offered him a magnificent and systematic explanation of the world and the role of human beings in it. From ecstatic exclamations in his diary we can see that Hegel gave Brandes an intellectual adventure of great intensity. He was deeply influenced by Hegel's philosophy of history and his dialectic method. When he came in contact with English empiricism later on, he was partly emancipated from German metaphysics and realized that Hegel's ingenious castle was built on sand. If it had not been for his extensive study of Hegel, Brandes might have become a Christian. Now he drifted farther and farther away from the Christian faith of his friends. Another German philosopher was of great importance for this emancipation: Ludwig Feuerbach, one of Hegel's left-wing disciples. The best-known books by Feuerbach are *Das Wesen des Christenthums* (*The Essence of Religion*) and *Das Wesen des Glaubens*, (*The Essence of Faith*) which the young Brandes studied very closely. Feuerbach can be regarded as one of the originators of the psychology of religion. To him, God is a product of man, of his fears and hopes—for example, his longing for a life after death. One of Brandes' excerpts from *Das Wesen des Christenthums* (*The Essence of Religion*) read: "The belief in the existence of God is the belief in an existence separate from the human world and nature."[5]

Brandes could not in the long run accept a belief that did not harmonize with a rationalistic view of life. He was attracted by Spinoza's pantheism and wanted to see himself and man in general as a part of nature. As a young man he also believed in progress, in the human being's ability to create a better world, and he felt that it was his own duty to serve as a soldier in the continuing struggle for political and social freedom. This was also a sort of religion, but it is important to point out that the formative process described above isolated Brandes from many of his student friends, and when he made his debut as a critic he was very soon regarded as a dangerous enemy of Christianity. His studies of Kierkegaard did not make him Christian, but perhaps they taught him something else: One must not compromise. One must make one's own decisions: either-or.

III   *The Young Scholar*

Brandes' first book dealt with a theological-philosophical problem. It appeared in 1866 and was called *Dualismen i vor nyeste Philosophie (The Dualism in Our Newest Philosophy)*. Supported by a friend and young philosopher, Gabriel Sibbern, Brandes attacked his former teacher at the university, Rasmus Nielsen. He denied that it was possible, as Professor Nielsen claimed, to believe in the miracles of the Bible and at the same time to accept a theory of life based on modern science. Brandes' book was a contribution to a lively public debate that was going on in Danish magazines and newspapers. The battle may be regarded as a forerunner to the literary breakthrough that Brandes himself initiated in the early 1870s. It showed that the spiritual climate in Denmark had begun to change under the influence of modern science and especially because of a new critical view of the Bible initiated by Strauss, Feuerbach, and Renan and their Scandinavian followers. One of these was the Swedish writer Viktor Rydberg, whose book *Bibelns lära om Kristus (The Bible's Teachings about Christ)* Brandes had read.

At a rather early stage in Brandes' career at the University of Copenhagen, when he was only twenty years old, one of his teachers encouraged him to become professor of literature, or aesthetics, as the chair was called at that time. His studies during the 1860s were to a great extent preparation for this profession, even if one cannot neglect the possibility that he had plans for a career as a writer or critic. The critical method he was taught at the university derived mainly from Hegel and from his disciples Johan Ludvig

Heiberg and Friedrich Vischer. Heiberg had introduced Hegelian aesthetics in Denmark and had created a system of his own based on Hegel. He was a skillful playwright and along with Kierkegaard and Hans Christian Andersen he made postromanticism a great period in Danish literature. Brandes admired him very much as a critic. His clarity of ideas, his wit, his elegant polemics were a good school for Brandes. Like Hegel and Vischer, Heiberg considered drama, or rather the specific type of drama he himself wrote, the vaudeville, the most important genre. Influenced more by Hegel and Vischer in this case, Brandes took a great interest in drama during the sixties. The reading list mentioned above contained a great many plays, and from 1867 to 1870 he made contributions as a drama critic to Copenhagen newspapers. His first literary studies were also mainly devoted to drama, and his approach was typical for the kind of criticism developed on the basis of German aesthetics. Like the Germans, Brandes preferred to deal with a work of art as a closed totality without any connection to its creator or the society he lived in. He applied a category, for example the comic or the tragic, to the literary work in order to see to what extent such a category was fulfilled. It is significant that his second book, which appeared in 1868, was entitled *AEsthetiske Studier* (*Aesthetic Studies*). The title refers to two such studies: "On the Term: The Tragic Fate" and "Two Chapters on the Theory of the Comic."

In this book is also found Brandes' first essay on Ibsen. His reading of Ibsen went back to 1864, when he was very impressed by *The Pretenders*, which had just come out. For several years this was his favorite Ibsen play. Brandes' critical instrument was not yet ready for plays like *Brand* and *Peer Gynt*, which received rather harsh treatment in his essay. He was not completely negative to *Peer Gynt*, but the weakness of the play was obvious to him:

It would be unfair to deny both that the book has some great and beautiful elements and that it tells us all, and especially the Norwegians, some great truths; but beautiful and true elements are of far less value than Beauty and Truth, and the work of Ibsen is neither beautiful nor true.[6]

This is harsh judgment on the most charming and witty of Ibsen's plays, and Brandes changed his opinion later on. But this essay shows that Brandes still had a long way to go before he could step forward as the spokesman for the young literary generation in Scandinavia.

IV   *The New Critical Method: Naturalism*

Georg Brandes received his master's degree in aesthetics in April 1864. His professors had to make up a new degree to adequately evaluate the work of the talented student, and he received *admissus cum laude precipua*.[7] Up to this time his university education had primarily been oriented toward Germany, but French literature began to interest him more and more in the years immediately following his exam. Decisive for this change in taste was a trip he made to Paris at the end of 1866. He remained in France three months, and one of his most important experiences there was his meeting with the French philosopher and literary critic Hippolyte Taine. Brandes was inspired to study the writings of Taine by the author Émile Zola, who was at that time almost completely unknown outside France. Zola had just published a collection of essays, *Mes Haines*, (*My Hatreds*) which Brandes bought and in which was included an essay on Taine.[8] Thus the young Brandes was influenced by two of the leading men in French naturalism at this early stage of his development. There is no indication that he had read Zola's novels at this time, though he had studied the writings of Taine, with whom he was already somewhat acquainted, before leaving Copenhagen. He also attended Taine's classes at the École des Beaux Arts, and in one of his letters home he sketched a portrait of the French critic as he looked at the podium. It is a good example of Brandes' ability to portray the people he met in his life:

Entered with feverish haste and sat down. Forty-year-old man, noble head, short neck, broad shoulders. Average height. Wearing full, blond beard, short, thin, shining hair, dark. Large, beautifully shaped nose, handsome mouth and beautiful white teeth. No eyes at all, a look as dead as the emperor's, eye-glasses, which made it impossible to see through him. Very winning smile. Rather weak but unusual voice. Overwork and exhaustion in his personality and in the expression on his pale face. He has worked like a fool and has probably endangered his health. Speaks without the least gesture, immovable, no facial expression, a cold, blasé, superior and impressive calm, as if the subject didn't concern him.[9]

Brandes' confrontation with Taine's writing, which he read extensively during his three months in Paris, led to a radical reorientation of his critical method: he abandoned the aesthetic categories he had earlier used. Up to this time he had treated a poetic work as an autonomous unit without regard to the society the work reflected or in which it was created. Taine was one of the first sociologically oriented literary historians. Here he stood in debt to Balzac and the French positivists. He also borrowed some of his concepts from the natural sciences, especially biology and geography, such as the concept of milieu, which played a central part in his criticism.

After his return from France Brandes once again took up his academic studies and received his doctor's degree from the University of Copenhagen in 1870 for a thesis on the criticism of Hippolyte Taine: *Den franske Æsthetik i vore Dage (Contemporary French Aesthetics)*. His book became important for literary research and criticism in Scandinavia because he, like Zola in France, used analogies from the natural sciences when dealing with the working methods of the critic. In the spirit of Taine, he often made references to the natural sciences in expressions such as "the natural sciences give us the answers," "the critic is the natural scientist of the soul," and so on. The opening chapter of his book was devoted to Taine's term *"faculté maîtresse,"* dominant faculty, mentioned in his book on Livy. According to Taine, Livy's dominant faculty was his gift for rhetoric, a trait common to the classical historians in general. Brandes' objection to the concept of *faculté maîtresse* was that while the personality may consist of unities, something that Taine advocated on the basis of his scientific comparisons, he doubted that these unities were made up of one special characteristic. Brandes revealed that Taine had too few *facultés maîtresses* since he used the same ones to characterize both Livy and Victor Cousin, orators, and Shakespeare and Dickens, who were distinguished for their unusual imaginative talents. Brandes therefore found the term too comprehensive. "The human spirit is not so simple as Taine will have it; its essence is manifold, contradictory, and variable."[10] He quoted Sainte-Beuve, seemingly a beneficial counterweight to the more dogmatic Taine, in support of his view of the complexity of the personality. Another reservation Brandes directed toward Taine in this context was that nowhere, not even in his *Histoire de la littérature anglaise, (History of English Literature)* did he attempt to describe "the developmental history of genius." Taine was more concerned with that which was common to different epochs.

Naturally, the section of Brandes' book on Taine that deals with the work of the critic is especially interesting. Here his radical departure from his former aesthetic views can clearly be seen in his discussion of Taine's teachings on causality and on the effects of milieu. Brandes said that the critic should not be satisfied only by studying the work of art, he should go further and, in the way of geneticists, should see how the work originated. The critic should investigate the fetal stage of the literary work, study the different drafts, and try to become familiar with the writer's work in general. From the individual writer he should move on to the group, the literary school from the same country and the same time. From there he should take still another step and broaden his perspective so that his investigation will include the spiritual and material conditions of the country in question at the time the work was written. The analogy with the biologist and botanist is clear. He also wrote:

As there is an external temperature which, by its fluctuations, determines the genesis of this or that plant species, so is there also a spiritual temperature which, by its fluctuations, determines the origin of this or that type of art.[11]

In this context Brandes emphasized that the modern critic he spoke of did not primarily evaluate or moralize. His personal taste was unimportant. Instead he ought to investigate contexts and relationships, drives and habits. He ought to understand and explain, not moralize and evaluate. Here Brandes approached a relativistic point of view in religious and moral questions: "We see everywhere only degrees and nuances, know no more Religion, only religions, no Moral, only customs, no Principles, only facts. Everything is conditional, yes, everything is relative."[12]

Taine wanted to see the literary work and its creator, the literary genius, as a product of external forces, of race, the environment, and *"le moment"* (the pressure of the past on the present). Brandes found it difficult to accept Taine's views on genius. He felt that genius consisted of something that could not be explained on the basis of these three forces alone. Above all, the fault with Taine's reasoning was that he confused conditioning with causality. Brandes returned to this point of contention in the extensive discussion of Taine's views on causality that completed his study.

One of the most interesting books for the understanding of Taine's aesthetics is, without a doubt, *Philosophie de l'art (The Philosophy of Art)*. It received a special chapter in Brandes' book on Taine. Taine was interested in reaching a scientifically valid evaluative norm for the appraisal of literary works. The task of the critic was not to judge but to explain and understand, and here, as Brandes correctly observed, Taine was a bit self-contradictory, though in actuality, neither Brandes nor Taine managed to avoid the problem of evaluation.

What characteristics of a literary work determine its greatness? Brandes began as a disciple of Heiberg's and Hegel's aesthetics and proceeded to Vischer, whose magnum opus was one of Brandes' authorities for several years.[13] Vischer, like Hegel, was of the opinion that it was the idea behind the work that was the determining factor. This was opposed by the Herbartians, who wanted to liberate aesthetics from metaphysics. Zeising, Köstlin, and Zimmerman, all Herbartians, stressed the formal aspects, and their studies on proportion and harmony made an impression on Brandes. He never totally freed himself from these men, the masters of his youth. While working as a critic he maintained a great interest in the form of the literary work, and he often went into extensive discussions of composition, style, and other formal elements.

In his book on Taine, Brandes had the opportunity to write an exposition on the above-mentioned aesthetics.[14] He then described Taine's plan to solve the problem of evaluation in aesthetics. Brandes called Taine's point of view "pure naturalism." "To make a notable character dominant: that is the goal of the work of art," said Taine.[15] As usual, Taine looked to the natural sciences, in this case to biology especially, to find support for his theories. Certain animal characteristics are less variable than others. The most important ones are the most stable. In the same way there are different levels in a human being. On the surface we have customs and mores more or less determined by the times we live in; farther down we have the characteristics that are determined by the race we belong to; and finally, farthest down we have the characteristics that are common to all people. Similarly there ought to be different types of literary and artistic works: those that appeal to their times and are in vogue only for a few years; those that appeal to a whole generation; and finally, those that embody a whole epoch such as the Middle Ages, the Renaissance, or the Classical period. That Brandes accepted this new "aesthetics of content," which he analyzed in his book on Taine, is obvious from a letter he sent a few years later to his friend, the German author Paul Heyse: "all good books are summaries of a period. . . ."[16] Similar expressions appear later on and build the foundation for the socially oriented literature for which Brandes became the spokesman, and that in his spirit was reflected in the plays of Ibsen and Strindberg.

V *"Race, Milieu, Moment"*

Race, milieu, and *le moment* were the three concrete tools that Taine passed down to his students. By race he meant, not only that which was significant for a whole people, but also the innate natural abilities of a human being in general.[17] He found support in Darwin and Prosper Lucas. In his history of literature he frequently attempted to determine the characteristics that an author inherited from his parents. Taine had a rather faulty view of these problems, as he shared the incorrect belief of his times that achieved characteristics could be inherited. It was not until the turn of the century, when Mendel's discoveries became known, that that question was answered. Thus, Taine's and Brandes' views on race and biological inheritance were for the most part incorrect. One therefore finds many strange statements about poets and peoples in Brandes' writing that he thought to be scientifically well-founded. This was especially true after his visit to Germany when he came in contact with a Jewish professor by the name of Lazarus who published *Zeitschrift für Völkerpsychologie und Sprachwissenschaft (Review of Racial Psychology and Linguistics)*. Many of his observations were perhaps correct, but in those cases that he attributed to racial conditioning, a contemporary sociologist or cultural anthropologist would instead speak of environmental influences.

As far as the concept of milieu is concerned, Taine, and to a certain extent Brandes, retained a good deal of its biological and geographical meaning. Taine spoke of such climatical factors as temperature and rainfall, of such geological and geographic factors as soil types and topography, and of the style and furnishing of housing. He also spent a great deal of time on the social and political conditions, and it is especially these latter two that Brandes incorporated into his critical method. Brandes was, to a certain extent, an eclectic, and he rejected or applied with a great deal of moderation much of the extreme and dogmatic, not to say naïve, in Taine's enthusiasm for scientific analogies. *"Le moment"* was altogether too vague a term for him, and without the independent force of factors such as race and environment. When Brandes occasionally applied the term, it was primarily as a description of that stage in the literary, cultural, and perhaps also political development of a country in which a literary work was created.

VI *Sainte-Beuve*

Brandes did not wholeheartedly accept Taine's naturalistic aesthetics. His study of the skeptical and much less dogmatic Sainte-Beuve was a healthy antidote. An essay on Sainte-Beuve in Brandes' book *Kritiker og Portraiter (Criticisms and Portraits)* shows that Brandes was familiar with him even before he began *Main Currents*. Brandes devoted special attention to Sainte-Beuve's method of comparative technique in his short essay. This is what he wrote about Sainte-Beuve's *Port-Royal:*

> But *Port-Royal* is only his point of departure, his castle. He departs on expeditions, from one sally to another, looking for parallels, developing analogies, sometimes from literature, sometimes from reality, convening and moving away and thus sketching in passing almost all of the greatest French authors from Corneille, Racine, Molière to Voltaire and Vauvenargues, yes even to Lamartine and George Sand.[18]

Brandes adopted this comparative technique. As the years passed he became extremely well read in European literature. One may even wonder whether there has ever been, before or after him, a critic with the same broad perspective on his contemporary literary panorama as Georg Brandes. He utilized this perspective to make continual comparisons and one of his goals was, as he stated in the first part of *Main Currents*, "to bring that which is strange to us close to us so that we can use it and to create a distance to that which is familiar to us so that we can get perspective upon it."[19] Not a bad program for the study of comparative literature, and it is as valid today as it was a hundred years ago.

Sainte-Beuve's special genre was the literary portrait, which also came to be one of Brandes' most favored forms of presentation. In imitation of Sainte-Beuve, he called his second collection of essays, published the same year as the thesis on Taine, *Criticisms and Portraits* (1870). It consisted for the most part of play reviews written while he worked as a theater critic for *Illustreret Tidende* in Copenhagen. But there were also some longer studies, such as those on Hans Christian Andersen and Mérimée. They are assembled together with other essays under the title "Character Sketches."

The author and his work were almost identical for Brandes at this stage of his development. He moved freely between the author and his work, and his character sketch was meant to illustrate them.

VII   *The Essay on Hans Christian Andersen*

Brandes began his essay on Hans Christian Andersen by attempting to find a common feature, a *faculté maîtresse* in the spirit of Taine, that he could use as an angle of departure. Hans Christian Andersen's dominant characteristic was his childlike quality. This corresponded not only to the naïveté of Andersen's personality, but also to something childlike in the Danish temperament. "The simplicity of Andersen's writing guaranteed him readers among all Danes. It guaranteed him even more among foreigners. The childlike is in its essence popular. . . ."[20] Brandes was the first Danish critic to give the great storyteller the place he deserved in Denmark's literary history. Andersen had been ignored too long. Brandes was aware that Hans Christian Andersen, by concentrating on the story as a genre and on children as a public, had staked his claim to a new area for the author: "it was something new, a real innovation to be the children's writer."

Brandes also made use of another of the Tainian basic concepts: race. The most basic characteristic of Andersen's philosophy of life was, Brandes said, that he put the heart first, a trait that was also typically Danish. The same was true of what Brandes called "the fantastic humor" and "the idyllic tone," which he said was typical of Andersen's stories and which he described as typically Danish. He used the concept of milieu in an analysis of the relationship between material and literary work, to which he devoted a good deal of space. The essay on Andersen can furthermore be said to be constructed according to the following Taine-inspired scheme: (1) the style; (2) the writer's *faculté maîtresse;* (3) the working method; (4) the general validity and permanency of the story; (5) the flora and fauna in the story; (6) the writer as the representative of his race; and (7) the stories from the point of view of genre.

Brandes had begun to find his form in this essay: the elegant spiritual article with a dash of the informal style inspired by Sainte-Beuve. The way he began his essay, with the aphoristic statement that "it takes courage to have talent," shows that he was also beginning to depend upon his own talent. He continued by relating an anecdote about Armand Carrel and in that way came to Andersen's special style, the storylike style. There is a directness and a tangibility about this composition that reminds one of Hans Christian Andersen's own writing. Brandes had read him extensively and had also known him personally. The essay is still worth reading today. In emphasizing the genre aspect Brandes was ahead of his time, and he thus anticipated later research in the field.

VIII   *Mérimée*

At this time, however, Hans Christian Andersen was not Brandes' ideal writer. The sensitivity and naïveté typical of Andersen's writing were foreign to him. He felt closer to the Frenchman Prosper Mérimée, which is clear from the beginning of Brandes' essay on him:

> If I were to mention one among all the writers of my acquaintance whom I assume it would be both profitable and a pleasure to know personally, one who I feel is free from the smallness and shabbiness which so often characterized poets and writers, I think I would name Mérimée.[21]

In Mérimée, Brandes found a completely different type of author, cool and reserved, attempting to hide behind the people he portrayed, an author who could tell about cruel and upsetting things without betraying the slightest sign of sympathy. Later Brandes would recognize the same trait in Flaubert, and these two authors paved the way for the objective style of narration so praised by the naturalists.

The essay on Mérimée was based more on Sainte-Beuve's comparative technique than on Taine's system of scientific concepts. The essay began with a series of extensive comparisons. The other members of the French romantic school, Balzac, George Sand, and Stendhal, were one after the other compared to Mérimée in character sketches that went on for many pages. The type of comparison in which Brandes excelled would now be called illustrative.[22] Brandes found no systematic angle of approach to Mérimée comparable to the childlikeness of Hans Christian Andersen. He painted a sensitive portrait of Mérimée, throwing light on many different aspects of his work and personality. He praised his strict scholarship and noted his reserve and tendency to mystify. Other traits he found praiseworthy were Mérimée's partiality to forceful and clearly defined characters, his sureness of style and form. Brandes also found a predilection for the documentary style, for a purely scientific foundation of the historical narratives especially; which would be more common with the advent of naturalism. Brandes moved away from the fantastic and unreal toward realism at this time, but he still had not come in contact with any true naturalists or realists. He turned to those romantics who wrote with a tangible realistic undercurrent. Mérimée's historical novel *La Chronique du règne de Charles IX (The Chronicle of the Reign of Charles IX)*, to which Brandes wrote an introduction, when, on his initiative, it appeared in Danish, is fairly representative of his literary taste about 1870, when he published *Criticisms and Portraits*.

CHAPTER 2

There Is Always a Troublemaker

IN 1870 Georg Brandes was twenty-eight years old and a fairly well-established critic and literary scholar in Copenhagen. He had just received his doctorate for his dissertation on Taine, which was well received and which was a beautiful ending to a brilliant career at the University of Copenhagen. His studies were mostly oriented toward aesthetics and philosophy. Politics and social questions had played a subordinate role in his development thus far, with the exception of his translation of John Stuart Mill's *The Subjection of Women* in 1869. The latter became an important impulse and stimulus for the debate on the emancipation of women in Scandinavia, a debate that gave birth to plays like Ibsen's *A Doll's House*, Bjørnson's *A Gauntlet*, and several contributions from Strindberg, to name a few examples. The translation of Mill's paper had led to a correspondence between Brandes and the English philosopher. In April 1870, Brandes began an extensive trip around Europe that lasted almost a year and a half and took him to France, England, and Italy. It was the final stage of his education and was of great importance for the role he would come to play as a stimulus for the flowering of Scandinavian literature, usually termed "the modern breakthrough" and represented by such figures as Ibsen, Bjørnson, Strindberg, and Pontoppidan. One wonders whether this breakthrough would have had such a modern and international character without Brandes' help. This is a question impossible to answer satisfactorily. One can only remark upon the fact that Brandes made a radical break away from national self-satisfaction and provincialism and opened the door to modern, radical Europe. It is for this reason that his travels in 1870–1871 were so important.

I *Abroad*

In Paris Brandes was welcomed with open arms by Taine, who maintained a central position in the cultural life of France as professor at the École des Beaux Arts. Taine introduced his young Danish follower to another of France's leading cultural personalities, the philologist, religious historian, and philosopher Ernest Renan. The result of this meeting was a short essay on Renan.[1] Brandes had already studied Renan's papers on the history of religion in the middle of the 1860s and had noted his variegated prose. Renan became one of the most important spokesmen for the relativism and skepticism that characterized the literature of the latter part of the nineteenth century. Anatole France is without doubt the most typical representative of this philosophy. Brandes had expected Renan to be a quiet scholar, but such was not the case. Renan lived in very poor circumstances since he had lost his professorship at the Collège de France because of his outspokenness with regard to religious questions. Renan was one of the "free spirits" who chose to swim against the current, and he would not sell his opinions for the sake of a job. This was the path that Brandes himself would come to follow. However, the shock Renan received because of the Paris Commune drove him toward the right. Behind his conversations with Brandes lay an unlimited contempt for the masses, mediocrity, and the uneducated. Renan believed only in the aristocracy of intelligence. Brandes was to come to the same point of view during the latter part of his life.

If Renan pushed Brandes in the direction of aristocracy, John Stuart Mill, whom he also met in Paris, pushed him toward democracy. Brandes' meeting with Mill was totally unplanned. Mill was passing through Paris and dropped in to visit Brandes at his hotel. Brandes had never met the philosopher and thought it was the watchmaker coming with his watch:

I opened the door and outside stood a tall, thin, elderly man in a long black coat buttoned at the waist. 'Come in,' I said without looking at him any more closely and went for my wallet. But the man remained standing where he was and, taking off his hat, said my name uncertainly. "That's correct," I said, and before I had a chance to ask again, I heard the softly spoken words: "I am Mr. Mill." If he had said he were the king of Portugal, I couldn't have been more surprised.[2]

Mill's visit marked the beginning of a long friendship, which culminated in a trip to England for Brandes and a visit at the home of the English philosopher. On this occasion Brandes had the opportunity to discuss Mill's philosophy in depth and to relate it to his own point of view, which was strongly influenced by Hegel. John Stuart Mill, as a representative of English empiricism, was extremely critical of Hegel. Mill was surprised that Brandes was so familiar with Hegel and admitted that he had not read the German philosopher himself, neither in the original nor in translation, and said that he knew of his work only through English references to it. When Brandes asked him what impression he had of Hegel's philosophy, Mill answered that there was perhaps something to it, but everything he wrote about metaphysics was pure nonsense. When Brandes somewhat surprisedly replied that he couldn't really mean such a thing, Mill said that this was exactly what he meant. He then asked Brandes whether he had really read and understood the writings of Hegel, and when Brandes answered that he had, at least the main points, Mill said: "But is there really anything to understand?"

Thus Brandes received a strong dose of empiricism to counteract the German metaphysics he had been brought up on. Later, when Brandes returned to Denmark, he plunged even deeper into studies of Mill's works. A concrete result of this was his translation of the little thesis *Utilitarianism*, to which he also wrote an introduction. The greatest advantage of utilitarianism for Brandes was that it showed that it was possible to create an ethic not based on a divinity or a life after death. Brandes never completely left the core of utilitarianism as it was expressed in Bentham's principle of the greatest possible happiness for the greatest possible number, but he later had difficulties uniting it with his teachings, inspired by Nietzsche and Renan, on the great man as the source of culture.

Upon his return to Copenhagen, Brandes attempted to write a philosophical work in the spirit of Mill with influences from Spencer, Bain, and Taine, whose book *De l'intelligence (On Intelligence)* (1870) was published during Brandes' visit in Paris. But Brandes was no philosopher. His attempt resulted only in a compendium on Mill's *Examination of Sir William Hamilton's Philosophy*, and he was self-critical enough not to publish it. But Mill's theory of the association of ideas had left its mark on him. Instead of a dualistic division of man into soul and body, he was given an acceptable explanation for the structure of the personality.

The orientation of the modern breakthrough toward reality and political life, toward a reformation of society, toward a non-metaphysical view of man, are all in the spirit of Mill. Mill was one of the great innovators of the last century, and perhaps more than anyone else he contributed to the fact that Brandes dropped some of the metaphysical ballast that still remained with him when he began his trip to France and Italy in April 1870.

Brandes' long stay in Italy and especially his study of Renaissance art helped to sharpen his contempt for ascetic, Christian morals, and to encourage his attraction to the sensual. His previous view of antiquity, influenced by Winckelmann and Thorvaldsen, was replaced by a more realistic view via impressions received from such things as the wall paintings in Pompeii. He no longer saw Italy through Goethe's and Winckelmann's eyes, but rather through Stendhal's and Taine's.[3] But on many occasions it was direct observation that helped to alter his views on art. In one of his letters to his parents from Italy Brandes wrote:

There is no other art than Greek art. No other people have come so naturally to art as the Greek people. It's no use denying it. All that is modern is only imitation, which is not comparable. These people seem more and more to be the only ones who understood life, straightforward, naïve, honest without fear, stupidity, superstition, or ugliness. Look at all the wedding scenes. These people knew what Man, Woman, Beauty, and Happiness are. They never came to truth by taking shortcuts. What did the Jews know? They knew how to say "thou shalt not." The poorest, emptiest, coldest and most negative formula.[4]

These lines contain much of the philosophical rebellion behind Brandes' literary program. It was a question of liberating the senses, of a totally new way of looking at the relation between the sexes. Here Brandes' art and literature experiences went hand in hand with John Stuart Mill's program for the emancipation of women. What we now call a woman's nature is to a great extent an artificial product—the result of a forced oppression. In reality a wife is her husband's slave. That is what Mill claimed in his book *The Subjection of Women*, which Brandes had previously translated. It was not only institutions and laws that had to be changed but, even more, attitudes, values, and conventions.

But when the revolutionary trumpeters showed they were deadly serious in the Paris Commune of 1871, Brandes was more than a little shaken by their progress. A revolution is no tea party and when the Communards set fire to public buildings and triumphantly toppled the Vendôme column during the final days, Brandes' reaction was somewhat divided:

They have thrown down the Vendôme column. It is not necessary to speak of the raw barbarity of this. It is France's shame that it wasn't prevented. But still, still there is something great in the action. What other people would do it? There *is* a great idea behind it.[5]

Later it became clear that some of the reports from Paris on the progress of the Communards were exaggerated. The Louvre had not been burned and all of its art treasures were intact. However, the wave of destruction hit the Tuileries, and Brandes was at first shocked when he heard this. But it was obviously Brandes' opinion that a great idea lay behind the revolution. It must be remembered that when he returned to Denmark in the summer of 1871 and began to prepare his lectures, it was the uproar of the Communards, which by then had ended in tragedy and could be viewed with some perspective, that gave them the challenging tone that many of the establishment felt was dangerous and revolutionary. Brandes himself seemed to be somewhat surprised by the effect of his lectures. "I'm not advocating anarchy, I only want Truth, Clarity, and Knowledge," he wrote to one of his friends in August 1871. The truth, however, can be revolutionary dynamite.

II *The Lectures*

On November 3, 1871, in a small amphitheater at the University of Copenhagen, Brandes delivered an introductory lecture to his great work *Main Currents in Nineteenth Century Literature*. There were so many listeners at his second lecture that there was not room for them all. He was a great success, but it was not long before complaints began to be heard. In his autobiography Brandes wrote that rumors were circulated that twisted what he had said. They said he had spoken negatively about society and the home. Thorvaldsen, the sculptor who was something of a national hero, was said to have been called an old fool. That Brandes did not mince his words was clear from a letter from one of his most faithful friends: "Thanks for the lecture yesterday, it was brilliant, but I think you were a bit hard on the audience. Don't you think so yourself? If only you could refrain from putting the cat among the pigeons!"[6] Brandes' way of

looking at things, as he said himself, was based on the claim to
freedom of thought and the belief in free research. This seems obvious today, but it was not at all a common viewpoint in Scandinavia
at that time. The universities were still strongholds of theology and
one could not base any opinions on rationalism, as Brandes did,
without taking risks. He maintained that rationalism had not yet
come to Denmark other than in a rather washed-out theological
form.

Brandes wanted to use the method of comparative literature to
describe the main currents of European literature and to relate
them to the situation at home. The outline of the work, which he
sketched in his introductory lecture, clearly bore the mark of Hegel.
Brandes attempted to apply Hegel's dialectics, with the idea of
thesis-antithesis-synthesis, which is then the point of departure for a
new thesis, to historical and literary events. The first stage was a
reaction to the ideas of the French Revolution in the "emigrant"
literature represented by Chateaubriand. Here, Brandes said, the
reaction is only in an initial phase. It went a step farther in the "half
catholic romantic school" in Germany, and culminated triumphantly
with Joseph de Maistre, the early Lamennais, and the young Victor
Hugo. But then the tide turned with a group of romantic poets in
England with Byron at the head, and, finally, the opposing movement reached its peak with the liberal group proceeding out of the
July revolution in France: the later Hugo, Lamartine, Musset, and
George Sand, but above all with "the young Germany," with Heine
and Börne in the lead. Brandes came to devote a volume of his work
to each of these six groups.

It need hardly be said that Brandes based his history of literature
on a fairly weak foundation. His thesis was that Scandinavia and
especially Denmark had come in contact with the reaction to the
ideas of the French Revolution, but not with the opposing movement that he described in the last three parts of *Main Currents:
Naturalism in England* (Byron, Shelley, Keats, etc.), *The Romantic
School in France* (Hugo, Musset, George Sand, Balzac, Stendhal),
and *Young Germany* (Heine, Börne, Gutzkow, Laube). Brandes was
of the opinion that Danish romanticism had strong reactionary
traits. As examples he mentioned Ingemann's poems, Oehlenschläger's poetry, Grundtvig's sermons, and Mynster's speeches.

According to Brandes, literature thus far had been very little in
the service of progress. This was true not only of the romanticists,

such as Oehlenschläger, Ingemann, and Hans Christian Andersen, but also of the postromantic writers, such as Hostrup and even the young Ibsen. Brandes asked himself whether Ibsen's *Brand* was revolutionary or reactionary, and added that he could not answer that question since the work contained equal parts of both.

Brandes felt that contemporary Danish-Norwegian literature was in a state of atrophy. It had become too abstract and idealistic. It no longer dealt with our lives, he said, but with our dreams. It had landed in sterile discussions about morals. If one lived up to the moral in Ibsen's *Brand*, it would mean that half of humanity starved to death for love of an ideal.

III *The New Literary Program*

What type of literature did Brandes advocate instead? Here it may be fitting to quote the words most often cited as the kernel of Brandes' literary program: "That literature lives in our time is demonstrated by the fact that it takes up problems for debate."[7] Brandes may have gotten this idea from a preface that Dumas *fils* wrote for his drama *Le fils naturel (The Natural Son)*.[8] Brandes' program was gratefully adopted by Ibsen, Bjørnson, Strindberg, and the other writers of the breakthrough. It was in accord with what was already implicit in his criticism of the postromantic period, namely, that literature ought to be at the service of progressive forces. It ought to analyze the outdated bourgeois society of the 1800s. The following topics were especially emphasized in Brandes' literary program:

1. *Marriage.* The nineteenth-century marriage of convenience was only a façade behind which vices, crimes, double morals, and especially the spiritual oppression of women were concealed. At this time Brandes himself had tangible experience of what such a marriage was like. His first great love, Mrs. Caroline David, lived in a marriage that Brandes had good reason to believe was incestuous. He mentioned George Sand as an example of a writer who discussed the problem of marriage.

2. *Religion.* During his studies, Brandes had been somewhat influenced by religion, primarily through the writings of Kierkegaard, but Feuerbach, Strauss, and Renan definitely turned him away from Christianity. While he was in Italy he saw how the church could dominate social life and become a negative factor. He considered Jesus "a very beautiful being, a kind of male Joan of

Arc," but he was totally opposed to Christianity and to the church as an institution.[9] He heartily agreed with the words of Voltaire, "écrasez l'infâme (crush the infamous thing)." The theologians had already dominated Danish literature too long. One could almost say that the whole of nineteenth-century Danish literature was written by baccalaureates of divinity, and one need only to point to names like Grundtvig, Hostrup, and Kierkegaard to demonstrate that there was a good deal of truth in this. The same was true of Sweden. Names like Franzén, Wallin, and Tegnér, all bishops, may be mentioned to give an example of how the church set its stamp on cultural life. Voltaire, Byron, and Feuerbach were writers who took up the question of religion.

3. *Property.* When speaking of property, Brandes referred only to Proudhon, and there is no reason to believe that he was familiar with Marx, Engels, or Lassalle at this time. They came later. It is, however, noteworthy that as early as 1871 Brandes was interested in airing the question of property in literature purely on principle.

4. *Society.* To Brandes, society was primarily a combination of laws and customs—most of them out of date—that the individual was forced to accept. The individual was confronted with this society, which he saw as an extremely complicated suit of prejudices he was expected to don early in his youth. Brandes wished to have this society reformed and debated with the help of literature. He wanted to achieve some kind of balance between the individual and society.

It is clear from the above that Brandes was primarily interested in the ideas and content of the new literature. He became the spokesman for an aesthetics of content, and when he discussed the gallery of literary types, it was obvious that he preferred to subordinate them to the socially critical or revolutionary program. He chose two figures from the older romantic literature, Werther and Marquis Posa. The problem with these two was that they were dreamers and not men of action, types that had been models for Danish literature. Brandes wanted to make them men of action:

One beautiful day when Werther was, as usual, walking around suffering from unrequited love with Lotte, he realized that the bond between Albert and her actually meant nothing, and he seized her away from Albert. One fine day the Marquis Posa got tired of preaching freedom in the court of Philip II to the tyrant's deaf ears, and he stabbed him through the heart with his sword.[10]

Can it be said more clearly? There is a pronounced revolutionary tone in such statements. But Brandes was also looking for a new type of author. His prototype for the romantic poet's ideal was Oehlenschläger's Aladdin, and he said that Aladdin was an attempt at portraying literary genius. Aladdin is a portrait of the idle dreamer who succeeds at everything without exerting himself. But, Brandes said, "Genius is not the brilliant daydreamer, but the brilliant worker, and the innate gifts are only the tools, not the finished product."[11]

Brandes' appearance with his first series of lectures entitled "Main Currents in Nineteenth Century Literature" was both a scandal and a success. The purpose of the lectures, held in November and December 1871 at the University of Copenhagen, was to pave the way for a job as a teacher at the university. Brandes had influential patrons in the university such as Carsten Hauch, professor of literature, who had hoped that Brandes would be his successor, and Hans Brøchner, professor of philosophy. Five hundred people were gathered in a room meant for two hundred, and they applauded Brandes' attacks on all that was sacred in Denmark. One of the members of the faculty who had been present at Brandes' lectures reported to his colleagues that Brandes preached "complete negation of eternal life . . . the absurdity of marriage and its closely related vow of fidelity . . . unmotivated ridicule directed toward a worldwide historical power such as Christianity . . . no respect for those institutions which the nation regards as sacred. . . ."[12]

This report is rather typical for the situation in which Brandes appeared. Denmark of the 1870s was fairly representative of Northern Europe. Christianity had a very strong position and had the character of a state religion. The universities were primarily educational facilities for officials who would work in the government and in the church. Ministers were considered public officials. Kierkegaard had challenged the Danish state church from a totally different point of departure than that of Brandes and had finally chosen to go his own way. The society of the nineteenth century was composed of a number of institutions, each of which preserved its own traditions. The state was the principal structure, with the church at its side. Marriage was not an agreement based on the free will of two people who loved each other but rather a legal and religious contract between two partners in which the economic side of the question was every bit as important as the emotional, and in which the woman almost always was the weaker partner. She had to take what was offered. The man could satisfy his emotional needs outside of marriage. Lower class women were suitable sex objects.

When Brandes appeared with his lectures in 1871, he regarded this society from the point of view of an outsider. He was born in a Jewish home and had come to terms with religious questions at an early age. Thanks to his alert intellect and enormous appetite for books, ideas, and people, he could quickly absorb the new views on man and society that were propagated by Darwinism, English empiricism, and German Hegelianism, among others. These views lay behind his preaching, but the powerful institutions in Denmark—the state, the church, and the university—found their existence challenged by Brandes' ideas. One wonders if it must not always be so in times of rapid development. In any case, the distance between Brandes' ideas and the ideas the establishment was based on was so great that it was impossible to incorporate him into the power structure.

CHAPTER 3

But Woe to the Troublemaker

CRITICISM of *Emigrant Literature* was aimed from three sides: the literary, the moral, and the social or political.[1] As a scholar, Brandes was accused of being subjective and unoriginal. Instead of being an aesthetic investigation, his book had a social purpose. People were used to seeing art as an autonomous world, unrelated to the society in which it appeared. Some of the debate centered on Goethe's *Werther*. The reason for Werther's destruction, in Brandes' opinion, was the clash between his individual desires and the demands of society. Brandes returned to this theme again and again in *Emigrant Literature* and later in *Main Currents*. Brandes' critics denied the existence of such an antagonism between the individual and society. They rejected his claim that literature should debate such problems.

A not unexpected interpretation of Brandes' demand that literature should throw light on the problem of marriage and the relation of the sexes in general was that he wanted to advocate immorality and free love. Brandes was quite simply without morals. When it was a question of his demand for the reform of society as a whole, Brandes was, much to his own annoyance, associated with the socialists who, in the beginning of the 1870s, had a weak footing in Copenhagen. Not only that, but the Paris Commune incident, which had recently taken place, had shaken people so that very little was needed to alarm them. "Has Mr. Brandes really declared war against society?" asked Carl Ploug, editor in chief of the most influential Copenhagen newspaper (*Fædrelandet*, February 2, 1872).

I Excluded from the Newspapers

The press was an important power factor in the battle that now began to rage between Brandes and the liberal national establishment. Before his trip abroad Brandes had been welcome in many of the leading papers, *Dagbladet* among others. He had begun to feel like a conquering hero after the first weeks of his popular lectures. The newspapers included notices about him. But his opponents began to gather their forces, and since they controlled all the leading newspapers, Brandes received massive unfavorable criticism when the lectures were published in the beginning of 1872. The remarkable thing about the situation was that he was denied the right to reply and was therefore forced on one occasion to send in an article as a paid advertisement in *Dagbladet*, for which he had previously worked. Even newspapers that had requested articles from him turned against him in the storm that now began to rage. An excerpt from his diary reveals his reaction:

Everything looks black. All the roads are closed. "There is no hope". *Dagbladet's* position. Delblanco's refusal of an article he had asked me to write: "The times are a changin'." It's obvious that the circle is closing in around me. One good thing now, when all else is going wrong—Old Hauch is dying. The day I become professor, I'm stronger than all of them . . .[2]

Brandes' hope thus lay in becoming professor after Carsten Hauch, who died in Rome in February 1872. The latter had left a letter recommending Brandes as his successor. Brandes attempted to have this document published in the newspapers, but met with little success. The two largest newspapers in Copenhagen refused to take up Hauch's "testament." It was at this point that Brandes, understanding the adamancy of the opposition, wrote in his diary: "Night. 4:00 A.M. A feverish night. Can't sleep. *Dagbladet* and *Berlingske* have *refused* to publish old Hauch's declaration. I will never forget this pettiness as long as I live."[3] And in his entry of July 9, 1872: "Such hate. From cabinet ministers down to the lowliest journalist. It's obvious. I just have to get used to the idea: I won't be accepted for the job. I have to plan my life in another way."

Brandes had previously supported himself by scholarships from the university and by what he could earn from theater reviews and occasional articles. Now these possibilities were denied him. A group of young authors and intellectuals gathered around him, and at first he had a forum for his ideas in *Nyt Dansk Maanedsskrift*. Two of the most promising young authors, Holger Drachmann and J. P. Jacobsen, were also contributors. Brandes also had an important

comrade in arms in his younger brother Edvard, with whom he
established a monthly magazine called *Det nittende Aarhundrede
(The Nineteenth Century)* in 1874. Originally they had planned to
start a daily paper, but that idea was not realized until 1884 when
Politiken began to come out. In 1882 Edvard Brandes was employed
on the editorial staff of *Morgenbladet,* so Brandesianism successively fortified its positions and eventually eliminated the repercussions of the blockade that resulted from the lectures of 1872.

II   *Explanation and Defense*

Brandes continued struggling for his ideas by using the channels
at his disposal: *Nyt Dansk Maanedsskrift,* and later *Det nittende
Aarhundrede,* and Gyldendal, his publishers. In response to the
negative reception of his lectures and the first part of *Main Currents,* Brandes wrote a booklet entitled *Forklaring og Forsvar (Explanation and Defense,* 1872). Here he discussed those statements
that had caused the greatest uproar and that had to a certain extent
been misinterpreted. He defended his method of relating literary
figures to the society in which they were created. One of the slogans
of his lectures was the demand for "free thought," an unprejudiced
testing of everything, regardless of dogmas or beliefs. One of his
opponents had declared that freedom of thought was really nothing
other than "free desire." Brandes' slogan for free thought was linked
to his claim that literature should discuss marriage, and the conclusion was that he was really arguing for immorality: "the free thought
is the dirty thought."[4] Brandes counter-attacked with a fairly self-
confident and well-planned explanation of what he meant by freedom of thought:

What is meant by freedom of thought may be said in a few words: It is the
conviction that there is no specific area either in nature or in history which
is not subject to the laws which otherwise govern nature and history. It is
the conviction that a part of western Asia, during a period of ancient history,
was not governed by totally different natural and spiritual laws than the rest
of the world now and earlier, and that it wasn't the stage for "supernatural
events" while the rest of the world, from the north pole to the south and
from ancient times until now, has only been the stage for natural events.

Brandes' situation was influenced by the fact that the process of
democratic development in Denmark was hindered by the Estrup
regime, a counterpart to Bismarck's unparliamentary regime in

Germany at the same time. In spite of the fact that the liberal party—the Left—received the majority in Parliament, it was powerless to influence governmental decisions to any great extent. When the breakthrough of parliamentarianism finally came to Denmark in 1901, Brandes received his professorship.

Julius Paludan was a fairly typical representative of the conservative Christian opinion against Brandes, and since he formulated the principal and legal objections to the hiring of Brandes by the university, his arguments are summarized below. The summary is based on a series of articles presented in brochure form and published in *Dagbladet* under the title "Lærefriheden og Demokratiet" ("Freedom of Teaching and Democracy").[5]

1. No one can say that the principle of teaching freedom was trampled on in the case of Brandes, since he was permitted to give his lectures at the university.
2. A man who is an enemy of the established society and who has as his goal the abolition of society ought not to find it suitable that this society give him a position.
3. The state cannot employ public servants to oppose it.
4. The university is a state institution, something scholars ought to be mindful of in their position as public servants.
5. The state ought to determine what is true within certain limits.
6. The state cannot favor anyone who is a violent enemy to everything established, especially to marriage in its present form, to religion in every form, and to all human and divine authority.

Paludan also dealt with Brandes as a scholar in a special series of articles.[6] Since he also referred to other people's objections to Brandes' scientific methods, these objections are summarized below:

1. All of Brandes' works are stamped with the hatred of religion and society.
2. He sets up English sensualism and positivism according to Locke, John Stuart Mill, and Condillac against religion.
3. The purpose of his research always overshadows its objectivity.
4. He thinks that the great heathen geniuses Pindar, Vergil, and Plato were the founders of European civilization.

5. He claims that our greatest religious genius, Kierkegaard, would have become a freethinker if he had lived longer.
6. His treatment of the romantic period is unsympathetic and he takes up only its negative sides.
7. Brandes' personality and all of his works are saturated with propaganda and for that reason he cannot be called a scholar.
8. His philosophy of life is ruthless individualism, an advocacy of the absolute freedom of the individual limited only by a subjective conscience but in open antagonism to society's traditions and authoritative restrictions.

III   New Interest in Germany

The reaction sketched above to Brandes and his program shows that it was a question of a confrontation between an authoritarian conservatism and a radical liberalism. He was refused a career as a public servant, but as an author he was not denied the right to work for his ideas. His works were favorably received in the other Scandinavian countries and in Germany. The first part of *Main Currents* was published in Germany as early as 1872, and the interest from that direction led Brandes to orient himself toward that language area. Ibsen may have shown the way. He had been living in Dresden since 1868 and moved to Munich in 1875. In 1872 Brandes visited Dresden for a month and spent a lot of time with Ibsen, with whom he had corresponded more or less regularly since the beginning of the 1860s.[7] Brandes went from Dresden to Berlin, and there lived with his German translator, Adolf Strodtmann. He found a gathering place for Berlin's intellectuals at his publisher's, Franz Duncker. A wave of new impressions washed over him and a new way of looking at Germany began to grow in him. He described his impressions in the following words in a letter to his parents:

First you must know that I feel more and more sympathy for the Germans. A wave of longing for freedom is sweeping across the nation and one breathes deeper in this air. It sometimes seems to me that this air is like the bear's blood which gave the strength of ten men spoken of in an old saga. There is room for progress everywhere. I would never have believed that *Dagbladet*'s Berlin correspondent was so cowardly and such a disgusting toady for the Danes as I now see he is. Everything that man says is a lie. Believe me. Bismarck means business in his struggle against the clergy.

And believe me, in what concerns education and social and political freedom, it is Bismarck who is the great man and who knows the spirit of the
times—in everything a man of progress.[8]

In part it was a painful reevaluation of his relationship to Germany,
which only eight years earlier had taken the southern provinces of
Denmark in a bloody battle. Brandes' praise of Bismarck as a man
of progress must be seen in the light of his struggle against the
Catholic Church. And Brandes' new love for Germany was also
connected to the fact that during his visit in Berlin in 1872 he met
his future wife.

Brandes' relations with women were always tinted by scandal. His
first great passion was a married woman by the name of Caroline
David. When Brandes made her acquaintance he caught a glimpse
of a marriage that was an even more frightening example of the
double morality of the nineteenth century than Ibsen's *Ghosts*. In
the case Ibsen described, it was a question of a half-brother and
sister who, unaware that they are related, fall in love with one
another. In the case of Caroline David, it was consummated incest.[9]
At the age of twenty-two she had married a thirteen-years-older
foster brother, a wealthy landowner, and there is good reason to
believe that he was also her half-brother. When Brandes met her
she had had six children with this man. The affair with Brandes led
to divorce after a tormenting struggle between the spouses. For
Brandes it was a question of liberating an enslaved woman who lived
in an impossible marriage. It was a frightening example of what he
could read about in John Stuart Mill's *The Subjection of Women*,
which he translated to Danish in 1869 when he was most involved in
his attempts at arranging a divorce for Mrs. David. Brandes' affair
with a married woman and the resulting divorce were well known in
that level of Copenhagen society in which he moved. The phrase
"free thought is free desire" received a special meaning as a result of
this knowledge.

When Brandes fell in love with the wife of his German translator
he caught a glimpse of a marriage that, behind its fine facade,
revealed an even more depressing reality. At the age of nineteen
Henriette had married the much older Strodtmann. The latter had,
as a young man, been infected with syphilis on a trip to Paris.
Because of this he lost the sight of one eye. The disease seems to
have been latent, breaking out only in certain periods. When estab-

lishing a motive for the divorce, Brandes questioned Henriette about her husband's symptoms and then consulted a friend who was a doctor. He later referred to the diagnosis in a letter to his future wife in which it was clear that it was one of the more serious types of syphilis.[10]

It is hardly likely that the young woman, who said that she grew up with no knowledge of sex whatsoever, knew from the beginning what disease her husband suffered from. The marriage was obviously a typical common-sense arrangement that took place on the advice of her parents. Mrs. Strodtmann lived, as she herself put it, like a daughter in the house, which implied that she had no sexual relations with her husband.[11] It takes a good deal of cynicism to tie down a young woman in this way. Or was Strodtmann representative of a time that was not willing to recognize the fact that women also had sexual needs?

Brandes arrived at this home with its "white marriage" in October 1872 and once again became the cause for a divorce. But the process took several years. It was not until 1876 that the formalities were arranged and Brandes married Mrs. Strodtmann. By doing so he also strengthened his ties with the German language. He took the final step the next year and moved from Denmark to Berlin. Until that time he had yearly spent long periods of time in Germany because of his acquaintance with Henriette Strodtmann. He believed it would be easier to support himself as an author from Berlin. The move there was an important step for Brandes on his way toward a position as a European critic.

CHAPTER 4

Main Currents

Main Currents was an attempt at writing a history of literature, including the contemporary literary developments of the main European countries: France, Germany, and England. Chronologically it dealt with the first half of the nineteenth century; politically, with the period between the French Revolution of 1789 and the February revolution of 1848. Considering the fact that Brandes began writing *Main Currents* in 1871, his proximity in time to the literature he dealt with in his lectures is clear. However, it took him about twenty years to complete his survey, and during this time his view of literature and society changed along with his literary methods. Nevertheless, his principle concepts were well established. Literature was a weapon in an ideological debate, an instrument for the continuous change of values and social situations. From this point of view it is obvious that literary works were judged in relation to Brandes' own radical way of looking at things, and to a great extent were evaluated on the basis of the degree to which they could contribute new arguments to the ongoing literary debate. While writing *Main Currents*, Brandes was also actively involved in the trends of modern literature as a critic and essayist. His two books on Poland and Russia may be regarded as a complement to *Main Currents*. His goal, a survey of the most important language areas of Europe, became even clearer.

I Emigrant Literature

Part one of *Main Currents*, published in Danish in 1872, was entitled *Emigrant Literature*. Here Brandes referred to the French emigrant authors, especially Mme de Staël and Chateaubriand. Both these authors were forced to emigrate during the revolutionary war and the Napoleonic era. Brandes meant them to exemplify a growing reaction, but this is actually valid only for Chateaubriand. In general, Brandes was not interested in authors as such nor in their works as structural units. Instead, he directed his attention to an assortment of fictional figures, or, as he put it, types.

As Wellek said, the concept "type" was of great importance for the advance of realism.[1] Schelling used the term to denote great universal figures of mythical proportions like Hamlet, Falstaff, Don Quixote, and Faust. This view migrated from Germany to France via an essay by Charles Nodier entitled "Des Types en littérature" *(Types in literature)* (1832). Balzac used it in the preface to *La Comédie Humaine (The Human Comedy)* (1842) in which he claimed that he studied social types. George Sand gave the term a similar meaning in the preface to *Le Compagnon du Tour de France (The Companion of the Tour of France)*. Taine's use of the term played a decisive role for Brandes, who, in accord with Tainian aesthetics, used "type" to mean a literary figure representative of his epoch. The scientific view borrowed from Taine was, however, clear in Brandes' use of the concept of type. The following passage, one of many in *Emigrant Literature* in which the term was used, is illustrative:

In the history of literature we move from one variety of epoch-type to another in much the same way as the natural scientist studies the evolution of the same basic form, from, for example, the arm to the leg, to the paw, to the wing, to the webbed foot, in different species. The next variation on a type which I would like to bring to your attention is Benjamin Constant's Adolphe.[2]

Here Brandes attempted to apply a purely evolutionary viewpoint to literary material. The literary type went through certain predetermined changes, following a basic pattern, in much the same way that a part of the body changed in the struggle for survival. The analogy is, of course, absurd, but that does not mean that Brandes' technique in itself was totally unfruitful. Many of the comparisons he made among different literary figures are justified and were noted both before and after *Main Currents*. In a way one could say that Brandes applied pure comparativism in the first part of his work.

Brandes' outline for his presentation is sketched below. Dates are included to give some idea of the chronology.

1. Chateaubriand, *Le Génie du Christianisme* (1802)
2. Rousseau, *La nouvelle Héloïse* (1761)

3. Goethe, *Die Leiden des jungen Werthers* (1774)
4. Molière, *Le Misanthrope* (1668), Shakespeare, *As You Like It* (1599?)
5. Chateaubriand, *Le Génie du Christianisme* (1802)
6. Senancour, *Obermann* (1804)
7. Constant, *Adolphe* (1816)
8. de Staël, *Delphine* (1802)
9. de Staël, *Corinne* (1807)

Brandes' subject was the French emigrant literature, but only five of the above works can be included in that school. His point of departure, as already mentioned, was not the work as a whole, but one or two figures in each work, and he began with René in Chateaubriand's book. René was a "main type." In order to find the genesis of this type, Brandes went back four decades in French literature to *La nouvelle Héloïse (The New Heloise)*. In turn this work traced its ancestry to Prévost's *Manon Lescaut* and the plays of Marivaux among others. Brandes' interpretation of *La nouvelle Héloïse* and the new way of regarding love that was expressed there led him to Goethe's *Die Leiden des jungen Werthers (The Sorrows of Young Werther)*. Goethe's novel was published thirteen years after Rousseau's, and here one could speak of a certain influence, but this was not what Brandes was interested in. Instead he wished to demonstrate that figures like Werther, Saint Preux, and René were all more or less examples of similar phenomena in society. A quote from his character sketch of Werther will clarify:

Werther is an invalid; what is it which he is lacking inside? He is uneasy and feverish, but, let it be understood, his uneasiness is based on apprehension and insecurity, on longing for the moment and longing for eternity, but not on hopelessness or desperation. He belongs to a time full of premonitions and superstitions, not to one of surrender and despair. We will see his counterpart in Chateaubriand's René. The basic cause of Werther's misery is the negative relation between the boundlessness of the heart and the boundaries of society.[3]

The continually returning theme of *Main Currents* is the individual versus society. Werther was rejected by a society that he denounced, and this opposition between the individual and society could not be resolved at that stage of historical development in which Werther appeared on the scene. According to Brandes, the result of this discrepancy between the individual and society is melancholy, so characteristic of the "types" he discussed. But melancholy itself was no new occurrence during the last part of the eighteenth century. Brandes therefore moved back a few more decades in time to Alceste, the melancholy hero of *Le Misanthrope*. Alceste in turn had many striking similarities to Jacques, one of the minor figures in Shakespeare's *As You Like It*, and here Brandes completed his genealogy of the melancholic figure and could finally go into his analysis of René.

It took Brandes almost thirty pages to sketch this background, and the figure of René was not the final product of this literary genealogy. He was a main type and was in turn the source of many variations. The melancholic, egocentric, blasé hero appeared fairly often in the literature of the nineteenth century. Among René's spiritual relatives Brandes mentioned Kierkegaard's seducer Johannes in *En Forførers Dagbog (The Diary of a Seducer)*, Byron's Cain and Manfred, and the poetic protagonist in Heine's *Buch der Lieder (Book of Songs)*. Here Brandes mixed fictional figures with their creators. He wrote about two Danish authors without ever mentioning their names: Kierkegaard and Grundtvig. The reason for these somewhat secretive references was obviously that there were many who would have taken offense if Brandes had mentioned these two in relation to René and Werther. About Grundtvig he wrote: "He jumps into the role of the Divine Prophet, lets himself be worshiped like the Pope, and, though an old man, lets young women come to him to kiss his shaking hands."[4] These were fairly profane words about the much disputed churchman, who in any case could not be regarded as a melancholic type. Kierkegaard, for whom Brandes never could hide his admiration despite a differing philosophy, escaped more lightly. For him, melancholy developed into a prevailing gloom.

One of the contributing causes of the new state of mind that marked the early nineteenth century and that produced such literary figures as René was, according to Brandes, the emancipation of the individual and the liberation of thought. Previously society had been more or less static, and the individual had a given place. With the advent of the French Revolution things changed. Napoleon's career also paved the way for the literary genius.[5]

Brandes dealt with woman as a literary type for the first time in his treatment of Constant's *Adolphe*. He had passed by the feminine figures in the earlier novels he touched upon, but Ellénore, the feminine protagonist of *Adolphe*, was the object of a rather profound investigation. She was an example of a new, modern woman in literature, one that Balzac would later make more familiar in his novels—*"la femme de trente ans,"* the thirty-year-old woman, the mature woman. To help us understand the novelty of Constant's creation, Brandes introduced his analysis of *Adolphe* with a discussion of two of Goethe's feminine figures, Gretchen and Clärchen. Brandes emphasized the dependence and immaturity of these two young women. They were not equal partners for their men, but rather adoring children who clung to them. They dissolved into uncritical adoration for the men they loved. Constant's Ellénore was different. She was no inexperienced, love-struck young girl. She was strong-willed instead of weak. Furthermore, there was a protectiveness and motherliness in her erotic passion that resulted from the fact that the relationship was one of two equal beings, both intellectually and emotionally. According to Brandes, Ellénore's development into such an important womanly figure depended upon the fact that Mme de Staël was her model. Later research has questioned the truth of this, but that is of less importance here. This is a good example of how Brandes, using sociological methods in literature, searched for fictional figures who could serve as sources of inspiration for the struggle for the emancipation of women going on in his own time. He wrote:

The woman's struggle in literature—struggle against the establishment and society—appears long before Balzac and long before George Sand. Ellénore represents this struggle because she is based on the most powerful woman of the century.[6]

But Constant's *Adolphe* was also an example of how an author satisfied Brandes' demand that marriage be debated in literature. He said that Constant's novel demonstrated the impossibility of finding happiness in marriage, but also the impossibility of finding it outside marriage. "Where then is happiness in modern society?" he asked himself. These problems were also discussed in Mme de Staël's *Delphine* and *Corinne,* which were extensively analyzed in the subsequent parts of the book. One of the most meaningful and noteworthy elements in the first part of *Main Currents* was the large amount of space Brandes devoted to such figures as Ellénore, Corinne, and Delphine. In discussing Mme de Staël's novels, he argued for the right of the personality of the woman to develop free from social pressure. Nowhere is the polarity between the individual and society so accentuated as in his analysis of these two novels, in which, by the way, he made incessant digressions. Brandes wanted his audience to realize that much of what was taken for granted in Western society was only relatively valid. He took the word *home* as an example. The Northern European in his hard climate thinks of his home in terms of warmth, coziness, and shelter while the word has totally different connotations for the Southern European. Brandes continued:

The word "domestic" comes to designate the woman's greatest virtue and duty, and this race would least of all permit itself to say that all of its greatest ideals, the home, kindness, domesticity, the family, stem from only one cruelly simple, cruelly low climatical necessity—the need for artificial warmth. [7]

It is hardly so simple as Brandes put it, but such statements to a great extent helped to make *Main Currents* dynamite in the literary debate. Brandes came to be regarded as a social rebel who wanted to destroy the very nuclear center of society—the family.

Mme de Staël's *Corinne*, which was set in Italy, gave Brandes the opportunity to make use of his impressions from his recent visit there. He did this several times in the book. He had also visited Switzerland and could describe the countryside in which *La nouvelle Héloïse* was set. This technique of sketching the environment in which the fictive action took place was one Brandes learned from the literary traveler Taine. He also took up his new, realistic view of antiquity in relation to *Corinne*, and compared it to those of Winckelmann, Goethe, and Racine. Here, too, are sections that were offensive to his contemporaries, such as his statement that the classic sculptor Thorvaldsen's relief *Natten (Night)* was an example of the watered-down, falsified, idealized antiquity. He wrote:

Thorvaldsen's *Night* is only night when one sleeps; it ought to have been called Sleep, not Night. Nighttime calm, not Night. For night as the Greeks saw it, night when people loved, night when people murdered, night which hid all lusts and crimes under his cloak, this night it is not. It is a mild summer night in the country. [8]

Brandes became the interpreter of naturalism's view of antiquity. His criticism of the accepted view of antiquity of his time was an expression of his attempt to arrive at a new view of reality behind clichés, conventions, and prejudices. It is difficult for a modern reader of *Main Currents* to understand how his writing could have been so revolutionary for his contemporaries. This is because many of his reevaluations are now generally accepted. Every epoch has its own gods. When they finally fall it is not without a crash.

II   The Romantic School in Germany

It is hard to overemphasize the influence, both positive and negative, that the German Romantic period had on the cultural life of Europe. Form-wise it meant a change from the aesthetic dogmatism of French classicism, which had reverberations up to the modernism of our times. But it also meant a break with the rationalism of the Age of Enlightenment and a developing political liberalism. It was primarily from this latter point of view that Brandes surveyed the German Romantic period when he began the second part of *Main Currents: Den romantiske Skole i Tydskland (Romantic School in Germany*, 1873). Both Denmark and Sweden were strongly influenced by the German romantics. Writers such as Oehlenschläger, Grundtvig, Kierkegaard, Hans Christian Andersen, and Heiberg were all in deep debt to the Germans, and one could even say that Denmark and, to some extent, Sweden were cultural provinces of Germany. And Brandes' own youth bore the mark of the German romanticism he would later denounce. He had also studied Shakespeare and Calderón, the initiators of the German Romantic period. His contact with the more realistic French romanticism had a liberating influence. Heinrich Heine, Brandes' favorite author, directed hard criticism toward the romantics in *Die romantische Schule (The Romantic School)*, which appeared in the form of lectures while he was in exile. Arnold Ruge came with another critical confrontation with romanticism in *Hallische Jahrbücher (The Halle Year Book)*. But Brandes also based his work on more balanced appraisers such as Hettner, Haym, and Julian Schmidt. Brandes' book is in parts very unself-reliant. One of Brandes' German critics, a Dr. Puls, has shown Brandes' dependency on Haym's classic work. In light of the fact that Brandes fairly openly plagiarized Haym, Puls allowed himself to be witty: "When one goes from Haym to Brandes, one feels at once so 'home-ish,' not to say "Haym-ish'—everything is so well-known, so familiar, and this feeling increases the more one gets into Brandes' book."[9]

Brandes had a suggestible nature and easily let himself be influenced by others. He was a typical eclectic. In spite of the fact that he took formulations and viewpoints to a great extent from earlier researchers in romanticism, his work nevertheless bore his personal stamp. As in the first part of *Main Currents,* Brandes was mainly concerned with characterizing the Romantic period by concentrating on a number of literary figures or types. They were primarily taken from the following works:

1. Tieck, *William Lovell*
2. Jean Paul, *Titan*
3. Wackenroder, *Herzensergiessungen eines kunstliebenden Klosterbruders*
4. Schleiermacher, *Briefe über Lucinde*
5. Tieck, *Franz Sternbalds Wanderungen* and *Der gestiefelte Kater*
6. Novalis, *Hymnen an die Nacht* and *Heinrich von Ofterdingen*
7. Eichendorff, *Aus dem Leben eines Taugenichts*
8. Fouqué, *Undine* and *Der Zauberring*
9. Tieck, *Leben und Tod der heiligen Genoveva*
10. Kleist, *Das Käthchen von Heilbronn, Der Prinz von Homburg, Penthesilea,* and *Amphitryon*
11. Werner, *Die Söhne des Tals* and *Die Weihe der Unkraft*

Naturally one could come with many reservations about the choices included on the list, but Brandes would answer that he was interested in describing the main currents in European literature. As is clear from the outline above, the work was not organized according to author but rather according to how the authors fit in under the different aspects Brandes attributed to the German Romantic period, namely; (1) a poetic aspect, (2) a social aspect, (3) a religious aspect, and (4) a political aspect.[10] None of these aspects of romanticism left Brandes satisfied. Poetically the movement ended up in "hysterical worship and blue mist," he said.[11] Socially one was limited to only one aspect of private life—the relation between the sexes. Religiously one noted none of the revolutionary tactics used in the renewal of form. And finally, politically, it was romanticism that lay behind the reaction at the Vienna Congress after the fall of Napoleon. In the end, the romantic poets personified much of what Brandes had devoted his life to fighting: escapism in literature and art, religious obfuscation, and reactionary politics. Here he really

seemed to have something that fit in the scheme he had planned for
his work.

Since Brandes hated the ideological foundation of romanticism,
the people who believed in these ideas also became suspect. Here,
of course, he had good teachers in Heine and Ruge. The romantic
school consisted of a group of, for all practical purposes, sick individuals:

A consumptive Herrnhuter with hectic sensuality and hectic longings for
the supernatural—Novalis. An ironic melancholic with sickly hallucinations
and sickly catholic tendencies. I mean Tieck. A poetically impotent genius
with the genius's need to rebel and the fainthearted's need to subordinate
himself to an external language of power—Friedrich Schlegel. A weak visionary with half-crazy opium fantasies like Hoffmann. A fussy mystic like
Werner and a genial suicide like Kleist.[12]

But such youthful outbursts were not typical of the book as a whole.
The idea of throwing light upon the Romantic period via the social,
religious, poetic, and political aspects was not without originality
and gave Brandes many opportunities to carry out his critical appraisal in the way he had planned and in the way that was so necessary. He took up the "negative" and "positive" preparation for
the Romantic period in two introductory chapters. According to
Brandes, the negative element in the early stages of romanticism
was its subjectivism, which he traced back to Goethe. The romantics
were interested in private life, the subjective ego, and for Brandes
there was something basically wrong with this since it prevented the
authors from describing the social and political situations and led to
the avoidance and falsification of reality. He chose Tieck's novel
William Lovell as a typical example of this subjectivistic line.

Brandes summed up the positive elements of the preparatory
stage of romanticism with the words "Freigeisterei der Leiden-
schaft" ("the passion of freethinking"). He painted a penetrating
portrait of Goethe's circle in Weimar and of the erotic freedom
they indulged in. But he could only conclude that they did not take
the social consequences of their praxis. Such was not the case with
Mme de Staël, who visited Weimar for a time. The German romantics paled in comparison to the socially and politically active Mme de
Staël:

For them everything is *personal*, for her everything is already *social*. She
has spoken publically, she is fighting for great social reforms. These German

women from the humanistic period are, even when most liberal, too much inclined toward the idyllic. *For her it is a question of altering life politically: for them it is a question of making life poetic.*[13]

For Brandes, the best attempt of the romantics to move in a social direction was the young Friedrich Schlegel's erotic autobiography, *Lucinde*. It was, however, only an attempt. Marital problems were debated, but the novel was nevertheless colored by romantic subjectivism. It could have had a revolutionary force, but Schlegel did not understand that he had to subordinate himself to a greater idea, namely, that of freedom and progress. *Lucinde* thus led to no practical results socially whatsoever. Brandes did, however, devote a good deal of space to it in his presentation, and he followed it up by describing what he termed the "reality corresponding to Lucinde." This method, inspired by Taine, gave him the opportunity to penetrate the problem of the relation between the sexes more deeply than a discussion of Schlegel's novel itself allowed. He sketched a pair of very favorable portraits of the two emancipated women who lay behind Lucinde: Dorothea Veit and Caroline Schlegel. In Brandes' eyes they were several steps above the male members of the romantic group. He attributed a real revolutionary political passion to Caroline Schlegel.

The extensive discussion of *Lucinde* was completed by an analysis of Schleiermacher's *Briefe über Lucinde (Letters about Lucinde)*, which Brandes considered important because it was, as he put it, "aimed at prudishness." He quoted parts of Schleiermacher's letters that could be interpreted as advocating free love. And the book gave him the opportunity to introduce a less ambiguous apostle for free love—George Sand. Her novel *Jacques* supplied him with a number of critical statements against marriage, such as: "Marriage is now and will always be for me one of the most odious institutions."[14] He also took advantage of the opportunity to go to Shelley's "Notes on Queen Mab" to find still more arguments for a more human or perhaps idealistic view of love than the marriage of convenience of the nineteenth century could supply. One of the quotes from Shelley:

Love withers under constraint: its very essence is liberty: it is compatible neither with obedience, jealousy, nor fear: it is there most pure, perfect, and unlimited, where its votaries live in confidence, equality, and unreserve.[15]

And another quotation reads like this:

Prostitution is the legitimate offspring of marriage and its accompanying errors. Women, for no other crime than having followed the dictates of a natural appetite, are driven with fury from the comforts and sympathies of society.

Another of the quotes from Shelley said that no one has been able to find a system more threatening to human happiness than marriage. Here, of course, Brandes hid behind George Sand and Shelley. And it can hardly be more clear that what Brandes was primarily interested in was the content or idea of the literary work. He wanted light thrown on the problem from all angles. Literature gave him the arguments he needed in his struggle for a change of the norms, customs, and moral ideas on which society was built. He hated marriage and the Victorian double standard of morality and did not hesitate to attack the problem. He struggled for the social, political, and sexual liberation of women. It was a central problem for him. In the same way Brandes' book on German romanticism supplied the writers of the modern breakthrough with material for their debate on the place of women inside and outside marriage. Ibsen had not yet written A Doll's House. Strindberg, Jaeger, and Pontoppidan had not yet made their contributions. The large group of now half-forgotten women writers who took up these problems during the 1880s and 1890s had not yet appeared on the scene. Many of them, such as Victoria Benedictsson and Ann Charlotte Leffler, were attracted to Brandes.

The social attempts of the romantics were thus not accepted, but what about the poetic aspect? Their attempts to bring language and music together were ridiculed, partly influenced by A. Ruge.[16] The sonnets, terza rimas, and ottava rimas badly hid the formlessness of the content.[17] Their tendency toward symbolism and allegory did not fit into Brandes' aesthetics of realism: "The thought returns again and again, that all true art should be allegoric—that is, with neither blood nor backbone."[18] Nor did he fall for the romantics' descriptions of nature, with moonlit countrysides the most common ingredient. Their understanding of the personality can be illustrated with the help of Hoffmann's Die Elixiere des Teufels (The Devil's Elixirs). Brandes felt that the romantics had a certain tendency to divide personalities into different "egos." He juxtaposed his own modern view, supported by Taine and Mill, of the personality as a product of idea associations.

Brandes chose Novalis as an example of the romantic position in religious and political questions. Novalis was a clerk in a mining company and, inspired by Ruge, Brandes took his readers on an underground mine trip through the German "Gemüt" *(mind)*. The romantics' love of the dark and of night, seen most clearly in Novalis' *Hymnen an die Nacht, (Hymns to the Night)* Brandes considered symptomatic. He himself worshiped light, and was the heir of the Age of Enlightenment more than any other epoch. This worship of night was thus deeply antipathetic to him: "Hatred of daytime and daylight is common to all the romantics."[19] After taking his readers with him into this unhealthy and dark world, a suitable breeding ground for religious mysticism and a sickly deathcult, he called out to them:

Now that I have told you about pleasure, glory, religion, night and death, about all the darkness which could throw a shadow on the brightest sunshine, don't you feel the way I do, that something inside of you cries: Air! Light! Yes, isn't it smothering?[20]

He let this passage run on into a long comparison between Novalis and Shelley in which the religious and political obfuscation of the former is contrasted to the worship of light and the open mind of the latter.

Brandes' analysis of the German romantics was thus very critical on every point. But his book still makes for good and engaging reading because Brandes, as a literary historian, took the authors' ideas seriously. He not only treated the works as aesthetic documents but also analyzed and examined the extent to which their inherent philosophy was reasonable and valid. This way of writing the history of literature has not been practiced nearly enough. It is difficult to deny, of course, that Brandes was a bit one-sided in his judgments and that he made a mistake in not correctly appreciating the contribution of the German romantics in the area of form and aesthetics. He set up the English and French romantics against the Germans in social and political questions and as a result, this part of *Main Currents* was not as well received by the German critics as the rest of the work. They felt wounded by the negative attitude toward the German romantics throughout the book. Alexander Jung reviewed the German translation of *Main Currents* and wrote as follows about the section on the Romantic period: "Is it not true, Herr Brandes, that you want to put that 'Taugenichts' [good-for-nothing] and the rest of the romantic school as well, under supervision?"[21]

When Brandes devalued the German romantic movement it was also because he wanted to aim a blow at its Scandinavian followers. And the powerful romantic movement still had a great influence on cultural life. This was true not only of second-class authors—neither Ibsen nor Bjørnson nor Strindberg had, in 1873, as yet quite left the late romantic period. It was not until the middle of the 1870s that they moved away from the historical subjects favored by the romantics and toward contemporary problems in the spirit of Brandes.

III   Revolution and Reaction in Nineteenth-Century French Literature

The third part of *Main Currents, Reaktionen i Frankrig (The Reaction in France,* 1874), was, as Brandes himself said in his autobiography, his most polemic work.[22] He also admitted that he wrote it with reference to his own times. During these first years of the 1870s he was strongly influenced by socialism as formulated in the writings of Lassalle. In this part of the book, the literary material gave way to the social, political, and religious. The literary works discussed received only surface treatment. It was only in the latter part of the volume that Brandes got into real literature: Chateaubriand's *Les Martyrs,* Lamartine's *Meditations,* and the earlier works of Hugo and Vigny. Mme de Krüdener and her now forgotten novel *Valérie,* which can hardly be said to belong to French literature, received a thorough presentation.

The composition of the book was, however, well planned and built up around what Brandes called the growth and dissolution of the principle of authority. According to Brandes, worldly and religious authority were crushed in the French Revolution of 1789, and when the monarchy was abolished, the power of the Catholic Church was crushed and religious freedom was introduced. Naturally, Brandes was sympathetic to these developments during the time of the revolution. In his struggle at home, the religious establishment was one of his main opponents. Robespierre was described as a sympathetic figure. Brandes also touched upon the revolutionary's view of property and noted that the Girondists regarded the right to property as something obvious, "an absolute and individual right," while it was relative and social for the Jacobians.[23] Robespierre's introduction of the cult of the highest power was seen as something naïvely moving, but at the same time impressive. It was a "naïve but honest expression of the religiosity of the eighteenth century."[24] The thaw that the revolution represented in the question of religious freedom came to an abrupt end with Napoleon's concordat with the pope in 1801. The Catholic Church was then reestablished, though under the strong protests of, among others, Napoleon's generals. The papal delegate had to be smuggled into Paris under cover of night for fear of attack from the masses.[25] Brandes could not refrain from turning this episode into an elegant polemic. When religion was reinstated it was, according to Brandes, in order to reinforce law and order. He claimed that Napoleon, who himself was religiously indifferent, spoke of "my prefects, my police, and my priests" all in the same breath.[26] The priests became police, only in different uniforms. Nor did Brandes miss the chance to point out that Chateaubriand's song of praise to the Christian religion, *Le Génie du Christianisme (The Genius of Christianity)*, just happened to be published at the same time that the concordat was signed. Napoleon saw to it that it was reviewed the same day that the Te Deum was sung over the religious restoration.

The restoration of ideas had, however, begun even earlier with Bonald's *Théorie du Pouvoir (The Theory of Power)* (1796), supplemented with *La Législation Primitive (Primitive Legislation)* (1802). Bonald was a true advocate of the principle of authority and his writings were treasure chests for Brandes when it was a question of finding the theoretic motivations for the authoritarian and patriarchal society. Bonald built a bulwark around marriage and the family. For him the family was the nucleus of society, and he was therefore against the liberal divorce laws passed during the revolution. Bonald argued for a pure patriarchal society. The man represented *le pouvoir*, power, and the woman, *le devoir*, duty. Naturally, children were serfs in this "mini-society." The goal of marriage was not individual happiness but the stability and continuity of society.

This was a totally unacceptable viewpoint for Brandes, the individualist. He wrote in opposition:

The principle of freedom in its different forms such as Liberalism and Socialism must be placed above the principle of authority in this area as in all others. If we forget for a moment the socialistic theories as they are put

by the Saint Simonists, then the liberal theory with its principle of individualism as it has been developed by the French and English and especially the American philosophers, is above the principle of authority. It is
this principle which is the basis for the above-mentioned project. The basic
idea is that it is not the family, as is generally accepted, but the individual
who is the bearer of society and that the individual is sovereign.[27]

Thus Brandes proclaimed the sovereignty of the individual. He referred to such American and English authorities as Samuel Warren,
Stephen Pearl Andrews, and John Stuart Mill, and clearly stood on
their side. Brandes was a fairly typical example of radical liberalism
of the nineteenth century. No sensible representative of modern
liberalism would dare to claim the sovereignty of the individual. But
these claims must be seen in the light of the patriarchal and authoritarian society that appeared, or rather reappeared, after the
brief period of the French Revolution. The patriarchal structure in
most of the countries of Western Europe, like a petrified shell,
remained untouched by the French Revolution. The psychological
consequences of the patriarchal family structure can still be felt in
our day and are the basis for Wilhelm Reich's theories, among
others.

In the last parts of the volume Brandes discussed Lamartine's,
Hugo's, and de Vigny's early poetry. Hugo was a man of the future
since he in time would drive through an aesthetic rebellion against
classicism. He is therefore treated in the chapter entitled "The
Dissolution of the Formal Principle of Authority." Brandes was a
great admirer of Hugo, at least after the latter emerged from his
religious and royalist period. The final chapter has the somewhat
optimistic title "The True Dissolution of the Principle of Authority,"
and it primarily traced Lamennais's path from a loyal and believing
son of the church to a rebel against papal authority in *Les Paroles
d'un Croyant (Words of a Believer)*. At the same time Brandes
moved forward historically to 1830, the year of the July revolution.
He saw the writing on the wall predicting changes in the reactionary
climate that characterized the Holy Alliance. One of these was
Byron's heroic death in Greece in 1824.

IV   Naturalism in England

When he began the fourth volume of his great work, Brandes was
forced to move on to a relatively new area. He had previously been

fairly well acquainted with only Byron and Scott among the English romantics. His research was thus demanding and took place in Berlin and Munich. He gave his first lectures on Byron in the spring of 1874, and the book was completed in April of the following year.[28] It may surprise the contemporary reader that Brandes chose to describe the English romantics as naturalists. The term *naturalist* became a key concept, which he applied to the whole group. The section on the Lake School was called "Naturalism Is Summoned"; Scott's works were characterized as "historic and ethnographic naturalism"; Shelley was under the label "radical naturalism"; and the whole presentation culminated with an apotheosis of Byron entitled "The Culmination of Naturalism." One may wonder how Brandes could include such totally different temperaments as Wordsworth, Coleridge, Scott, Shelley, and Byron in the concept of naturalism. The idea of using the word *naturalism* as a literary concept may have come from the German romantic scholar Haym, who put it this way in *Die romantische schule:* "We follow Tieck through the later stages of his development from his first naturalistic phase to his reflective and satiric phase and then to the fantastic creations."[29]

Zola's interpretation of the concept of naturalism had not as yet been generally accepted when Brandes wrote *Naturalism in England.* But both Zola and Brandes had already been confronted with a view that was fundamental for the conception of the book on true naturalism, namely, Taine's scientifically inspired literary criticism. Taine introduced his history of English literature by describing the countryside, the geological and topographical situation, and then proceeded to the political and social environment. Brandes took a similar approach in the introductory part of *Naturalism in England.* He began by speaking of "common traits in national character"— Taine's concept of race—and wished to consider what he called the Englishman's partiality for the worship, study, and adoration of nature as a racial characteristic. This predilection, he said, was especially noticeable in Wordsworth and Scott. This nature worship is also expressed in love of animals, and in a taste for sports and the outdoor life, which Brandes seemed to find in Byron and Scott. He claimed that Byron, as a boy in Newstead, was surrounded by a whole menagerie of animals.

Taine's concept of environment had been adapted from biology and geography, but it also included social relations. Brandes devoted a special chapter to the political and social framework of En-

glish romanticism, and this part was built around a critical portrait of
the prince regent, later George IV, who embodied the reactionary
politics then in control. This extravagant regent, who, with his love
of elegant clothes, set the style for the rest of Europe, was set in
contrast to the social misery among the masses: "While the weavers
in Glasgow and Lancashire cried to the heavens in hunger, he gave
great feasts with incredible pomp and received the exiled Bourbon
like Louis XVIII."[30]

Brandes was one of the first to place literature in its social and
political context. Writers were not seen only as "spiritual" beings.
Their political allegiance was noted, but was not always decisive for
the way in which they were evaluated. Wordsworth, Coleridge,
Southey, and Scott were conservative, but the latter was reactionary
in such a way that he was almost appealing to Brandes. Unlike
Southey and Wordsworth, Scott refused to sell his independence in
order to become the court poet. Brandes' writings are full of definite
sympathies and antipathies. He was clearly negative to Wordsworth
and especially Southey, but this did not prevent him from giving full
credit to Wordsworth's nature poetry. This was actually not so
strange, since here we are dealing with a type of democratic realism
that made Brandes think of Runeberg and his description of the poor
peasants in Saarijärvi. But Brandes' knowledge of English was
clearly not good enough to enable him to appreciate Wordsworth's
poetic diction. He reacted to what he called the formlessness in
Wordsworth's poetry and against his attempts at an everyday
language. He contrasted Wordsworth's "loose" form with Gautier's
famous sonnet "L'art." In ordinary company, conversation can move
around flexibly, he claimed, but when it is a question of poetry, the
form can never be too precise. So in 1875 Brandes, politically the
man of the modern breakthrough, was aesthetically still at the art-
for-the-sake-of-art stage.

While studying Taine, Brandes had been impressed by his criticism of Scott and the historical novel, a genre that had dominated
the nineteenth century. According to Taine, all of Walter Scott's
descriptions of the past were wrong. The clothes and countryside
and all the externals were correct, but the action, dialogue, and
feelings, and everything else, were refined and altered to suit a
modern public.[31] Brandes praised Scott for his precision in portraying the environment and the countryside. He claimed that Scott
studied the landscape as a painter would and again and again he

emphasized, in the spirit of Taine, that Scott was more than anything else interesting as a representative of his race and of Scottish nationalism. According to Brandes, Scott was ill-equipped to describe modern man as an individual, but he could capture the uniqueness of the clan, the people, the race. This illustrated how imprisoned Brandes himself was in the concept of race. In Brandes' eyes, Scott had some advantages as a character painter, but his novels, unlike Goethe's and Byron's, were not products of different stages of growth and development. In addition, they were often badly composed with numerous repetitions.

Keats, who was not one of the politically involved poets, was nonetheless treated with understanding. Brandes always knew when he met a great artist. Moore was slightly involved in the Irish liberation movement, and Brandes used this as an opportunity to write a historic exposition of the island. He found a true story that could be effectively told in the fate of Moore's boyhood friend Robert Emmet. Here, reality offered more exciting material than a novel.

The question has been raised as to whether Brandes knew enough English to really appreciate Shelley's poetry.[32] He seems to have had some difficulties in understanding the sound patterns of the words. His prose translations of Shelley's poems into Danish were hardly geared to giving the reader an idea of his musical verse. It is, however, possible that Brandes' aesthetic sensitivity was underestimated, in spite of language difficulties. His acquaintance with Shelley's poetry went back to the 1860s, and from his letters to his future wife, Henriette Strodtmann, it is clear that he felt a vibrant contact with Shelley's poems.[33] But even as late as 1873 it was obvious that he was not sure how to evaluate Byron's poetry in relation to Shelley's. The English author and critic Gosse found it necessary to write to him in 1874: "You know, do you not, that it is not Byron, but Shelley, who is the greatest—facile princeps—among our modern poets?"[34] Gosse had met Brandes on a trip to Denmark in 1874 and recited Shelley's poetry for him. Much in both Shelley's poetry and personality harmonized with Brandes' own aesthetic and ideological program. Shelley declared himself an atheist as a very young man, and linked to this was his revolutionary pathos for freedom, which was the central part of the picture Brandes painted of him. Concerning "The Skylark," Brandes wrote: "It creates the transition to a long line of freedom songs, the large group in which Shelley's genius is the herald of the coming revolutions. His song of freedom is one long battle cry clad in changing melodies."[35] Brandes had almost no reservations about the vagueness and abstractness that characterized so much of Shelley's work; he was no poet for the pronounced realist. Brandes' praise of *The Cenci* led to the play's being published in Danish. He himself wrote an introduction to this edition. In 1883, however, he admitted in a letter to the German poet Fitger that the drama was not very successful and that his criticism of it in *Naturalism in England* was altogether too favorable.[36]

But Brandes saw the radical rebel in Shelley, and that is why his works were described as "radical naturalism." Of the 525 pages in the original version of *Naturalism in England*, 170 dealt with Byron, who received the gigantic task of revolting against the authoritarian principle described in part three. The Hegelian principle of composition that lay behind *Main Currents* was clearly visible here. Brandes saw the authors as toys in the great dialectical game that Hegel sketched in his philosophy. To Brandes, this dialectical game was a developmental stage in a progressive direction in world history, and the writer was to be an active soldier in the struggle. This applied to Byron. Few poets had participated in world events as Byron had. It soon became clear to critics of *Main Currents* that Brandes had systematically built up a superhuman image of Byron. The first three parts of *Main Currents* were the base of the pedestal on which he placed the Byronic giant.

Brandes was influenced by the glorification of Byron that took place during the early part of the 1800s. Byron became an important source of inspiration for politicians and writers all over Europe. His influence on Slavic romanticism can hardly be overestimated, a thing that Brandes also noted when he directed his interest toward the east: Pushkin, Lermontov, Mickiewicz, and Krasinski had all been profoundly impressed by Byron. This was also true of Musset and Heine, who were the young Brandes' favorite authors. He was raised on the literature Byronism left in its wake, and by the 1860s he had already read most of Byron's poetic tales.[37]

The German historian Gervinus seems to have been the one who showed the way for Brandes when he let Byron's heoric death in Missolongi in 1824 be a turning point in European history.[38] Brandes' tendency to hero-worship became clear in his confrontation with Byron. The last pages of *The Reaction in France* give a good idea of the role he ascribed to the English poet:

When Napoleon died, greatness fell, the true hero of an era disappeared from the earth. Human admiration was empty, like a pedestal which has lost its statue. Lord Byron filled the empty space once again with the fantastic greatness of his heroes. Napoleon had replaced Werther, René, and Faust; Byron's desperate Promethean hero replaced Napoleon."[39]

It was with this attitude that Brandes went to work on his book, to give Byron his just place in world literature. Taine, the teacher of his youth, had begun to weed out some of the poetic tales that are now largely unreadable for us. Taine pointed out the false, the unreal, and the gimmicky in such works as *The Bride of Abydos, The Giaour, The Corsair, Lara, Parisina, The Siege of Corinth, Mazeppa,* and *The Prisoner of Chillon,* but he still could not hide a certain admiration for Byron's theatrical heroes: "Who could forget the death of Lara after reading it?"[40] Brandes skimmed over these works without comment in his chapter on Byron and instead concentrated on *Childe Harold, Manfred, Cain,* and *Don Juan,* a sample that has held its own well.

Byron was a fairly typical representative of romanticism in his earlier poems, which were populated with romanesque heroes and stereotyped beautiful women. He successively moved toward the satiric realism of Don Juan with its almost antiromantic bitter tone. Brandes placed *Don Juan* and *Cain* at the top of Byron's works. In his view, the author should not accept society as something static and once and for all given, but should forcefully attack prejudiced and out-of-date institutions. It was the rebel in Byron to which he was attracted. He was blind to Byron's naïve, flirtatious, *poseur* style. The important thing for him was that when the others kept silent, Byron dared to be ironic, to ridicule and challenge as in the many digressions of *Don Juan*. This poem was "the culmination of naturalism" for Brandes because here Byron openly took his position as a politically radical writer: "It is then Byron who initiates the radical opposition in Europe in the middle of the 1820s which broke with the political Romanticism and the Holy Alliance which was nothing more than European political hypocrisy systematized."[41] Byron thus became a kind of initiator of European radicalism and as such was admired for his civil courage by the forerunners of the real

naturalism with whose works his poetry had little in common. But
Brandes also felt a kindred spirit to the aristocratic Byron when he
too was accused of amorality and blasphemy in his struggle with the
ruling liberal national intelligentsia.

V   Romantic School in France

The first parts of *Main Currents* came out one by one with only a
year between publications (1872–1875). Part five, *Den romantiske
skole i Frankrig (Romantic School in France)*, was not published
until 1882, and the last volume, *Det unge Tyskland (Young Germany)*, not until 1890. They will, however, be discussed here in
order to give a complete picture of the work.

The first parts stirred up a good deal of attention all over Scandinavia and were also translated into German. But Brandes directed
his attention to other works as well. He published biographies of
Søren Kierkegaard (1877), Esaias Tegnér (1878), Benjamin Disraeli
(1878), and Ferdinand Lassalle (1881). Since he now devoted all of
his time to writing and had no employment that gave him a depend-
able income, Brandes was forced to support himself by his lectures
and his books. Thus the fifth volume of *Main Currents* came into
being as a result of lectures delivered in Copenhagen and Berlin on
a group of authors who were the focus of his interest at the time:
Hugo, Balzac, Musset, George Sand, Stendhal, and Sainte-Beuve,
to mention the most important ones. His lectures were also published in part in German publications such as *Deutsche Monatshefte*
and *Deutsche Rundschau*. Thus when the book was published as a
whole in 1882, it had already had a relatively wide distribution,
and Brandes had developed from a local Danish talent into a
European critic to be reckoned with. In 1879 he revisited Paris to
do some research for his book.

The Romantic School in France begins with a presentation of the
political background of the period between 1824 and 1848. The
Restoration and the July monarchy are described critically. Thus
even in this part of *Main Currents*, social and political characteristics
are accentuated. Brandes began by presenting what he considered
to be the basic conditions for French romanticism: a newly
awakened interest in Shakespeare, which influenced the historical
drama, and Walter Scott's novels, which also had offshoots in
France. In addition he mentioned the rediscovery of the poet

Chénier, executed during the French Revolution. But Brandes was very careful to distinguish between French and German romanticism. He wondered whether French romanticism was not just naturalism in disguise.[42] What Hugo demanded in his manifesto was simple nature, truthful descriptions, local color. In spite of the fact that Brandes was at this time familiar with French naturalism as Zola interpreted it, he used the term very generally, and gave it an almost Rousseau-like meaning: a unity with nature, a worship of nature and the natural. George Sand, he said, was the daughter of Rousseau, and Stendhal and Mérimée were "half brutal, half elegant nature worshipers." Nonetheless Brandes saw the French romantics largely through the eyes of a naturalist.

At the end of the 1870's, Zola had begun a reappraisal of the romantics, especially Hugo. Brandes was soon familiar with it.[43] Zola emphasized, among other things, Hugo's great dependence upon the classic rhetorical technique. Brandes wrote: "French Romanticism is, in spite of the many elements it has in common with Romanticism elsewhere in Europe, in many ways a classic phenomenon, a product of French classical rhetoric."[44]

Brandes devoted a good deal of space to the poetry of Victor Hugo, which he had read with avid interest since his youth. Brandes' writings were full of quotations from Hugo, and he was especially fond of the first poem in part three of *La Légende des Siècles (The Legend of the Centuries):* "Le Satyre." He even attempted to translate it. Hugo portrayed Pan as a challenger in this poem, a Promethean figure who embodied much of what Brandes stood for. His appreciation of the collection of poems *Feuilles d'automne (Autumn Leaves)* was also noteworthy. According to Brandes, Hugo staked out a new area in poetry with this collection. It is clear that Hugo's poems about his home life were regarded as a conquest for realism. The collection entitled *Les Orientales (The Orientals)* also received a good deal of space in the portrait of Hugo. Hugo's novels were not, however, included. The reason for this was, naturally, that two of the most famous novels. *Les Misérables*(1862) and *Les Travailleurs de la Mer (The Toilers of the Sea)* (1866), were not written in the period Brandes dealt with in his book (1824–1848).

Brandes discovered Musset at an early age, a discovery that fit in well with his worship of Heine. He translated one of Musset's most famous plays, *Il faut qu'une porte soit ouverte ou fermée (A Door*

Must Be either Open or Shut). It is possible that his first enthusiasm had paled somewhat by the time he wrote his chapter on Musset in *The Romantic School in France.* Taine had written a study on Musset that was filled with admiration and that culminated with the cry: "He, at least, has never lied." Brandes could no longer follow his teacher in his evaluation of Musset. A good deal of this section was devoted to a comparison between Musset and George Sand. It was a rhetorical show that certainly must have had an effect in the lecture hall. Once again Brandes made use of the comparative technique he had learned from Sainte-Beuve. In general, he willingly compared different authors to one another in *The Romantic School in France.* Hugo was compared to Musset, Musset to George Sand, Stendhal to Mérimée, Mérimée to Gautier. In spite of dutiful praise of Musset's short stories and plays, his portrayal was on the whole unfavorable. He felt that Musset in contrast to Goethe lacked the ability to develop himself. When he died in 1857, he had survived his work by many years. Musset was too weak, too subjective, and too one-sided in his interest in the erotic area for Brandes' taste at this time.

He felt closer to George Sand. One of his interpreters has said that after Hegel and Taine, there was no one who influenced Brandes more.[45] The right of passion, free love, the impossibility of marriage, all were discussed in George Sand's novels, most of which he had read before he presented his "breakthrough" program in 1871, in which the French authoress held a prominent position. His claim that literature should debate the status of women and marriage as an institution was made tangible by George Sand. What lay behind her novels was a questioning of society, of male society, and this became clear in Brandes' analysis of her novels. Brandes based his presentation on a fairly limited sample of her enormous production: *Indiana, Lélia, Jacques, Lucretia Floriani,* and the short story "La Marquise," which he called a masterpiece. Before he wrote his chapter on George Sand he read Zola's critical essay on her in *Documents Littéraires.* Zola cited what were said to be her last words: "J'ai trop bu la vie" ("I have drunk too much of life"), and went on to say that the statement was not reflected in her writing. He felt that she had ended up by observing life from the sidelines and by sacrificing too much to imagination. In other words, she lacked a "sense of reality," which Zola considered to be the most important characteristic of an author. He reacted against the falseness in her descriptions of people and environments and against her declamatory style.

Zola's criticism probably made Brandes more reserved in his appraisal than he would have been in 1871. He wrote:

These books are now almost totally uninteresting artistically: characterization is weak in its abstract idealism, the action is improbable, as in *Indiana*, or unreal, as in *Lélia* and *Jacques*. The presentation is, in spite of the harmony of style, often declamatory and overwrought . . .[46]

In spite of this, Brandes wished to attach a value to these novels as human documents, since "a plaintive song and a battle cry" could be heard from them. At the end of his essay Zola implied that the people who accused the naturalists of immorality could just as well have accused George Sand of the same thing. Her novels painted a twisted picture of reality. The women who read her novels might get the idea of saying they were just as misunderstood as her heroines. In the naturalistic novels, however, there was no place left for ephemerous dreams in their sober descriptions of reality.[47] Brandes countered Zola's attack. He said he was not satisfied with a record of the most common moral patterns of behavior given by the naturalists, especially Zola. He wanted writers to point the way toward a new morality, he wanted them to be the bearers of a vision of another, better society. Zola was not at all ethically radical. His concept of vice was the commonly accepted one, and he even tended to moralize. But Brandes dreamed of a society in which love between two people would be a personal matter, and it was here that he felt a kinship with George Sand.

Brunetière painted a somewhat more generous picture of George Sand and her influence on nineteenth-century realism and naturalism in his book *Le Roman Naturaliste (The Naturalistic Novel)*. Among other things he said: "Isn't it true that *Valentine*'s and *Jacques*'s appearance on the scene marked the introduction of social questions in literature?"[48] These words were indubitably true for Brandes, and that is why his portrait of George Sand is so important. He judged her work more from the point of view of social reform than from aesthetic considerations.

No author in *The Romantic School in France* was so well suited as a model and source of inspiration for the modern Scandinavian writers as Balzac. He, like George Sand, was introduced in the first part of *Main Currents*. Brandes had at an early age read Taine's and Sainte-Beuve's essays on Balzac. Later he also read Zola's study on him. Of the romantics, it was primarily Balzac and then Stendhal

with whom the naturalists allied themselves. What Brandes mainly
learned from Balzac was that the writer's task was to describe his
country and his times.[49] He even made it a golden rule that
whichever country and whatever period the writer chose to describe, he could only succeed in rendering his own times and his
own country. Here and now was the *signum* of realism, and it was a
central theme in Brandes' poetics. Balzac was too modern in
Brandes' view to develop the historical novel in the spirit of Walter
Scott, and thus was placed in a class of his own among the French
romantics: he alone dealt with the problems of his times, whereas
the others fled to other countries and other periods. Whereas the
historical novel was not very useful to those like Brandes who
wanted literature to be a weapon for challenging the established
society and its values and institutions, the sociological composition
of Balzac's *La Comédie Humaine* was eminently suited to the purpose. Brandes, like Taine, spoke of Balzac's similarity to a scientist:
"In comparison with scientists, he saw himself as a doctor of social
science."[50] Brandes emphasized Balzac's objectivity and honesty,
the fact that the latter never judged or moralized, that he never
refused to tell the truth because of disgust or enthusiasm, no matter
how uncomfortable it was. Brandes was thus attracted by Balzac's
realistic or naturalistic traits under the influence of Zola's and
Taine's analyses. But at the same time he was not blind to the fact
that the rich flow of impressions the reader was confronted with in
Balzac's novels could be tiring. He also noted the split in Balzac's
spiritual physiognomy that expressed itself in "Mysticism in Science
as in Religion" and in Balzac's leaning toward Catholicism, all of
which were strange to Brandes, the positivist.

Stendhal represented a somewhat different line in French romanticism. When he died in 1842, the same year Brandes was born, he
was not very well known to the reading public. The first studies on
him by Colomb, Bussière, Mérimée, and Sainte-Beuve show little
understanding for the uniqueness of his literary works. Generally,
his *La Chartreuse de Parme (The Charterhouse of Parma)* was considered his best book, but the publication of an essay by Taine in 1864
led to a reappraisal of his authorship. Taine was a warm admirer of
La Chartreuse de Parme, but his essay dealt primarily with *Le Rouge
et le Noir*[51] *(Scarlet and Black)*. Zola and Bourget then continued
along the same lines.[52] Actually, it was only when Bourget's essay
was published that the rest of Europe began to be interested in

Stendhal. To illustrate his narrative technique, Bourget took some of his examples from *La Chartreuse de Parme*, but the main part of his exposition was based on *Le Rouge et le Noir*.

One of the basic ideas behind Brandes' literary program was that the Scandinavian countries, and Denmark especially, had not yet been affected by the reaction against romanticism that had set in in the rest of Europe. He looked for a renewal of the rationalistic line from the eighteenth-century. French naturalism was a kind of renaissance for the idea of the Age of Enlightenment, which had, however, "hibernated" in a totally different way in France than in Scandinavia. Some of the romantics bridged the gap between the Age of Enlightenment and naturalism. Balzac was one such man, and Stendhal even more so. In his study, Sainte-Beuve emphasized Stendhal's dependency upon the radical thinkers of the revolutionary period, the "ideologists" Cabanis and Tracy. And, Sainte-Beuve added, "he proceeds purely and directly from the eighteenth-century."[53]

One of Stendhal's important rationalistic traits was his criticism of Christianity, and here he found complete favor with Brandes. It is not impossible that Stendhal inspired Brandes to study such eighteenth-century rationalists as Condillac and Cabanis, which his library card showed that he had. Stendhal's strength lay in his extensive knowledge of psychology, partially acquired by studying the eighteenth-century philosophers of the Enlightenment. Zola's novels, and with them the first wave of naturalism, were more physiological than psychological. With the late naturalists, including Bourget, the tendency leaned toward a stronger interest in the psychological novel. This wind shift came at the same time that Dostoevsky's novels were discovered. Earlier in his study of Stendhal, Brandes was struck by his psychological analysis. This was strongly emphasized in *Main Currents*:

He was a psychologist through and through—as an observant tourist, a historian, a novel and short-story writer, he was always a psychologist. He never ceased to study the human soul, and he is one of the first moderns for whom history as science was reduced to a psychological problem.[54]

Brandes shared the view that history was in actuality a psychological problem. He had, perhaps, adopted it from Taine, who in turn was in debt to Stendhal. Using literature as documentary material,

Brandes attempted, especially in the first parts of *Main Currents*, to reveal the psychology of the century. Later on he became more interested in explaining men than history.

Of the main figures in *The Romantic School in France*, only Gautier and Mérimée now remain. The former did not fit in very well in the breakthrough program with its demands on realism and social involvement. Art for art's own sake—"l'art pout l'art," the core of Gautier's aesthetic philosophy—was diametrically opposed to Brandes' ideas of art as an instrument in the changing of society. But Brandes had the ability to see constructive elements even in aesthetics that differed from his own. He was in complete agreement with Gauthier's demand that one should not judge works of art on the basis of morality or usefulness. He could therefore write the following about Gautier's theory of art: "It is true and incontestable in the sense that art is not subject to the same rules for what is fitting, which rightfully govern the rest of life, and even less to those which unjustly govern."[55]

Brandes' interest in Mérimée during the early 1870s, which resulted in the essay in *Criticisms and Portraits* (1870), was mentioned earlier. In a letter to his future wife in 1874 Brandes still referred to Mérimée as his favorite author.[56] And this was not so strange. Mérimée played a significant role in the growing wave of realism. He even seems to be the first author to whom the term was applied.[57] The critics spoke of his photographic method and of his taste for low subjects. Brandes himself wrote: "Strangely enough, this writer was originally taken for a pure naturalist."[58] The reason for such a conclusion was, he said, that there was a naturalistic element in romanticism in general. Here he was referring to attempts to describe different milieus as precisely as possible—even exotic ones—and of psychological realism. But even if Brandes could point out naturalistic elements in Mérimée's writing, he was not blind to that which was romantic and unreal. He praised Mérimée's short stories—undoubtedly his greatest contribution. There were not very many good short-story writers in nineteenth-century European literature, and Mérimée was one of the key figures in the development of this genre. The clear, objective, and sober narrative style he developed was long an ideal for Brandes. The author should be hidden behind his work, not comment upon it and, above all, not moralize. This was also Flaubert's ideal style. Brandes met it in Mérimée before he discovered Flaubert.

In a special chapter of *The Romantic School in France* Brandes took up what he termed the sociopolitical ideological movement and its relation to poetry. Here he primarily examined pre-Marxist socialism stemming from Saint Simon. Several members of the romantic school were strongly influenced by it, especially George Sand. It was through her that Brandes himself came in touch with utopian socialism—in that way and also through his study of Sainte-Beuve's biography of Proudhon.

The Romantic School in France is the most substantial volume of *Main Currents*. Here Brandes wrote about authors he knew well, and his preparation for this book was more thorough than for the earlier volumes. Furthermore, it dealt with writers who had a decisive influence on the realistic and naturalistic literature of Europe in the 1870s and 1880s.

VI Young Germany

The last part of *Main Currents* was written with a great deal of inner resistance on Brandes' part.[59] It was not published until 1890, almost two decades after his outline of the work as a whole. The European literary scene had changed very quickly during these years, especially because of the emergence of naturalism. "The young Germany," including Heine, Börne, Immermann, Gutzkow, Laube, and Mundt, had aged very rapidly, and only Heine remained vital and important and still widely read. Originally the plan was that *Main Currents* would end by paying homage to that group of writers who created the literary and ideological basis for the revolution of 1848, the chronological endpoint. Seen literarily, *Young Germany* was an anticlimax. Nevertheless, Brandes maintained the political-revolutionary perspective that characterized the book as a whole. As in the earlier volumes, he began with a political exposition of the reactionary atmosphere in Germany during the years before the July revolution. Then the revolution came in 1830 and, with a sense of the dramatic, Brandes described how some of the authors in the "young Germany" group reacted to the news from Paris that the July revolution had broken out. In this way the reader was introduced to three of the most important authors later discussed: Gutzkow, Börne, and Heine. Later, in the last pages of the book, the outbreak of the February revolution was described along with its repercussions in Germany. The presentation was thus

framed by these two revolutionary outbreaks, and this gave the last
part of *Main Currents* a definite social and political character.

The dominating figure of *Young Germany* was Heinrich Heine.
The part dealing with him was so extensive that Brandes later ex-
tracted it and, with only a bit of retouching and a few additions,
published it as a separate book. There were few authors with whom
Brandes had so much in common. When, as a young man, he
thought of becoming a poet, it was Heine who was his model. He
read so much of his poetry that one day he was satiated and could
not read any more.[60] After this youthful infatuation he achieved a
certain degree of perspective. He discovered the looseness and
sometimes carelessness of Heine's informal style, and this criticism
was taken up in *Young Germany*.

During these years Heine was almost as well known outside
Germany as at home. Evidence of this can be found in the many
investigations of his influence in Europe.[61] He was a source of irrita-
tion for the Germans during his lifetime. From his secure place of
refuge in Paris he lashed out at his countrymen. During his long stay
in Germany, Brandes observed that Heine was not at all favorably
received there. Anti-semitism had influential proponents in German cultural life—such as Treitschke. Brandes emphasized the visionary, the bitter, and the vitriolic in Heine's poetry. He compared
him to Rembrandt and found that he had something of the same
color treatment and "clair-obscur." Heine, he stated, is no romantic, but neither is he a realist. He had, of course, taken over much of
the romantic language, but with his clashing dissonances, breaches
of style, and leaps of thought, he moved away from romanticism.
Brandes thus appreciated in Heine that which made him into a great
artist. For the most part, Brandes appraised Heine's works aesthetically. It was not easy to figure out Heine politically. In spite of his
political radicalism he could praise the Russian czar as the flag-
bearer of freedom. How to balance that equation? Brandes said that,
while it obviously was an example of political naïveté, Heine was a
worshiper of freedom and at the same time an affirmed aristocrat.[62]
In other words, Brandes found the same conflict in Heine as he felt
in himself at the time he published *Main Currents* and while under
the influence of Nietzsche: How to unite the worship of genius with
a radical progressive view of society? Brandes, influenced by
Nietzsche and Renan, thought he had found a means, which he
called aristocratic radicalism, and he seemed to find traces of the

same in Heine. There is not a drop of conservative blood in Heine, he said, but he also continued by saying that neither did he have a drop of democratic blood. He wanted Genius to be recognized as leader and ruler.

In his portrait of Heine, Brandes more than ever made use of the comparative technique he had developed. The method suited a hero-worshiper like Brandes perfectly. Heine was so great that he could be compared with only the truly influential figures in human cultural history, with Aristophanes, Rembrandt, and Goethe, and systematic comparisons with these three were included in the section on Heine.

Many of the authors Brandes discussed in *Young Germany* were of Jewish descent. This was true of Heine, Herwegh, Henriette Hertz, Rahel Varnhagen, Johann Jacoby, and Moritz Hartmann. Another central figure in this part of *Main Currents* was also Jewish, namely, Ludwig Börne. Börne's most influential work was *Briefe aus Paris (Letter from Paris)* (1831), which Brandes had read in his youth. It was a report from France during the July monarchy, written with a bit too much political naïveté for Brandes to let it pass without criticism. Furthermore, Börne took every opportunity to scorn Goethe, who came from the administrative aristocracy in Frankfurt whereas Börne had grown up in the ghetto of the same city. At the time of writing the last part of *Main Currents*, Brandes was in a period of Goethe worship. All were compared to the great poet from Weimar, and in this comparison Börne could not measure up to be placed on a pedestal with the real greats.

A fairly extensive part of the sixth volume of *Main Currents* dealt with three female figures who wrote no fiction. Their names were Rahel Varnhagen, Bettina von Arnim, and Charlotte Stieglitz. They interested Brandes as typical figures of their times. Here Brandes obviously meant that he did not do justice to the period by discussing male authors alone. These women had not devoted themselves to pure fiction, but still they contributed to the cultural climate by their letters and personalities, and it was this, the psychological atmosphere of the period, that Brandes tried to capture.[63] Thus he established a kind of balance of the sexes in his work, for the fact that these women did not appear as writers but rather, in the case of Rahel Varnhagen and Bettina von Arnim, as admirers of Goethe, only demonstrated the sexual handicap that women of that time had to overcome.

The weakness in the design of *Main Currents* becomes clear in the last volume of the work. Poets like Hebbel and Mörike were left out of the mainstream of European literature. But *Main Currents* was not a history of literature in its ordinary meaning. Instead it was something between literary history and political history, something that functioned in the border area between these two, and that revealed tendencies toward the history of ideas and personal history. Pjotr Kogan, the Russian critic, stated in a valuable characterization that what Brandes had achieved was really what could be called the history of European intelligentsia.[64] Brandes was interested not only in books but in the fruitful development of dynamic thought. From this point of view it was justifiable to include such figures as Schleiermacher, Gentz, de Maistre, Bonald, Lamennais, Börne, Jacoby, Rahel Varnhagen, Bettina von Arnim, and Charlotte Stieglitz. They could give an indication of the intellectual climate.

The last volume of *Main Currents* was well received in Germany. One of the experts on *Young Germany*, Bölsche, on whom, by the way, Brandes based a part of his presentation, thought that it was the best work as yet on that period.[65] Brandes also received positive reviews from other places. *Preussische Jahrbücher* said that the book had the same weaknesses and strong points as the previous parts.[66] Brandes was good at characterizing, at tracing the exchanges between countries, and his knowledge was extensive. But he was tendentious, unsure about details, and nonchalant in his choice of what was frequently anecdotal material. The part on Börne and Heine was judged best —a fairly accurate appraisal.

CHAPTER 5

The First Biographies: Lassalle, Kierkegaard, Tegnér, and Disraeli

AT the time of Brandes' appearance on the scene, the literary biography was not particularly common, even though the genre as such is an old one with roots as far back as the Bible and Plutarch. Boswell's *Life of Samuel Johnson* (1791) is usually considered to be the first true literary biography, but William Roper had written the biography of Thomas Moore as early as 1626. Brandes' point of departure was Sainte-Beuve. He had previously written shorter biographies inspired by Sainte-Beuve, such as the essays on Hans Christian Andersen and Prosper Mérimée. The books discussed here were his first attempts on a larger scale, and we will begin with the portrait of Lassalle. The book on Lassalle was not published in Danish until 1881, though it appeared in German in 1877, and as early as 1874–1875 in article form in the Brandes brothers' magazine *Det nittende Aarhundrede*. Brandes himself says that with this book he wanted to achieve something similar to Sainte-Beuve's portrait of Proudhon.[1] His preparations involved, among other things, interviewing as many people as possible who had been in contact with the socialist leader in order to get an idea of what he was like psychologically.

I *Lassalle*

Brandes' interest in Lassalle began on his visit to Berlin in 1872. He was fascinated by his inflamatory pamphlets. He also read Spielhagen's romanticized portrait of Lassalle in *In Reih' und Glied (To March in Rank)*. He became personally acquainted with Spielhagen and was able to acquire a good many facts from him. Brandes was more impressed by Lassalle's unflagging audacity than by his ideas, and said in his autobiography that he had never been terribly interested in German economy—it was rather the personality behind the writing that fascinated him: ". . . hard as iron, therefore unyielding, superior in knowledge and clarity, thus he was able to meet both public and private opposition and come away unscathed, as if it never existed . . ."[2]

When Brandes came in touch with Lassalle, he had just recovered from the effects of the negative reaction to his first series of lectures at the university, and in Lassalle he felt he had found a kindred spirit: scholar and agitator, a man who was strong enough not to be defeated by the opposition he had created. In Lassalle, Brandes thought he recognized a combination of defiance, chivalry, high self-esteem, and passionate involvement, which Brandes felt characterized him himself:

His burning love of science and knowledge, his thirst for truth and justice, his enthusiasm, his unbending self-esteem, his great vanity, his courage, his love of power: all have the same burning, consuming character. He was a lantern-bearer—a torchbearer who gladly placed himself in the center of the light beside the torch with which he brought clarity.[3]

Brandes gladly thought of himself in the same way, and sketched a self-portrait written along similar lines. In a letter to a French friend he wrote that there were also private similarities between Lassalle and himself.[4]

Brandes' admiration of Lassalle tends to make the book fairly naïve and uncritical at times. This is especially true of the young Lassalle's sophisticated, not to say dandyish conduct, his affairs and his extravagant habits in society. But there is no doubt that Brandes was sincerely interested in his political program. In December 1872 Brandes wrote in his diary: "Deeply impressed by Lassalle. The bourgeoisie is completely rotten and extinct. One ought absolutely to turn to the workers." In 1872 Brandes was on the side of radical European liberalism. It was a clear revolutionary radicalism, primarily influenced by the ideas of John Stuart Mill, but it was not at all socialistic. Brandes had shielded himself from any relations with the socialism that was beginning to make progress at the time. In *Forklaring og Forsvar (Explanation and Defense)*, he stated his case decisively against socialism:

The reason that I have not joined with the socialists is simply that I am not a socialist. By that I do not mean that there is something wrong with being one. I have never expressed my opinions of socialistic ideas and find no reason to do so now either.[5]

This was, however, written before he left for Berlin and began to study Lassalle at the end of 1872. During the rest of the 1870s he studied both Marx and such other socialist theoreticians as Proudhon and Alexandr Herzen. *Die Arbeiterfrage (The Labor Question)* (1865), written by the German professor of philosophy Albert Lange, also meant a great deal to him and was often referred to in the book on Lassalle.

In principle Brandes seemed to agree with Lassalle's criticism of economic liberalism. Lassalle said that it was impossible to eliminate the consequences of what he called the "iron hard law of wages," that is, the fact that the owners of capital never paid more wages than would keep the workers living on a minimum standard with the help of savings funds, insurance policies, and so on. Lassalle claimed that the only solution was to let the state intervene and to stimulate the workers to form production unions with a state guarantee. Lassalle was a Hegelian leftist and, according to Brandes, it was from Hegel that he adopted his reliance on the state. Brandes was doubtful as to whether the production unions Lassalle had sketched could function if they were not formed from the inside, democratically.[6] He was much more suspicious of the state than Lassalle and was afraid that the bureaucratic organization Lassalle considered necessary would hinder rather than favor the worker's independence. He also had reservations about the workers' taking over the financial risk that the owners of capital had thus far been responsible for. Nor could he accept Lassalle's philosophy of equality. "The apprentice shall and ought to have more than the novice, the supervisor shall and ought to have more than the apprentice, and the master ought to have the most."[7] Brandes thus had several reservations about Lassalle's socialism. He regarded his ideas as contributions to a debate, but was favorably disposed toward the discussion of such issues as the question of private property and the situation of the working class.

In 1883 Brandes gave a lecture on Lassalle for a group of workers in Copenhagen. He received a letter from the man who arranged the lecture, V. Pingel, who wrote:

Tomorrow there is something which the workers will be very interested in hearing, and that is whether you yourself believe in Lassalle's theories. In my opinion, the only correct thing to do would be to state your position clearly on this point.[8]

One understands from this that the readers of Brandes' book were unsure as to where he actually stood in relation to socialistic ideas. Brandes can hardly be accused of being an opportunist, but it is possible that he hesitated to openly declare himself a socialist. But in spite of the reservations, the book filled an important function at this time in spreading socialistic ideas in Scandinavia. Both Bjørnson and Strindberg read the biography of Lassalle. Strindberg thought that Brandes had been too impartial and too aesthetic.[9] He probably was referring to the linguistic and stylistic analyses of Lassalle's inflammatory pamphlets. He had observed Lassalle's preference for militant expressions. Like Bismarck, he loved to use the word "iron." Brandes admired Lassalle's sharp logic, and his ability to see reality behind illusion. Brandes' study of Lassalle seems to have led to his acceptance of the role of agitator given him, and even his satisfaction with it for a time.

II *Kierkegaard*

In the fall of 1876, Georg Brandes went on a lecture tour in Norway and Sweden, and the subject of his lectures was Søren Kierkegaard. One might expect that Brandes the atheist would have little in common with a religious figure like Kierkegaard, but Brandes had gone through a Kierkegaard period in his youth during the first part of the 1860s.[10] It was difficult for an intellectually aware person to grow up in Denmark and miss someone like Kierkegaard. His influence on the cultural life of Denmark and Scandinavia as a whole had increased after his death. In 1876 Brandes was representative of a philosophy that was in many ways diametrically opposed to Kierkegaard's, and he stated in his autobiography that he felt a need to clarify for himself and others his position in relation to Kierkegaard.[11] At the end of his life, the author of *Either-Or* and *The Moment* had stood in direct opposition to the Danish church, but in 1876, when Brandes once again tackled Kierkegaard, he was not only on his way to being accepted but also to becoming a power in the church.

The book on Kierkegaard may be seen as a continuation of the inventory of the bankrupt estate of romanticism that Brandes had begun in *Main Currents*. Romanticism was not dead in Denmark. Kierkegaard is included in his gallery of examples as an illustration of the negative side of romanticism in *Main Currents*. One of the basic romantic types is the introspective melancholic, such as Chateaubriand's René. A Danish counterpart is mentioned in the same context, unnamed but with obvious reference to Kierkegaard:

Melancholy is most characteristic of the fourth one. The essence of his vocation, the source of his life and even of his work as an author. And this melancholy deprives him of any common sense when judging reality. The least little thing that happens to him swells up into something Meaningful, something Definitive, and Predestined, which he returns to time and time again, while the same thing would be a trifle for someone less inclined to melancholy.[12]

The romantic poetic ideal as it appeared in Oehlenschläger's *Aladdin*, the "do-nothing," the contemplative, vegetative introvert exemplified by the figure of Johannes in *Either-Or*, was condemned in *Main Currents*.[13] Like Zola, Brandes now wished to encourage its complete opposite, an active, extroverted, socially oriented type. Kierkegaard's aesthetics was of the same flesh and blood as Tieck's William Lovell and Eichendorff's Taugenicht.[14] Kierkegaard was thus included among the German romantics as their kinsman, and when the light was on him, as it often was in the first parts of *Main Currents*, it was always an unfavorable light. On the basis of such comparisons it is not easy to understand what incredible power Kierkegaard had had over Brandes. As a nineteen-year-old he wrote in his diary: "Isn't he the greatest man in Denmark, or the world?"

Thus, when Brandes began his study in 1876, he had a fairly clear picture of Kierkegaard. There was no earlier serious biography of the philosopher. His collected works were not yet published, but Barfoed's and Gottsched's publication of his posthumous papers had already begun in 1869 and was completed in 1881. Brandes' book was written using the same method he had developed under the influence of Taine and Sainte-Beuve. In the spirit of Taine, he attempted to establish the determining faculty of Kierkegaard's personality, his *faculté maîtresse:* piety and contempt.[15] In this basic conception of Kierkegaard Brandes could include both the man who accepted his father's religion with its conservative view of society and morals, and the later rebel against the state church and the religious establishment. Brandes' angle of attack was completely biographical: the definitive factors in Kierkegaard's development were his relationship to his father, his broken engagement, and "the *Corsair* feud." Brandes wanted to explain the phenomenon of Kierkegaard psychologically, and thus give him more reasonable proportions. He explained why the highly talented young man chose to study theology. It was because of his father's overshadowing influence, his dark, Old Testament religion. In this context he described the event that Kierkegaard himself in his diary called "the great earthquake." When Kierkegaard was twenty-five years old his father told him about the terrible "religious crime" he had committed as a young man. At the age of twelve he worked as a shepherd boy, watching the sheep and suffering from both hunger and cold. One day he went up to the top of a hill and cursed God. Even at the age of eighty, his father could not forget this blasphemy. This was one of the reasons for the father's melancholy, which the young Søren Kierkegaard inherited. His father's confession served only to increase his devotion and to bind him even more to Christianity.

Brandes could only hypothesize about Kierkegaard's relation to his father's experience as a young boy in the first version of his book, but his guess was confirmed when Kierkegaard's posthumous papers were published. Brandes was especially fond of some of Kierkegaard's writings and did not attempt to conceal his sympathies and antipathies. He naturally found the first part of *Either-Or* far superior to the second part. Johannes, the demonic seducer, would have fit in well with related literary figures who were among the favorites of his youth, Lermontov's Pechorin, Byron's Don Juan, and Goethe's Faust.[16] When, as was mentioned earlier, Brandes condemned this figure, it was a coming to terms with his own past. When it came to Johannes in *The Diary of a Seducer*, Brandes could only admit to his former fascination: "Never before in Danish literature had I met such spiritual superiority, such forceful thinking and (as I thought at the time) such worldly experience."[17]

But the mature Brandes could no longer accept the sexual views expressed in *The Diary of a Seducer*. He was only the shadow of a seducer, he says; here is nothing of the beauty and happy sensuousness of the Greeks. Both Byron's and Goethe's views of love are preferable to Kierkegaard's. Kierkegaard's view of marriage in the second part of *Either-Or* was even less acceptable to Brandes. Moving from the first part to the second is like going from a magic garden to a deserted heath, he wrote. For Kierkegaard, marriage was an institution ordained by God. This is exactly the opposite of Brandes' attempt to make the life shared by two people a nonreligious question. Brandes thus regarded Kierkegaard's thesis on the "Aesthetic Validity of Marriage" as the worst thing he had ever written.[18] Kierkegaard's view of women in general was extremely reactionary in Brandes' eyes. He referred to Paul's words that women must quietly and humbly receive men's teaching.

In Brandes' opinion, the key to Kierkegaard's philosophy lay in its anti-Hegelian existential element. Kierkegaard's preaching on the need to be subjective found response in the individualistic Brandes. That is why he also felt that Kierkegaard's great discovery was the category of *Hin Enkelte (the individual);* this was "the precious pearl he gave to his times."[19] But according to Brandes, Kierkegaard made a mistake in his appraisal and use of this category. He had discovered the "great independence of America," but he mistook it for the old storyland of religious tradition and equated "Hin Enkelte" with the Christian. Thus Brandes embraced the existential individualist but felt nothing for Kierkegaard's dogma of paradox. He had settled the score with that in his first polemic paper, *Dualism in Our Newest Philosophy* (1866). This did not prevent Brandes from highly valuing Kierkegaard's purely religious writings. He felt that *Afsluttende uvidenskabelig Efterskrift (Concluding Unscientific Postscript)* was the middle point of Kierkegaard's life's work, literarily valuable because of its special style or blend of styles. *Practice in Christianity* was, in his opinion, Kierkegaard's best book because of its passion for truth and its penetration. The Christ figure presented there is not Rafael's or Thorvaldsen's, but rather a "Christ as Rembrandt painted him, the simple man, the friend of the worker and the oppressed," the one who said "come to me all ye who labor and are troubled."[20] Here Brandes' and Kierkegaard's view of the Bible had a common meeting ground.

Brandes was even more able to appreciate and admire Kierkegaard's last books, in which he violently attacked the Danish state church. He quoted him extensively on the different religious rites: baptism, confirmation, communion, marriage. Kierkegaard, according to Brandes, claimed that confirmation was only maintained because the priests themselves were perjurers and wanted the society as a whole to be perjurers.[21] His judgments on baptism and communion were just as harsh.

The book on Kierkegaard was written by someone very familiar with the philosopher's way of thinking and with the ability to understand him. Between Brandes' first infatuation with Kierkegaard and his monograph lay an intensive study of the English empiricists. Brandes reread Kierkegaard through the eyes of John Stuart Mill before beginning his work. With this book he lay the foundation for research on Kierkegaard, and when it later was translated to German it became an important factor in Kierkegaard's growing influence on the cultural life of Europe. Brandes had expected the publication of his book to result in a certain amount of public debate; to his surprise, none took place. He wrote a friend about this:

When I describe Kierkegaard as only an inferior spirit, with a personality to a lesser extent religious and to a greater extent narrow-minded, no one can say anything against this—even though the opposite view was propounded yesterday. And so it is with everything.[22]

III *Tegnér*

During a lecture tour of Sweden in 1876, Brandes met Esaias Tegnér's grandson Elof Tegnér, who had written positive reviews of *Main Currents*. Elof Tegnér encouraged Brandes to write a biography of his grandfather, and at the same time gave him some unpublished letters to use as source material. At this time Tegnér, along with Bellman, was regarded as the greatest Swedish author, and he was worshiped as something of a national saint. He had achieved a certain reputation outside Sweden with his narrative poem *Fritjofs saga*. This work was especially popular in Germany, and Brandes said that it was the obligatory confirmation present for young girls. Naturally this says something about the degree of realism in the erotic descriptions of the book.

It must have been a stimulating challenge for Brandes to tackle this book. He had the same passion for ripping off masks as he attributed to Sainte-Beuve in the chapter on him in *Main Currents*. And the book on Tegnér was written as a psychological portrait in the spirit of Sainte-Beuve. At the time Brandes wrote this biography, nothing had been written about Tegnér's life and work other than semiofficial panegyrics. It was thus Brandes' task to find the man behind the official picture of the public servant, bishop, professor, and national poet.

Brandes was actually well equipped to write a book on Tegnér. He had gone through a "Nordic period" early in his youth when he had studied both the Icelandic sagas and the Swedish romanticists, Tegnér and Atterbom included. He had also just finished the two volumes of *Main Currents* on German and English romanticism when he began his biography of Tegnér. Brandes obviously had a negative opinion of German romanticism. On the other hand, he was very positive about Shelley and Byron among the English romanticists. He especially remarked upon Tegnér's antiromantic traits expressed in his struggle against the German-influenced Uppsala school. Tegnér developed a wittiness in this struggle that was not far behind the German romantic critics Heine and Börne.

In Tegnér Brandes saw the enlightened man, the rationalist, the worshiper of light. He described Tegnér as a very unconventional bishop who in reality was skeptical of dogma and who had accepted his position because of purely economical reasons. He cited Tegnér's words to his colleague Franzén when the latter accepted the same position: "If you have to be a clergyman, I think it is better to be a bishop than an ordinary minister."[23] Brandes used the unpublished letters to throw a new light on the big crisis of Tegnér's life. Like Kierkegaard, Tegnér also experienced his "earthquake," referred to in his well-known poem "Mjältsjukan" ("Spleen"). With the help of these letters Brandes discovered that this poem had come in wrong chronological order in the official publication of the writer's works. It was placed between a poem from 1812 and one from 1813, but should have come somewhere in the middle of the 1820s. Brandes attempted to explain the reason for the writer's crisis and, supported by information from his grandson, came to the conclusion that it had to do with erotic failures.[24] Brandes thought the poem was purposely dated wrongly for reasons of discretion.

Of all of Tegnér's works, *Fritjofs saga* was dutifully discussed most extensively. It was compared to the Old Nordic version, which Brandes felt was superior in its realism. Otherwise the poems and speeches both in verse and in prose were only superficially discussed. Tegnér's fury against the Holy Alliance could only impress Brandes, but it is more his personality, as it was revealed in the letters, that Brandes really appreciated. Tegnér had something of the same witty, bitterly ironic temperament Heine had, and this made a hit with Brandes, a hero-worshiper like Tegnér, even if they otherwise had very different ideals. Tegnér's *faculté maîtresse* lay in his metaphoric ability, to which Brandes devoted a special chapter.

The book on Tegnér was published at about the same time in German, Danish, and Swedish. It was first published in Germany as a series of articles in the respected magazine *Deutsche Rundschau,* to which Brandes had contributed regularly since moving to Berlin.

IV   *Disraeli*

In 1878 the Berlin Congress was held and Brandes sent reports on it to the Norwegian newspaper *Dagbladet,* for which he had been writing articles. The English prime minister, Disraeli, played an important role at the congress, which was meant to lead to a settlement after the recently terminated Russian-Turkish war. Disraeli's diplomatic skill earned him headlines, and Brandes caught a glimpse of the statesman on one occasion during the summer of 1878:

The other day when I went out at the time of the Congress and walked across the Kaiserhof Place I saw Disraeli in the distance; I passed him so closely that my sleeve touched his. He looked sick, old, and ugly. He leaned on the arm of his secretary, Montague Corry, and walked very slowly in a dignified manner. Behind them, a comical servant carrying a red box with the papers. Almost everyone raised their hats to them and bowed down low. The Germans are very respectful. D. greeted them in somewhat the same way as Napoleon III—wearily.[25]

This is an exquisite period picture from the Berlin of 1878 and says a lot about both Disraeli and the Germans. Later Brandes used this glimpse as the concluding vignette of his book. Perhaps it was this brief meeting that decided Brandes to write his biography of Disraeli the same year. Brandes the hero-worshiper was under the spell of a great man. Previously, while working on *Main Currents*, he had read Disraeli's *Venetia,* a novel *à clef* on the life of Byron. During the summer and fall of 1878, Brandes made an intensive study of Disraeli's novels and of the existent biographies and decided to accomplish the impossible by finishing the book the same year. Edmund Gosse, the English author, helped him with the material.[26]

It may seem strange that Georg Brandes, who had previously

written a well-disposed biography of the socialist leader Lassalle, could shortly thereafter eagerly devote himself to a conservative politician like Disraeli. What was unique about Disraeli, however, was the strange mixture of aristocrat and democrat. In his novel *Sybil*, Disraeli had described England as "two nations," and he had subtitled the novel *The Rich and the Poor*. He described the poverty and exploitation both in the countryside and in the new industrial cities. As a young member of Parliament he also backed the first manifestation of the pre-socialist workers' movement, the Chartist action. But Disraeli thought that the aristocracy ought to help the poor. He was also the brain in the Tory party radical group called "the young England." Brandes wrote that there were parts of *Sybil*, Disraeli's most influential novel, that were reminiscent of Lassalle.

Brandes was not, however, blind to the faults in Disraeli's works and personality. The novels were not very good and would not have been worthy of deeper interpretation had they not been written by a politician with the fame of Disraeli. In Brandes' opinion, Disraeli was not well educated and had no respect for science. In the battle between the Darwinists and representatives of the church he backed the religious side. This was in reality the same battle Brandes had fought, a bit late, at home in Denmark. Disraeli supported the church because it was "the only Jewish institution that remains." Such a statement could only depress Brandes. Otherwise Disraeli's pride in his Jewish background was something that fascinated Brandes. In one of his novels, *Tancred*, Disraeli wanted to show what important contributions the Jewish race had made to European culture. In the episode partially quoted above, Brandes somewhat pathetically called Disraeli the "last Jew" and said that "almost against my will I felt a sympathy for him take over my soul."[27] In contrast to many other Jews active in cultural life, Disraeli accepted his Jewish heritage and was proud of it.

Brandes' biography is primarily an analysis of Disraeli's novels, but it also describes the parallel between his literary works and his political activity. In his biography of Lassalle, Brandes had been captivated by the style of the polemic brochures and speeches. Disraeli also interested him as a speaker. One of the most brilliant parts of the biography is the description of Disraeli's maiden speech in Parliament. But Brandes did not neglect the pathetic elements of Disraeli's speeches and his tendency to play up to the audience. The book was written in a few months at a furious tempo and in a journalistic style. This was probably because for once Brandes saw a chance to publish a book with good possibilities of becoming a best seller. It was soon translated from German to English, and was also published in the United States in pirated versions. Brandes therefore did not earn as much as he could have, but it helped to spread his fame outside Northern Europe and Germany.

CHAPTER 6

Exile and Homecoming

IN 1877 Brandes settled down in Berlin with his German-born
wife and remained in the German capital until the beginning of
1883. He was soon included in a circle of liberal authors, artists,
politicians, and scientists, all of whom influenced his way of looking
at things. One of the most influential was Wilhelm Loewe, who
belonged to the revolutionary group of 1848. He had been condemned to death because of this, and had spent several years in
exile in the United States. He was one of the leading men in the
Progressive party during the Bismarck era and a member of Parliament. Loewe was sometimes taken into Bismarck's confidence and
this meant that Brandes could get inside information on the political
situation in Germany, information he made use of as a correspon-
dant for the Norwegian *Dagbladet*. Gerda (Henriette changed her
name to Gerda when she married Brandes) and George Brandes
were accepted as members of the Loewe family and thus made
many valuable contacts in the cultural life of Berlin. One of these
was Friedrich Kapp, a lawyer who also had been forced into exile in
1848 and who had been made a member of Parliament upon his
return. Brandes wrote articles about both these liberal politicians in
*Berlin som tysk Rigshovedstad (Berlin, Capital of the German Reich
1885)*, a sample of the articles he had sent home to different Scandinavian newspapers. He contributed to the Swedish *Göteborgs
Handels–och Sjöfartstidning* and the Danish *Morgenbladet*.

I Berlin

Brandes was also well acquainted with a great many university
teachers, several with Jewish backgrounds, such as Lazarus, professor of psychology; Steinthal, professor of philosophy; and Bernstein,
professor of law. The latter, a very wealthy man, lived in a big house
not far from the Brandeses in Tiergarten, and his home was the
meeting place for scientists, writers, and artists. Here Brandes

could meet Max Klinger, the young artist à la mode; Siemering, the sculptor; Ernst Curtius and Theodor Mommsen, key figures in German historical research and described at length in *Berlin, Capital of the German Reich.*

In his autobiography, Brandes cited some melancholy reflections from his diary at the time of his arrival alone in Berlin in October 1877.[1] He had spent an evening walking through the empty streets and asking himself if he would ever make a name for himself in this world capital. The German translation of the first parts of *Main Currents* had given him a reputation in certain circles. His importance in the Scandinavian countries was of a quite different degree. But he was soon noticed both in Germany and in other parts of Europe through his articles in *Deutsche Rundschau.* In March 1881, he was extremely pleased with a clipping from the English paper the *Nation* in which *Deutsche Rundschau* was compared with *Revue des deux Mondes* and in which he was called its best writer. The editor of the paper, Julius Rodenberg, wrote him a letter in which he gushingly expressed his appreciation of his articles.[2] Thus Brandes came to play the same role in Germany as he played in Scandinavia. He introduced foreign literature, especially Nordic and French, and to a certain extent English.

In 1881 the Frankfurt-based publishing company Rütten and Loening asked Brandes to collect a number of his essays for publication. The result of this was *Moderne Geister (Eminent Authors,* 1882), which included essays on Paul Heyse, his special friend among the German authors, Hans Christian Andersen, John Stuart Mill, Esaias Tegnér, Gustave Flaubert, Frederik Paludan Müller, and Bjørnstierne Bjørnson. In a second publication from 1887, he eliminated the essay on Paludan Müller and instead added essays on Ibsen, the Goncourt brothers, Turgenev, and Max Klinger, the painter. In 1894 he published another collection of essays in German, *Menschen und Werken (Men and Books),* which included his lengthy paper on Nietzsche.

Brandes, however, was especially known for his lecturing talents in Copenhagen and elsewhere in Scandinavia, and it was not long before he was also lecturing in Germany. He gave five lectures in January 1880 at the newly established Humboldtakademie, and received good publicity for them in the Berlin newspapers. Later that year he received the honor of being one of the twelve chosen every year to lecture at the Singakademie, which was under the patronage of the court. This could almost be considered a social event with the queen as the most prominent member of the audience, and it was followed by a small dinner party at the castle. It was a moment of triumph for Georg Brandes. He who had been opposed by the Danish government and its head of state, he who had been driven into exile and refused all official recognition in his own country was treated with the utmost respect in Germany. In any case, there is no doubt that Brandes succeeded in winning a place for himself in German cultural life during his stay in Berlin, and if he had chosen to remain, he could have become a German author. He later extended his lecturing to include several of the larger German cities. Thus in 1884 he visited Darmstadt, Karlsruhe, Mainz, Hanau, Frankfurt, Brunswick, Bremen, and Vienna. On these occasions he spoke of "junges Deutschland," not a very controversial subject.

Berlin, Capital of the German Reich (1884) was thus a kind of summary of Brandes' years in exile in Germany, and was one of the most colorful things he wrote. Here he revealed himself to be a great journalist through his graphic pictures of German social, political, and cultural life. A historian wishing to describe the Bismarck era would find a lot of material in these observations. Brandes wrote like a curious, often dispassionate observer, often admiring, sometimes ironic and bitter. He admired Prussian discipline, the police, the fire department, the German universities, which he thought to be the best in the world. He sighed about the political immaturity of the German people, their subservience. He described the attempt on the life of the kaiser, the calling out of the police and blocking off of the streets. But he also described Bismarck's outlawing of the social democrats after the assassination attempt. He sympathetically portrayed the social democratic leaders who were expelled from Parliament because of the backlash after the attempt. He wrote about newly published literature, about art exhibitions, about new plays. He could give an account of how it was when Ibsen's *Doll's House* was presented in a shorter form with a new "happy ending," but also about the pessimistic philosopher in fashion, Hartmann, who served a reactionary cause in his criticism of Bentham-Mill's ideas about the greatest possible happiness to the greatest number of people.

II   *Return to Denmark*

But Brandes did not lose touch with the cultural life of the north nor with his friends in Copenhagen during his years in Berlin. He was a guest lecturer in Denmark and Norway. Friends in Copenhagen had not given up hope that he would return some day and in some way or other be connected with the university. This became a vital issue for the liberal faction of the Left. In 1880, his brother Edvard Brandes was elected a member of the Danish Parliament as a representative of the radical segment of the left-wing party. Thus he was also able to work for the return of his older brother. At the end of June 1882, Edvard sent him a message that a number of anonymous contributors had assured him a sum of four thousand crowns yearly if he would return to Copenhagen and agree to do a certain amount of lecturing there. The letter from this group read:

During the past five years since you left your native country to live abroad, there has been a growing opinion that the contribution which you could make to the furthering of Danish intellectual life is so great that one can only feel the greatest regret that you, because of the circumstances, are forced to expend so much of your working energy in a foreign literature. We are more and more aware that you are the man eminently suited to awaken and to nourish a feeling for knowledge and for scientific life in our studying youth through your lectures and through your personal influence.[3]

We are not sure of the real motive behind the request of this group of Danes—it was probably different for different donors—but it must be remembered that Brandes was still not officially hired, and it was not a question of a privately financed professorship. He was still outside the establishment. And judging from his reply, it was only after much hesitation that he gave up his position in Germany to return to Denmark.

Thus from the new year of 1883 Brandes once again lived in Copenhagen, and now Brandesianism was on its way to becoming a powerful factor in the cultural life of Denmark and of Scandinavia. The two Brandes brothers along with Viggo Hørup, a newspaper-man, founded the daily paper *Politiken* in 1885, thus giving the radical phalanx a platform. The two brothers corresponded with most of the influential authors in Scandinavia at the time, and the influence they exerted can be studied in *Georg og Edvard Brandes Brevveksling med nordiske Forfattere og Videnskabsmænd*, published in eight large volumes. Here one can read their correspondence with Bjørnson, Ibsen, Kielland, Lie, Strindberg, Fröding, Heidenstam, Ola Hansson, and J. P. Jacobsen, to mention a few of the most well known. Georg Brandes' correspondence with Pontoppidan was published separately.[4]

III *The Men of the Modern Breakthrough*

Shortly after his return, Brandes made a survey of the writers who could more or less be described as adherents of the realistic, social-problem literature he wished to stimulate. He did this in a collection of essays entitled *Det moderne Gjennembruds Mænd (The Men of the Modern Breakthrough,* 1883). In it were included seven essays dealing with Bjørnson, Ibsen, J. P. Jacobsen, Drachmann, Edvard Brandes, S. Schandorph, and Erik Skram. In this book Brandes called the writing of the 1870s and 1880s in Scandinavia the modern breakthrough. One could naturally criticize his choices, such as his brother Edvard, who at the time had written three plays along the lines of Ibsen and Augier. However, Edvard Brandes had made an important contribution as a critic and as the actual editor of *Det nittende Aarhundrede.* Later on he was editor of *Politiken* for a while, and he made a career in politics that culminated in his being appointed minister of finance. This man of many talents was a valuable support for Georg Brandes, less original perhaps, but more practical and politically knowledgeable.

The three most important essays in *The Men of the Modern Breakthrough* dealt with Bjørnson, Ibsen, and J. P. Jacobsen. Brandes had followed Bjørnson's authorship since his early youth, but they had gone different ways and ended up in different philosophical positions. The young Bjørnson with his religious-nationalist pathos had little in common with Brandes' radicalism. But during the 1870s Bjørnson moved closer to Brandes both religiously and politically. When the latter was forced to leave Denmark in 1877 he was very upset. "Aren't you ashamed to let that man go into exile because of lack of possibilities to earn a living?" he wrote to one of his Danish friends.[5] This attitude was the beginning of an extensive correspondence between the two. Bjørnson's peasant short stories were actually fairly foreign to Brandes' tastes, but he described them in depth and compared them to George Sand's descriptions of the countryside and to the German agrarian author Auerbach. He attributed greater importance to the modern realistic period of Bjørnson's writing beginning with *Redaktøren (The Editor,* 1874), and *En Fallit (A Bankruptcy,* 1875). Both may be said to have been inspired by Brandes' own ideas. They are important because they are, along with Ibsen's contemporary plays, the origin of modern bourgeois drama in Europe.

Ibsen and Brandes shared a more even development. I do not

know of any other writer whose path Brandes followed as closely through all its phases as Ibsen's, and they influenced each other mutually. Their correspondence began in the middle of the 1860s and was not terminated until the beginning of the new century.[6] In 1870 when Brandes lay sick with typhus in Italy, he received an encouraging letter from Henrik Ibsen that seemed to have a very stimulating effect upon him. Brandes especially remembered a few lines toward the end that he later returned to again and again. Ibsen wrote to the convalescing Brandes: "It is a question of the revolution of the human spirit, and you must be up there among the leaders."[7] Brandes felt as if he had received the call to a life's work with those words, and he quoted them in his Ibsen essay in *The Men of the Modern Breakthrough*, which was partly based on the letters from Ibsen.

Brandes was one of the first to really understand the scope of Ibsen's greatness. In 1872 Brandes had visited Ibsen, who then lived in voluntary exile in Dresden. He had followed Ibsen's challenge and begun the intellectual revolution. Behind him were fresh impressions of modern French literature, especially the dramatists of the Second Empire. Thus it was an expert on modern French drama who visited Ibsen, and this must have had some effect on his writing.[8] The concise character sketch of Ibsen, the man and conversationalist, was written on this visit and, somewhat altered, was included in the essay in *The Men of The Modern Breakthrough*. The original version from a letter from Dresden in 1872 reads:

He's not very tall, but athletically built, large head, great neck, *handsome*, powerful shoulders, he looks like you'd have to club him down in order to be able to deal with him. He doesn't say much, and what is unusual about his speech is its calmness and slowness, and the fact that he never smiles, never, even if the person he is talking to smiles first. He almost seems anxious sometimes. If I should in general try to describe him in one word, I would say that he is *threatening*. He looks like an authority, like a man who is used to putting people in their place, like a headmaster used to inspiring fear in his boys.[9]

Some of Brandes' statements about Ibsen are still valid today, others are surprising. He claimed, for example, that Ibsen was the born polemic. That was his *faculté maîtresse* as Taine used the term. Brandes also strongly emphasized the fact that Ibsen did not think of himself as the spokesman for a group, a class, or a people. He thought of himself as the "genial individual." According to Brandes, the inheritance from Kierkegaard and his idea of "the individual" was deeply rooted in Ibsen. Another typical characteristic of Ibsen's writing was, for Brandes, his pessimism. This is something that a later observer does not feel so strongly. But his pessimism is not reminiscent of Schopenhauer or Hartmann, both of whom regarded life itself as something evil. Brandes claimed that Ibsen's pessimism was not metaphysical, but moral. People are base and the times are base. Brandes' image of Ibsen, based on a study of his works, on their long correspondence, and on their meetings, was that of a radical individualist. "The state must be abolished." The revolution he wished to encourage had to be aimed at the authoritarian state. Ibsen was a lonely revolutionary, unwilling to back any political parties or theoretical isms. Of the plays he had published up to the time of the publication of Brandes' essay (1883), Brandes seems to have preferred *Ghosts*, the most naturalistic and perhaps most radical of his works. In his writing Brandes often referred to Mrs. Alving, the main character.

Schandorph and Skram were among the most faithful of Brandes' supporters, but neither of them managed to go down to posterity. J. P. Jacobsen was, on the other hand, a significant writer, although the scope of his work was not very extensive as he died when only thirty-eight years old. He developed a great deal of independence in relation to the Brandes brothers, but was no contentious personality. Jacobsen was interested in Darwin and translated him into Danish. He was not a one-sided tendentious writer, and in his essay on Jacobsen Brandes remarked upon the fact that he left it up to the reader to form his own opinions: "Not one little comment, not one wink of the eye reveals to the reader who the author thinks is right. . . ."[10] This type of narrative technique, practiced and preached by Flaubert and the French naturalists especially, was completely in accord with Brandes' own poetics at this time. Jacobsen's two main works were *Mrs. Marie Grubbe*, a historical novel from the 1600s, and *Niels Lyhne*, a contemporary novel about "weak freethinkers," as Jacobsen himself described it in a conversation with Brandes referred to in the essay. Thus, here too there is a similarity with the essay on Ibsen, since Brandes to a greater or lesser extent had discussed the works with the author, whom he had known, supported, and encouraged.

The essay on Drachmann, who at this time was moving away from

Brandes' European radicalism toward a popular national romanticism, was the cause of a rift between the two. In addition, Herman
Bang, one of the better young writers, criticized the essay collection
for bias and partiality. After his return to Copenhagen, Brandes had
planned to write a summary of the literary movement he had helped
to initiate in Scandinavia, but instead he found himself rather isolated in his own country, something that understandably enough
made him bitter. He had paved the way for the new movement,
received blows and paid the price, but he had also been disap-
pointed by some of his friends from the first years of struggle. The
fault was more his brother Edvard's than his own. Edvard was "the
whip" who attempted to keep the literary and political Left together
in Denmark. But writers do not voluntarily allow themselves to be
trapped into political folds.

The same year Brandes published *The Men of the Modern Breakthrough* he also published another collection of essays of a slightly
different character: *Mennesker og Værker (People and Books*, 1883).
This was a collection of articles on foreign writers only, with the
exception of Kierkegaard and Schack Staffeldt. The essay on Kierkegaard was a previously published review of the philosopher's
Posthumous Works. Brandes felt he had found evidence that
confirmed the fact that he had portrayed the man correctly in his
biography. He recognized Kierkegaard's bitterness over the lack of
understanding of his contemporaries and his complaints at being
forced to write for such a limited language area as Denmark. It was a
cruel fate to be a genius in a small town, and Brandes began to feel
the same way after his return.

The introductory essay in *People and Books* was an extensive and
scholarly investigation of the subject "Goethe and Denmark," originally written for the *Goethe Jahrbuch* of 1881. It is evidence that
Brandes' interest in Goethe, stemming from his youth, was still
strong. His description of the interpretation of Goethe in Denmark
was the background of the history of his own education as he discussed his own teachers Brøchner and Hauch in whose homes he had
been a frequent and welcome guest. He said that in Hauch's home
there was hardly ever an evening when Goethe's name or one of his
works was not mentioned. It was the yardstick by which others' art
was measured.

The other essays in the collection dealt with Tegnér, Snoilsky,
Auerbach, Paul Heyse, John Stuart Mill, Renan, Flaubert, and the

Goncourt brothers: two Swedes, two Germans, an Englishman, and three Frenchmen, all figures of the nineteenth century. Brandes thus revealed an admirable breadth and we obviously cannot deal with the essays in depth here.

Brandes had a personal relationship with the two German writers, Auerbach and Heyse. He had met them before during his stay in Germany in 1872, but he had been familiar with Auerbach's writing previously. He especially appreciated his novel *Neues Leben (New Life)* for its open-minded and pedagogical program. It had served as a bible for many enthusiastic nineteenth-century liberals, the young Leo Tolstoy among others. Brandes had long planned to write an essay on Auerbach, and in his introductory lecture in 1871 he implied that he would be discussed in the later parts of *Main Currents*. However, this was not to be the case. Perhaps he saw too much of Auerbach in the "salons" of Berlin where he was not taken so seriously.[11] Apart from *Neues Leben,* Brandes also appreciated *Barfüssele (Little Barefoot)* and "Die Frau Professorin" ("The Professor's Wife"). The former is an unbelievably sentimental story of a young orphaned girl, an incredibly noble and pure-hearted creature who struggles against miserable circumstances and vile intrigues and who finally receives virtue's reward—a rich farm boy. "Die Frau Professorin" is on a somewhat higher artistic level, but it is still very clear that Auerbach was already passé when Brandes met him. The reason for Brandes' finally writing about him at all seemed to be that he was charmed by the writer's lovable personality. It was Auerbach's sudden death in 1882 that led to the study.

Brandes became interested in Paul Heyse through his novel *Kinder der Welt (Children of the World),* which stirred up a great deal of attention in 1872 during Brandes' stay in Germany because of its anticlerical tendency. He thought he had found a kindred spirit in Heyse in his battle against the clerics in Denmark and took the initiative to an acquaintance with Heyse via letters that resulted in a lifelong friendship.[12] Brandes' letters to Paul Heyse are of special value since they are unusually openhearted even in questions of aesthetics.

Time has not been kind to Heyse's numerous short stories and novels. He belonged to the period between romanticism and true realism, in the same generation as Bjørnson and Ibsen, but without their ability to develop a social philosophy and philosophy of life. He was a Biedermeier figure with all that that implies of "petit bourgeoisie" and devotion to the existing norms and social relations. Heyse's development led to his moving away from Biedermeier, but it was a movement without any notable force. His literary figures were too passive and noble to satisfy Brandes' demands for realism and social involvement.

Thanks to Brandes' initiative, *Kinder der Welt* was translated into Danish, as were a number of Heyse's novels and short stories. Brandes' essay, first published in *Det nittende Aarhundrede*, helped to spread Heyse's fame in Scandinavia. He was so highly thought of and appreciated that he was awarded the Nobel Prize. Brandes was especially impressed with him as a short-story writer. Some of his stories are among the classics in world literature: "L'Arrabbiata" ("The Furious Girl") and "Die Stickerin von Treviso" ("The Embroiderer from Treviso"). His stories had, as Brandes observed, a few simple factors, a few characters, and an action that was compact and clear and planned so that at a given moment something unexpected happened. Heyse was thus an author with a great deal of technical skill and artistic awareness, not least when it was a question of the poetics of the short story, which especially interested Brandes in his long conversations with Heyse and in their correspondence. In his novels and short stories he denounced bigotry in sexual love—a good deed in Brandes' eyes. But Brandes was irritated by his sentimental narration and advised Heyse to read the coolly unsentimental Mérimée. When Brandes published his essay from 1875 in *People and Books*, his admiration for Heyse had begun to wane, and in a letter to another German writer, Fitger, he said that Heyse was hardly the greatest German writer.[13] It was more fitting that this honorary title be reserved for Gottfried Keller.

IV *Flaubert*

Flaubert's novels were a more representative expression of Brandes' literary tastes in 1883 than those of Heyse and Auerbach. It was not until the early 1870s that Brandes discovered Flaubert, but in 1875 he reviewed *Madame Bovary* in very favorable terms in *Det nittende Aarhundrede*. The following lines reveal the strong impression the novel made upon him, he who was more used to the sentimental narrative style in which Auerbach and Dickens excelled: "An icy chill emanated from the book. It was as if this author had finally drawn up Truth from the deep, cold well where it had been dwelling and put it on a pedestal, freezing, and spreading the chill and coldness of the depths."[14] This was the shocklike effect Flaubert had upon his readers at his appearance on the scene, and one can see that it was his abrupt break with the prevalent narrative technique that quickly made the earlier literature seem old-fashioned. Flaubert's way of working on a novel was also in contrast to that of the romantic, who, without preparation, could sit in front of a blank piece of paper and let his imagination flow. Brandes described how extremely carefully Flaubert prepared his novels, how he read ninety-eight volumes before he wrote *Salammbô* and over a hundred before he felt ready to write the section on farming in *Bouvard et Pécuchet (Bouvard and Pecuchet)*. Flaubert satisfied Brandes' criteria for a methodically working writer who retained his artistic demands. Brandes dwelt appreciatively on the carefully wrought detailed scenes in *Madame Bovary*. Flaubert picked and chose words as Brandes as a young man had claimed that writers ought to do. He was not satisfied simply to enumerate, but wanted to give the color, size, and other describable characteristics of a thing. For Flaubert the world existed to be described.

Brandes' essay was written after a careful study of Zola's, Brunetière's, and possibly also Sainte-Beuve's essays on Flaubert. The aesthetics of naturalism colored his view of some of the more romantic examples of Flaubert's authorship, such as the historical novel *Salammbô*. Sainte-Beuve had expressed the opinion that Flaubert was unsuccessful in making the historical characters believable. Flaubert had energetically defended himself and Brandes was on his side. As late as 1902, when Brandes reviewed a new translation of *Salammbô*, he wrote: "not one trait is reminiscent of the modern world."[15]

V *The Goncourt Brothers*

Like Flaubert, the Goncourt brothers were forerunners of true naturalism. In a sketch of his breakthrough program that Brandes sent home from Paris in 1870, he included the Goncourt brothers along with Flaubert and Dumas *fils* as exponents of what he called "the physiological and ethnographic-realistic school."[16] The two brothers' novels had later become popular via naturalism and were associated with Zola, who was their direct heir. Brandes began to read them seriously during the first half of the 1870s and discussed their works on a lecture tour he made in Norway. In a letter to Edmond de Goncourt he claimed that he was working to make them known in Norway. He wrote to Bjørnson in 1878:

I would like to direct your attention to the *Goncourt* brothers in French literature. (They are two novelists who have always worked together until just recently when the one brother died.) Read their "Renée Mauperin," "Germinie Lacerteux" and then all their novels, if you like them.[17]

In the same letter he encouraged Bjørnson also to study Zola. It is hardly likely that Bjørnson was familiar with any of these writers at this point, but he replied:

No, you overestimated me or got me wrong when you thought that I wanted more of *Zola* and the other two brothers (even worse) than a taste of them, even less to steal from them for my own purposes. No, damn it!—and that goes for this page and the next one too![18]

Bjørnson did not exactly want to call the brothers immoral, but he was repulsed by their rank descriptions of reality. "It is ugly, disgusting, and above all false in its psychology—in spite of certain natural parts." In 1879 Brandes suggested to another writer of the breakthrough generation, Alexander Kielland, that he study the Goncourt brothers, and this time he obviously had somewhat better luck. He especially wanted his Nordic colleagues to learn the French authors' methodical, goal-oriented working method. Before Brandes wrote his essay, he wrote to Edmond de Goncourt with some inquiries as to how the two brothers had worked together technically and made use of this information in his essay:

"As soon as we agreed upon an outline," he wrote, "we spoke for an hour or two about the section or part which now would be written, and we each wrote a version by ourselves in separate rooms. Then we read what we had written for each other and we either chose the best one without any discussion or we put together a new part, leaving out the weaker sections."[19]

In his essay, Brandes described the Goncourt brothers' novels as something radically new. Actually, the word *novels* does not adequately describe them. Brandes considered *Germinie Lacerteux* to be the masterpiece of their works. A simple servant girl became the heroine of a novel. It was one of the first attempts in world literature to bring the lower social classes into literature, not as comical figures, but as deep and honestly tragic characters. Zola went farther on the path with *L'Assommoir (The Dram-Shop)*. But the Goncourt brothers, art collectors and connoisseurs of Japanese art and French art of the eighteenth century, also appealed to Brandes because of their exquisite style and refinement. With reference to their position in relation to reality, to ugliness, and to truth, Brandes quoted Sainte-Beuve's polemic against Cousin's motto of the true, the beautiful, and the good. Sainte-Beuve said that if he were to have a device it would be the true, only the true, and the good would have to take care of itself. This was basically Brandes' view as well. He was not repulsed by the fact that Edmond de Goncourt had taken up the problem of prostitution in *La Fille Elisa (The Girl Elisa)*, but he said, with reference to the artist's relation to reality, "that the artistic spirit always modifies and individualizes 'the Truth.'"[20] It is possible that Brandes was recollecting Zola's well-known thesis that a work of art was a corner of reality seen through a temperament.

The essay on the Goncourt brothers was first written in German and read as a speech in Berlin in 1882 for three hundred people. Brandes later gave the same lecture in other parts of Germany and in Scandinavia. It is thus indisputable that Brandes actively helped to make the life and works of the brothers known outside France. He came to know Edmond de Goncourt personally on a visit to Paris in 1889, and when Edmond died in 1896 wrote a reverent obituary that was filled with melancholy. Shortly before Edmond's death, Brandes had met him at the home of Daudet, and he had also been invited to his famous home in Auteuil.

CHAPTER 7

The Discovery of East European Literature

IN the middle of the 1800s, little was yet known of Eastern European literature, especially Russian and Polish, in Western Europe. The simple fact of the matter was that these languages were not so well known. In 1840 a professorship in Slavic languages was established in Paris. Copenhagen was first in Scandinavia to open a department of Slavic languages in 1859 with Caspar Wilhelm Smith as docent and, six years later, professor. The first survey of Russian literature, Koenig's *Literarische Bilder aus Russland (Literary Pictures from Russia)*, was published as early as the 1830s in Germany. In 1843, Wolfsohn published his *Die schönwissenschaftliche Litteratur der Russen (Russian Literature)*. Brandes received his greatest help, however, from Reinholdt's *Geschichte der russischen Litteratur (A History of Russian Literature)* (1882) in his investigation of the Slavic language area. Otherwise it was Vogüé, a Frenchman, who primarily helped to draw attention to Russian literature with his *Le Roman russe (The Russian Novel)*, published in 1886. In France, Mérimée had been a forerunner by learning Russian and translating Gogol's writings into French. Leroy-Beaulieu, another French Russian scholar, wrote for the distinguished *Revue des deux mondes*. He was an acquaintance of Brandes' old friend Noufflard, who served as a link between the two of them.

The writings of Pushkin, Lermontov, and Gogol were all available in Scandinavia during Brandes' student days. In the beginning of the 1870s, Turgenev began to be a big name on the literary market in different places in Europe, including Scandinavia. He was the first of the great Russians to play an important role outside his native country, but was followed by Dostoevsky and Tolstoy in the middle of the 1880s when one may speak of a Slavic movement in European literature at that time, and in this pan-European movement, Brandes played an important part.[1]

I *Poland*

Interest in Poland came first, and the Scandinavian writers expressed a special sympathy for this country when Russian oppression was at its worst. In 1888 Brandes published two works on Slavic literature—twin books entitled *Indtryk fra Polen (Poland: Study of the Land, People, and Literature)* and *Indtryk fra Russland (Impressions of Russia)*—and with these he staked out a new territory for himself and for most of the Scandinavians. While it is true that the books were published two years after Vogüé's *Le Roman Russe*, one could speak of two pioneers following parallel paths, since Brandes visited Poland for the first time in February 1885. He received his first impulse to study Polish cultural life in 1881 when lecturing in German-occupied Posen. He was invited by a German-speaking association, but caught a glimpse of the Polish people's struggle to retain their language and cultural identity and wrote an article about this, later included in *Berlin, Capital of the German Reich*. In Copenhagen in 1884 Brandes received a visit from a Polish doctor, Karol Benni, who invited him to lecture in Warsaw, which he did the following year.

Because of *Main Currents*, which was read both in the German translation and in Polish excerpts, Brandes was well known among literary and culturally interested people, and was introduced in the leading newspapers and magazines. *Prawda*, whose editor was the radical positivist Swietochowski, placed Brandes beside Taine in first place as a contemporary aesthetic philosopher, researcher, and literary critic.[2] *Tygodnik Ilustrowany* wrote that the whole of his literary career to date had been one long struggle for freedom of thought in science and literature, and he was similarly praised in other publications.[3] Brandes' struggle for freedom of ideas was especially popular with the Poles, and it was for this they needed him.

Brandes delivered three lectures in the Warsaw city hall. According to the long article published on the front page of the *Kurier Codzienny*, the first lecture dealt with the intellectual life of Scandinavia during the 1800s. Brandes seems to have dealt primarily with Oehlenschläger, Grundtvig, Hans Christian Andersen, Kierkegaard, Ibsen, and Bjørnson, especially emphasizing the latter

two. The second and third lectures were taken from the fifth part of
Main Currents and met with some criticism since this material was
already familiar from the German translation. Brandes became
prized prey in Warsaw society.[4] The radical camp, which had previously introduced and translated Brandes, made cutting remarks
about the conservatives' enthusiasm over him. Even the leading
families did not hesitate to invite this atheist and man of progress to
their homes. They saw him only as a European celebrity. The conservatives did not know which god they were worshiping.[5]

Brandes delivered his lectures in French, which emphasized
even more the societal character of his appearances. He wrote to his
mother about his overwhelming reception.

If the Goddess of Freedom had become human and visited this unhappy
country for twelve days, she could not be received better than I. I live in a
whirlwind. I haven't been to bed before 4:00 A.M. and am up again between
nine and ten—I don't need any more sleep here. You should have heard my
last lecture. Such violent applause that I had to return to the hall two times.
And now, after the lectures, they're competing with each other to honor
me. The most famous portrait painter, Horowitz, is doing my portrait in
charcoal in order to sell photographs of it.[6]

It is not so strange that Brandes began to feel a certain partiality
toward Poland after such a reception. With this Polish appearance,
his career as a European lecturer began in earnest. Was there any
other critic with his perspective on contemporary European literature? Taine had been limited to the English and French languages
and could barely read German.

After returning to Copenhagen, Brandes made use of his Polish
experiences to give lectures on Poland, especially its romantic literature. It was not until after his second visit to Poland in 1886 that he
decided on the final form of his book on Poland and its literary
culture. In January of that year he once again traveled to Warsaw,
and this time was bold enough to lecture about the country's own
writers. It was with a certain amount of difficulty that his manuscript
passed the Russian censors. He was forced to visit the Russian
governor-general personally in order to get it accepted in time.
Since Polish romantic literature was very nationalistic and anti-
Russian, he had to balance his steps carefully.

This time even more than before, Brandes' appearance was an aid
in the inner resistance to the Russification of Poland, being carried

out by the Poles. A special method for this type of struggle develops in most occupied countries. Passages that more or less openly refer to the oppressor are not applauded—one waits a few minutes and then applauds for apparently no reason at all. By taking up the national literature of oppressed Poland Brandes helped to strengthen its inner resistance and national self-esteem. Once again his lectures were received with wild cheers and he was, as he put it himself, forced to pause several times and was called back again and again at the end of the lecture. They pounded on tables and benches and he heard some cry: "Let's raise a statue in his honor!"[7]

Poland: Study of the Land, People, and Literature was based on three visits to the country, the last in 1887, on which occasion, Brandes wrote in the preface to the book, he found nothing changed. The strongest impression on the contemporary reader is made by his description of how the Polish language was suppressed and how the Polish peasants were kept in ignorance and illiteracy. The common European division into groups was not necessarily applicable to Poland. It did not necessarily follow that a radical was a socialist, since socialization would only help the Russians, the oppressors. Nor did it follow that the intellectuals were anticlerics, since the Roman Catholic Church was one of the bastions against the attempts to Russify the country.

The book on Poland was made up of three sections, of which two were called travel impressions and were based on observations from Brandes' visits, some of a rather dubious racial-psychological character. He presented glimpses of the history of the country, of censorship, of the position of the church, of the influence of the theater, which was great since it was the only platform allowed for the Polish language. The final part was a summary of the romantic literary movement in Poland. Brandes concentrated his presentation upon three great names in Polish romanticism, Mickiewicz, Slowacki, and Krasinski. This concurred with the principle Brandes had applied in *Main Currents*, that is, of dealing with the leading figures. As far as contemporary authors were concerned, he met Sienkiewicz, later a Nobel Prize winner, whose earlier realistic writing he had noted favorably. In the beginning of the 1880s, however, Sienkiewicz had begun to write historical novels in the style of Dumas. These stories brought him millions of readers all over the world. Brandes seems to have thought little of them.[8] Poland's leading woman writer at that time, Eliza Orzeszkowa, was exiled from Warsaw, but Brandes read her unusual novel *Meir Ezofowicz* and spoke favorably of it.

Since *Poland: Study of the Land, People, and Literature* was soon published in German, English, and Swedish, Brandes must have made a great contribution to the awakening of European interest in Poland's situation and its literature.

II *Russia*

Main Currents had begun to be published in Russia in 1881, though not without complications. The third volume, *Reaction in France*, was publicly burned in Moscow.[9] As in Poland, Brandes soon had a good deal of influence and a relatively wide distribution in Russia and was considered to be one of Europe's foremost critics. In an early review of *Main Currents*, he was characterized as a brilliant talent who could summarize the different elements of an idea in a few words.[10] During his stay in Warsaw in 1886, Brandes received an invitation to visit Saint Petersburg. Peter Weinberg, a journalist and translator, seems to have been the motivating force behind the invitation. Brandes traveled to Saint Petersburg in April 1887 and there delivered three lectures in French: one on the Russian novel, one on literary criticism, and one on Emile Zola. A fourth lecture on Danish literature during the 1800s, probably the same he gave in Warsaw, was forbidden by the censors. Instead Brandes gave his old parade number, the comparison between Musset and George Sand from the fifth volume of *Main Currents*.

While in Saint Petersburg Brandes was also invited to Moscow, but before this he took a side trip to Helsinki and Viborg, where he also lectured. As in Poland, he was the center of a great deal of attention, and he spent some time at the manor of the Tenisev family in southern Russia. As so often happened with Brandes' female friends, his relationship with the princess Tenisev developed into a love affair. She became one of the many who learned Danish for Brandes' sake, and she translated some of his writing into Russian. Their correspondence was extensive but is still unpublished.[11] Brandes' Russian trip lasted three months, and it was primarily on the basis of this stay that he wrote and published *Impressions of Russia*. Like the book on Poland, it is not free from loose hypotheses and arbitrary generalizations. Brandes' tendency to make popular psychological generalizations led him to make such statements as "the main trait in the Russian national character is the tendency to 'go to extremes.'" Evidently it was not clear to him that the reason for these extremes was the unusually large class differences.

As in his book on Berlin, to which the two Slavic travel volumes must be compared, Brandes attempted to give a comprehensive picture of the theater, the press, and cultural life in general. But it was a difficult task since he could not speak the language. About half the book dealt with Russian literature from Nestor's *Chronicle* up to the modern Turgenev, Tolstoy, and Dostoevsky.

Brandes became familiar with Turgenev's books as they were translated into Danish during the 1870s. Turgenev was, to be sure, a tendentious author in the spirit of Brandes, but he was forced to write so that his works could pass censorship. Therefore his tendency could never become too explicit in his novels. *The Diary of a Hunter* had been an important factor in the abolition of serfdom. For the first time serfs were described sympathetically and given human value. This work was a typical example of how literature could intervene in social and political life as prescribed by Brandes' breakthrough program.

The section on Turgenev was completed as early as 1883, the year in which Brandes' real interest in Slavic literature was awakened. For Brandes, Turgenev's dominant traits as a writer were sadness and melancholy. Turgenev's technique as a novelist was developed under the influence of the French authors Flaubert and the Goncourt brothers, whom he knew personally and visited frequently on his long journeys to Paris. He advocated an objective, nonmoralizing attitude, which Brandes also argued for at this time. The essay on Turgenev is one of those most often translated. It was included in *Moderne Geister (Eminent Authors of the Nineteenth Century)*, also published in Polish, Russian, and English.

Brandes' relation to Dostoevsky was a special one. Attempts were made to introduce Dostoevsky in Germany in the 1860s with *Memoirs from the House of the Dead*, but the book sold only a few copies. In 1882 the Leipzig publishers made a new attempt, this time with *Crime and Punishment*. To overcome the resistance to the book, the publisher sent the novel to Brandes, among others, and encouraged him to make a little propaganda for it. Brandes read the book and was very impressed. He wrote to Schandorph, a Danish author: "I am very preoccupied with Dostoevsky's unusual novel *Raskolnikov*, which I once recommended to Edvard and which I will write about sometime. It is in its own way no less new and remarkable than *L'Assommoir*."[12] He wrote in similar terms to Paul Heyse in Germany.

Brandes' first article on Dostoevsky appeared in the Danish *Morgenbladet* on April 22, 1882, and was followed by two more articles. These were later sent to other Scandinavian newspapers and to a Vienna paper, *Neue Freie Presse*. The essay was also published in Polish in *Nowa Reforma* (1891) and in Serbian in *Zvezda* (1899). After that it was even published in Bulgarian and Russian in a collection of Brandes' literary character sketches, and appeared in several of the translations of *Impressions of Russia* including the American edition (1889). Brandes' articles on Dostoevsky had their greatest effect in Scandinavia. One immediate result of his contacts with *Morgenbladet* was that *Crime and Punishment* began to run as a serial. It appeared in book form in Norwegian the same year and in Danish and Swedish in 1884. There is hardly any doubt that Brandes helped to make Dostoevsky famous in Germany and Northern Europe.

Actually, Brandes' first reaction to Dostoevsky was not totally favorable, but he was aware that here was a unique and great writer. In a letter he stated that he had no sympathy for descriptions of madness in otherwise healthy people. Asceticism and Christian mysticism were also foreign to him.[13] But as Dostoevsky's works were translated into Western European languages, Brandes could broaden his knowledge of him. He also read Vogüé's important introduction in *Le Roman Russe*. Brandes' section on Dostoevsky in *Impressions of Russia* dealt primarily with *Crime and Punishment*. He simply included his article from 1883. As far as *The Brothers Karamazov* is concerned, he spotted the story of the Great Inquisitor, which is still one of the high points for many of Dostoevsky's admirers.

While in Russia, Brandes met Orest Miller, the first Russian biographer of Dostoevsky, and it is possible that their conversations helped to paint a more diversified picture of the author than what was possible on the basis of the meager amount of existing literature in German and French. Vogüé portrayed Dostoevsky as a barbarian, a stranger, in contrast to the more Western-oriented Turgenev. Brandes was of much the same opinion:

Whereas Turgenev's writing could almost be considered to be emigrant literature, with Dostoevsky it is clear that we remain on Russian soil; he is an autochthonous writer, "the original Scythian," a true barbarian without a drop of classic blood in his veins.[14]

Brandes was also a victim of the misunderstanding that Dostoevsky's novels lacked a planned composition. In *Literarische Streifzüge durch Russland (Literary Wanderings through Russia)*, which was one of Brandes' sources, Zabel wrote that Dostoevsky knew nothing about the technical composition of the novel, of the main action and the secondary action. And Brandes continued in the same vein when he claimed that Dostoevsky let his books be printed "before the ink dried on the page." Dostoevsky's strength lay in the depth of his psychological perception, that was very clear to Brandes. His portrait of Dostoevsky was original and diversified.

Tolstoy, the third great Russian, became well known in Western Europe at about the same time as Dostoevsky, and when Brandes wrote *Impressions of Russia,* a good deal of his work was already translated into Danish: *Sebastopol Tales* (1884), *Childhood and Boyhood, The Cossacks, War and Peace* (1885), *Youth* (1886), and *Anna Karenina* (1886–1887). The suddenness and concentration of these Tolstoy translations is noteworthy. One could really speak of a wave of Russian literature at this time. Brandes had no personal contact with Tolstoy during his stay in Russia, but he gave a speech on Tolstoy in Moscow and Mrs. Tolstoy and her daughters were present on this occasion. He was also invited to the Tolstoys' home in Moscow, but in the author's absence. He refrained from making the pilgrimage to Tolstoy's manor, Yasnaya Polyana, but described the situation there on the basis of a report from a "rather hard-boiled lawyer."[15] The owner himself went around dressed in ragged clothes like a poor peasant and was plagued with visitors, whom Brandes' reporter divided into three categories: the half-crazy, who saw what they wanted to see in the writer; the parasites, who came to take advantage of Tolstoy's love of mankind; and the journalists, who wrote about him according to the different political views they represented.

For Brandes, the most pronounced trait in Tolstoy's writing was his "faithfulness to reality." He was struck by Tolstoy's detailed realism, which was on a par with Flaubert's. But Tolstoy's Christian morality, which became quite fanatic at the end of his life, was foreign to Brandes. And he returned to his strange opinions on art and science several times—for instance, his inability to see Shakespeare's greatness. When *The Kreutzer Sonata* was published with its puritanic view of marriage, Brandes reacted with a sharp attack in his essay "Dyret i Mennesket" ("The Animal in Man").[16]

CHAPTER 8

Nordic Literature and the Debate on Morals

AFTER his return to Copenhagen in 1883, Brandes tackled Scandinavian literature with renewed interest and published two books with special national ties: a biography of Ludvig Holberg, the great Norwegian-Danish comedy writer of the 1700s, and *Essays: Danske Personligheder (Essays: Danish Personalities,* 1889), which was one of a pair of books in a collection with the same title, though the other was subtitled *Foreign Personalities,* also from 1889.

I *Holberg*

The biography of Holberg was written in haste, on order, and published in connection with the bicentennial of the author's birth. Its point of departure was the influence of heritage and environment, the formulas Brandes had previously applied in imitation of Taine. Thus he began with a description of Bergen, the Hansa city that was Holberg's place of birth, and then went on to the characteristics Holberg could have inherited from his father: "From him [the father], the son could probably have inherited his taste for travel and adventure; since he had served in both the Maltese and Venetian military service. . . ."[1] But environment in its broader meaning of the atmosphere and spirit of the times is most dominant in the book on Holberg. More than one-third of the book is devoted to a description of the intellectual and general cultural atmosphere in Denmark and Europe in which the young Holberg traveled. Brandes called it a time of wigs and boots, with wigs as a symbol of the unnaturalness and artificiality of the epoch. He claimed that not less than 45,000 pounds of flour was used to powder wigs in Denmark, and the book is full of such sensational information.

According to Brandes, the dominant trait of Holberg's literary profile was determined by classicism as a doctrine.[2] It followed that Holberg was a rationalist and actually a freethinker too, as was Brandes.[3] His hatred of pedantry was emphasized as well as his distaste for scholarly specialization. Brandes thus sought out such traits as were in accord with his own personality. Holberg was also portrayed as someone underrated, a martyr whose greatness was unappreciated by his countrymen. His plays received little space in the volume, but still the reader was presented with a very well-oriented guide. Brandes had known Holberg backwards and forwards since his student days and Paul Rubow, one of Denmark's foremost Holberg scholars, wrote in 1928 that Brandes' book was still the best introduction around to Holberg's writing.[4]

When the jubilee issue of Holberg's works was published, Brandes was impelled to write a short character sketch of the playwright, which was included in *Essays: Danish Personalities*. The article is interesting because the introductory section is an example of Brandes' first open declaration of his hero-worship. It also was an indication that he was moving away from the aesthetics of naturalism. One could say that naturalism was democratic in that it gave the lower classes access to literature. Zola pronounced sentence on the idea that imagination was the writer's most important instrument and instead spoke of the necessity of being able to observe reality, of the necessity of a *"sens du réel."* Brandes had previously agreed to this. In 1887 he wrote in his essay on Holberg:

Lately much has been spoken and written against the worship of genius. It has been found that the critic's analyses of genius have liberated him [the genius] from the burden of gratitude since they attributed much in each work to other writers than the author. They have meant to lessen genius, to reduce it to a product of its time and an expression of its culture. The influence of greatness was said to be overestimated. Everything would have come into being even without genius, only more slowly.[5]

In the continuation of the above-quoted passage Brandes spoke of the tendency to what he called "an intellectual ostracism of genius," which was said to have received nourishment via a study of the natural sciences. Brandes argued against the belief, stemming from Taine, that new ideas and points of view actually originated in the masses, and instead asserted that such ideas originated in a few who were far above the masses.

Similar attempts to rationalize his hero-worship can be found in Brandes' diary from the same time. He cited one such passage in his autobiography.[6] According to Brandes, Holberg was one of these great creative persons who in no way was a spokesman or collective voice for his country or fellow citizens. He acquired the most advanced and liberated way of thinking for his time via contact with progressive personalities all over Europe—exactly as Brandes felt he himself had. His education was not national and local, but universal. According to Brandes, Holberg hated Denmark with its pedantry and its stiff social and cultural pattern. Since he was so far ahead of his countrymen in education and culture, he became an educator for the future.

Brandes wanted to divide creative personalities into two types: the breeders and the bearers. The breeders were male, metaphorically speaking; and it was they who fertilized their time, while the bearers were "female," and it was they who received ideas from the breeders and gave them artistic form. It would not be unreasonable to try to fit Brandes himself into this pattern: he had a fertile intelligence, which supplied the Nordic authors of the modern breakthrough with ideas and suggestions to which they later gave an artistic form. He thus gave critics of his own type a greater dignity in the artistic hierarchy than purely fictional writers. Seen in this light, Holberg was both a breeder and a bearer. The basis for this way of looking at things seems to have been inspired by Brandes' first study of Nietzsche.

II *Oehlenschläger*

The other long study in *Essays: Danish Personalities* was devoted to Oehlenschläger, the writer long regarded as the greatest representative of Danish romanticism. Strangely enough, Brandes never wrote a longer biography of this key figure of nineteenth-century literature in Denmark. The article in *Essays: Danish Personalities* was, however, an extensive character sketch, and it took up somewhat the same problem as the essay on Holberg—the breeding genius as opposed to the bearing genius—though Brandes used other terms and angles of approach.

In his play *Aladdin*, Oehlenschläger painted a picture of the romantic genius as a naïve, lazy youth who found happiness and riches without any drudgery or methodical work. Noureddin, the methodically working seeker in the play, was described in dark colors as an almost repulsive figure. Brandes was very displeased with this. With Noureddin, Oehlenschläger had lampooned his friend and critic Steffens, the man who had introduced romantic philosophy and aesthetics in Denmark. Steffens sowed the seeds for romanticism in Denmark in the same way that Brandes did for the men of the modern breakthrough, and Brandes recognized the kinship. Throughout his career, Brandes struggled against the view of artistic creativity as expressed in *Aladdin*, and in his essay on Oehlenschläger he expanded the character sketch of the literary figure to include the entire Danish population, who, he said, bore the mark of the same naïveté that characterized the figure of Aladdin.

In the continuation of his essay, Brandes traced the fate of the Aladdin motif in Nordic literature, especially its influence on Ibsen. He pointed out that it was seen for the first time in Ibsen's *Kongsemnene (The Pretenders)*, in which Håkon corresponded to Aladdin and brooding Skule to Noureddin. In *Peer Gynt* Ibsen pronounced final judgment on the purely imaginative man, and thus on the romantic ideal. It was a phase in Ibsen's inventory and settlement with his romantic heritage. As Brandes pointed out, the similarities to Oehlenschläger's *Aladdin* were also striking in other respects, especially the mother figures. Thus Brandes' essay on Oehlenschläger was both a profound and an extensive analysis of a central motif in Nordic literature, and it therefore has a special position in his writings on the literature of his own country.

III *Heiberg*

A third study in *Essays: Danish Personalities* dealt with J. L. Heiberg, a postromantic who had something of a key role in Danish cultural life when Brandes himself was a young student. Now Heiberg is remembered mostly for his charming and perhaps overlooked vaudevilles, of which *En Sjael efter Døden (A Soul after Death)* is best known, but for the young Brandes and his generation he was also the *great* critic and aesthetic lawmaker.

Heiberg was very dependent upon Hegel and worked with a similar arsenal of categories. Brandes had unlimited confidence in and admiration for Heiberg's aesthetics during his first years of study, and when the master died in 1860, he wrote that he had loved him like a father.[7] Heiberg was the classic example of how one man can exert a decisive influence on the cultural life of a small country. Brandes stated in his essay that he was caught in Heiberg's grip until the middle of the 1870s. There are no biographies of any of the authors in the first parts of *Main Currents*—instead Brandes went directly to the literary work in a way that was reminiscent of Heiberg.[8] The essay was written in 1889, and at this time Brandes was able to regard Heiberg's system from a certain ironic distance. He did not deal with Heiberg's plays at all.

The rest of *Essays: Danish Personalities* consists of an obituary in honor of J. P. Jacobsen and a number of studies of less well-known names in nineteenth-century Danish literature. One of these that was especially interesting was a study of Karen Blixen's father, Wilhelm Dinesen, who published many travel and nature books under the pseudonym Boganis, which were praised by Brandes in spite of the fact that Dinesen represented a genre that was fairly foreign to him.

IV   *The Debate on Morals*

Throughout his career as a writer and debater, Brandes gave special attention to the oppressed situation of women in society. In his foreword to his translation of Mill's *The Subjection of Women* in 1869 he wrote:

We treat our women's spirits the same way the Chinese treat their women's feet, and like the Chinese, we perform this operation in the name of beauty and femininity. A woman whose feet have grown freely and healthily seems unfeminine and ugly to a Chinese, especially a Chinese woman. In our bourgeois little China, a woman who has been allowed to develop freely also seems to be an ugly and unfeminine malformation, and the narrow-mindedness of our authors and poets has probably accepted and defended the judgment of this bourgeois mass. Only freedom and the free are truly beautiful.[9]

In a new foreword to the second edition of Mill's book in 1885 Brandes disclaimed several points in Mill's theories about the existing situation of marriage and the weak position women had in it. The crux of the situation was, he stated, the introduction of the right to inherit after the father, which he related to Engels' work *Der Ursprung der Familie, des Privateigenthums und des Staats (The Origin of the Family, Private Property, and the State)*. At about the same time that this second foreword was written Brandes became involved in a long debate on the situation of women in which he defended the point of view behind the passage above, namely, that nothing that is natural for the human being in general ought to be suppressed, and that was true for women as well as men. The sexual instinct is a naturally conditioned factor in both men and women and ought to be accepted and affirmed. But general opinion was not nearly ready to accept the fact that woman's sexual instinct was as justified as man's and that in neither case was it a question of sin or immorality.

One could, however, speak of immorality when it was a question of the double morality of men and of the widespread prostitution. Bjørnson brought these questions to debate in his play *En handske* (*The Gauntlet*, 1883), which was about a woman who discovered that her fiancé had had sexual experiences before he met her. She broke the engagement because of this. Thus Bjørnson introduced what he termed "the demand for moral equality," which meant that women had the right to demand the same abstinence from men before marriage as men demanded of women.

Several Scandinavian writers took up Bjørnson's "gauntlet," thus initiating a pan-Nordic debate on morality.[10] Strindberg wrote one of his funniest short stories, "Virtue's Reward" in the collection entitled *Giftas* (*Married*, 1884), in reply to Bjørnson's play. Brandes entered this debate on sexual morality because of a short story by a Norwegian named Arne Garborg. The story is entitled "Ungdom" ("Youth") and in it the main character receives a copy of Bjørnson's *Gauntlet* from his betrothed. Garborg's short story was an ironic disclaimer of Bjørnson's puritanic view of sex. Brandes discussed this in his essay on Arne Garborg, which appeared in a publication entitled *Tilskueren* in 1885 and later in his collection *Essays: Foreign Personalities* (1889). He wrote:

Here there is a glimpse of the same reaction as in Strindberg's "Virtue's Reward." This seems to be the meaning: Nothing whatsoever is won by continually setting greater and greater demands on chastity. It takes no great talent to demand chastity. And it is not because of love for vice that mature people shake their heads at it. It is because they know that frail virtue is always much more natural and healthier than an unnatural vice, and as things are now for us human beings, the choice is usually between these two. Let education, with a natural and open presentation of the relationship between the sexes, help to force the instincts inside natural limits; but let us not fool ourselves that they can be suppressed or eliminated without making people defective or stupid. Asceticism, which at the moment is practiced by the great number of unmarried upper-class women, is a miserable thing, an unnatural thing, a sacrifice which is often accompanied by worthless prejudice. The life of the instincts is and will continue to be earthbound for the blossoming of fantasy and beauty as well as for smelly, poisonous plants. If spiritual credit is sometimes too dearly paid for with the sacrifice of purity and innocence, then true purity, no less than apparent, can also be paid for too dearly when it is accompanied by consuming regret and narrow perspectives for goodness and suppressed longing.[11]

Brandes' views on sexuality were in accord with the arguments of George Drysdale, an English doctor whose book *The Elements of Social Science; or, Physical, Sexual and Natural Religion* was published in Swedish in 1878 and widely read. Bjørnson wrote in a letter to Brandes that he did not like it at all, but the latter found it "honest and good."[12] Drysdale claimed that every person who had too little sexual contact lived an unnatural life, and this was true of women as well as men. He also claimed that hysterics in women and all that followed along with it was a result of abstinence or a twisted view of sexuality. With all his faults, Drysdale was something of an early Freud, and he was very important in introducing a more open view of sexuality in Scandinavia. Brandes took sides in the "morality question" in a series of articles during the period 1885–1887. He wrote, among other things, an article on Luther published in *Tilskueren* in 1885 and later in *Essays: Foreign Personalities.* He scratched the polish off the theologian and reformer and found underneath a thriving, life-loving Renaissance man. Luther quite simply revolted against the asceticism of the Catholic Church.

Luther claimed that neither man nor woman was created for chastity, and the commandment ought to have been: Be fertile and increase your numbers. It became apparent that Luther's writings were a gold mine for arguments against an ascetic and puritanic sexual morality. Luther was so determined in his opposition to sexual abstinence that he said that if a couple for some reason did not want to divorce because of a lack of satisfaction in their·marriage, then the wife, for example, ought to find a lover, with her husband's permission, either a stranger or her husband's brother, and any children should be regarded as her husband's.[13]

In 1886 Brandes found another occasion to take up the problem of sexual relations once again when Hans Jaeger, a Norwegian author, was sentenced to sixty days in prison and fined for his book *Fra Kristiania-Bohêmen (From the Bohemians of Kristiania)*.[14] While it is true that Brandes thought the book unartistic and raw in its tone, he said that its strength lay in the fact that the description was true. It was the social situation—the prostitution of women in Kristiania—that was really raw.

Brandes' actual leap into the debate on morality was based on a meeting of the cause of women in Copenhagen, which had inspired Elisabeth Grundtvig and two other women to express their opinion on Bjørnson's demand for "moral equality" and against the above-quoted section in Brandes' article on Garborg. The contribution was published in a magazine entitled *Kvinden og Samfundet (Woman and Society)* and stated that a woman's sexual instinct was not so strong as a man's and that, because of her finer nature, her "sexual instinct was expressed in a spiritual manner," as one of the ladies put it.[15] They denied that a woman's sexual abstinence would lead to negative consequences for her health. But one of the articles ended with the words "for in any case, none of us are angels." One of the unmarried ladies quite frankly said: "There is nothing at all wrong with me, not even a little tummy ache." Brandes justifiably felt himself attacked and wrote a reply under the pseudonym "Lucifer" in *Politiken,* in which he was bitingly ironic toward both the puritanic ladies and Bjørnson:

The point of departure for all of the ladies is the same: "women of culture" (one of them prefers the expression "normal women") are extremely moral people: men of culture or normal men are on the other hand immoral people. What to do with this miserable situation? Should women "now be like men" (immoral) or men "like women" (lilies)? And the question is answered, as is expected of pretty ladies, in the same way as all ladies, in favor of morality. Men ought to be *like women,* it is clear: pure creatures, what in modern language are called *Gloves* (in old Danish: hand stockings [untranslatable pun on *Haandstrømper*]).[16]

It is clear that Brandes, as a practiced polemic, had no problem in his game against the ladies in *Dansk Kvindesamfund (Danish Women's League).* He elaborated his point of view in a number of subsequent articles in *Politiken.* He refused to approve of the prevailing silently accepted order of things, which was built on the two cornerstones of prostitution and marriage, and where the upper-class women abstained from sexual relations before marriage while the young men frequented brothels. He wrote that he was not impressed by these "marriages of habit where half the women give birth to the children of men for whom they feel absolutely nothing."[17] In general he refused to define virtue in the way Miss Grundtvig defined it. Thus, as far as Brandes was concerned, it was a clear confrontation on the question of morality. When he wrote, and after publication of the first article it was under his own name, Brandes was fully aware that there were few others who dared to or were able to. What would happen to a female headmistress or doctor who opposed Miss Grundtvig in these questions? This was still such a burning issue that they would quite simply become socially impossible.

Brandes' open references to Bjørnson's drama in the quotation above when he spoke of "gloves" challenged Bjørnson to reply in a Norwegian newspaper, but at first he thought that someone else wrote under the name "Lucifer." This led Georg Brandes to write a new article, the style of which ought to have revealed to Bjørnson who lay behind it:

I am actually none other than the true good old Lucifer himself. My story is well enough known. Since the days of my youth I have been living in the best of company. When I wrote about *angels,* warmly and sympathetically as I did, it is because I myself am one. Of course a *fallen* one—which is naturally not true of the ladies, heaven forbid!—but still an angel. My specialty was from the beginning *Light, the greatest enlightenment*—this is my contact with *Politiken*—but this wasn't looked upon so well from people in higher places, and so I fell down from heaven, just like Danebrog [the Danish flag, which was said to have fallen down from heaven.].[18]

He concluded by saying that he got emotionally involved every time he heard virtue praised, no matter by whom: "from *Scavenius'* lips in Store Heddinge or from *Bjørnson's* lips in Paris, or from Miss *Grundtvig's* and the other *angels'* lips in the angelical city of Copenhagen." In the last sentence Brandes made a connection that upset Bjørnson very much. The Scavenius mentioned was the minister of culture, who had been interrupted while making an election speech in praise of morality and asked how his opinions could be consistent with the fact that he frequented the brothels in

Copenhagen. The person who asked the question had seen the minister of culture go into one of Copenhagen's notorious brothels. With this incident, the prevalent double standard of morality received a fairly concrete illustration.

Bjørnson aimed at Brandes' attack against Elisabeth Grundtvig, which he saw as incredibly shabby. Brandes replied with an article in *Politiken* entitled "Bjørnson as a Polemic," in which he spoke of the latter's preference for generally accepted truths. Being the son of a clergyman had set its roots in him, Brandes said, as well as the tendency to preach. The public debate between Bjørnson and Brandes continued with a few more articles. Brandes claimed that he had been suffering the shame of being the apostle of immorality for over a decade and that he was sick and tired of it. In his private correspondence with Bjørnson he demanded that the latter publically declare his friendship and take back his accusations of shabbiness and rawness. Bjørnson, to be sure, wrote in one of his contributions that he regarded Brandes as

one of the richest intelligences of all those working in Scandinavia; his artistic skill is surely the greatest. And he is a personality; few have his warmth and clarity: his picture remains etched on the soul of those who have seen him.[19]

But he still refused to take back his words.

On September 4, 1887, Brandes concluded a letter to Bjørnson with the following words: "I ask you once again: Will you take back your words? If not I hereby write my name for the last time, yours, Georg Brandes." Bjørnson's reply began with the word "No." And thus, because of the debate on morality, Brandes was forced to break his contact with one of Scandinavia's most influential and appreciated writers. He had tried to avoid it as long as possible, but finally their controversy was brought to a head. As Brandes was once again pestered by morality preachers with a new series of pamphlets aimed at him, he could well have used Bjørnson's friendship.

The great debate served to increase Brandes' isolation in Denmark, and several of his old friends severed their relations with him. He wrote to his ever-faithful friend Paul Heyse in Germany about Bjørnson's campaign and the speech on "monogamy and polygamy" with which he was touring Scandinavia:

I don't know, dear friend, if you have been following the strange moralizing plague which has been spreading throughout the north ever since the publication of Bjørnson's *Gauntlet*. All the old syphilitics infatuated with the idea of male virginity! All the old virgins proclaiming their demands for equality! And Bjørnson, the old goat, seems to have come into something which resembles a woman's "critical period," traveling all around the countries, giving the same speech day out and day in, in eighty different cities in Scandinavia, preaching the new gospel, that we should not kiss the girls. And the three Scandinavian tribes are moved by this while the only true profit to be had is the thousands and thousands of crowns which are jingling into Bjørnson's pocket.[20]

The isolation that resulted from the morality feud was increased by private worries at this time caused by pressures on Brandes' own marriage. In 1885 he had begun an affair with a young lady whose family was one of the wealthiest and most influential in Copenhagen and who strongly disapproved of her contact with Brandes. His love affair with Bertha Knudtzon led both to controversies and threats from her family and to suspicions and jealous scenes with his wife. Later on his marriage failed completely.

One of the many who wished to make his acquaintance was the promising Swedish authoress, Victoria Benedictsson. Brandes' aura of apostle of emancipation and his power as a critic tempted many to come to Copenhagen. Victoria Benedictsson, who lived in an unhappy marriage with a much older man—a much more common occurrence than we now can imagine—fell in love with Brandes. He had been spoiled with women's favors and did not return her feelings but exploited her need for tenderness in weak moments. Their affair ended when Victoria Benedictsson committed suicide in 1888. She described her life with Brandes in a diary published after her death. It is a tragic and moving document of the times, one of the most remarkable in Swedish literature.[21] There were many reasons for her suicide, one of which was that her novel *Fru Marianne (Mrs. Marianne)* received unfavorable criticism in a review by Edvard Brandes. The novel appeared at an unfortunate time in the literary political situation and was meant as a defense for traditional marriage. At the same time that the authoress published a book in defense of marital fidelity, she herself took the initiative in a love affair with Brandes, who represented the opposite point of view. It was an illustrative example of the consequences of suppressing a woman's right to sexual and emotional expression. Victoria Benedictsson did not have the strength to bear this conflict and so took her own life.

CHAPTER 9

Once You Discovered Me, It Wasn't Hard to Find Me

INCLUDED in *Essays: Foreign Personalities* was an essay on Nietzsche, which was significant in that it helped to make his philosophy known all over Europe. In a way this was one of the paradoxes in Brandes' ideological profile, that he could write favorably about such totally different figures as Mill, Lassalle, and Nietzsche. It may also seem strange that Nietzsche's works could have had such a great influence on European cultural life during the end of the nineteenth and the beginning of the twentieth centuries. When Brandes began his work on Nietzsche, the latter had already completed the major part of his work, but without creating any special attention. Brandes knew of Nietzsche's existence and activity while he was in Berlin. There he had met Lou Salomé and Paul Rée, who both played an important role in Nietzsche's life. Elisabeth Förster-Nietzsche stated that Brandes had made inquiries about Nietzsche during his stay in Berlin in 1883.[1] A Viennese visiting Nietzsche in Sils-Maria in 1886 told him of Brandes' interest, which led the philosopher to send one of his books to Brandes. Brandes stated that his interest in Nietzsche was awakened when he read his pamphlet against Strauss in 1872.[2] It seems that Brandes read Nietzsche's *Jenseits von Gut and Böse (Beyond Good and Evil)* with no apparent reaction at first. It was not until he read *Zur Genealogie der Moral (Toward a Genealogy of Morals)* that he became seriously interested in him. In his letter of thanks to Nietzsche he used the term *aristocratic radicalism* to describe Nietzsche's philosophy, and Nietzsche replied that that was the most intelligent thing that had thus far been said about his way of thinking.[3]

I *Lectures on Nietzsche*

Brandes was struck by Nietzsche's attack on ascetic morality in *Zur Genealogie der Moral,* and felt he had found a kindred spirit in the debate on morality. But he was also attracted by Nietzsche's contempt for democracy. The idea that the development of humanity was dependent upon a few creative individuals who ought to have the possibility to function in peace was one that Brandes, as well as many other contemporary intellectuals, soon caught on to. The introduction of general elections had not immediately led to the social changes many had hoped for. The masses were still for the most part illiterate. This was probably one of the reasons for this backlash of distrust against democracy. Reading Nietzsche released many of the ideas that Brandes had been thinking about without daring to express. To be sure, Nietzsche made a chaotic impression on Brandes at first with such works as *Also sprach Zarathustra,* about which he wrote to Heyse:

He has sent me an allegorical collection of stories: *Thus Spoke Zarathustra* (Part 4) which I can hardly understand. Some parts behind the perplexing mask are basically well known and trivial. Other parts are dangerously close to madness.[4]

In December 1887, Brandes wrote in a letter to Schandorph, the Danish writer, that Christianity represented a slave uproar in morality and that the same was true of the Reformation and the revolution, and in April 1888 he wrote another letter to Schandorph in which both the thought and the style bear the mark of Nietzsche:

I have again been studying philosophy for a long time. I am studying a German philosopher who is living in Italy. His ideas and mine agree so completely that I find him excellent, the only philosoper alive that I have any use for. We have been in touch with each other a few years. His name sounds strange and he is still unknown. His name is Friedrich Nietzsche. But he is a genius. Lately I have cast off one of my snakeskins. I have turned from the Englishmen back to the Germans in philosophy. English philosophy seems to me to have reached its peak. But my friend N. has the future ahead of him. I am also becoming more radical, less historic and continually more aristocratic in my aesthetic and historic viewpoints. I don't believe for one minute that great men are a concentrate of the mass, are created from below, are expressions of the flock, etc. Everything comes

from the great ones, everything is sifted down from them. I am happy for
the strong inner life I am living and for the fermentation of my ideas.
Stagnation is terrible and shedding skins is real and essential youth.[5]

The essence of Brandes' view of Nietzsche is contained in the
above-quoted passage. There is his questioning of the utilitarianism
of Mill and Bentham, which is sometimes summarized in the
phrase: the greatest happiness to the greatest number. This motto
was one of the cornerstones for both the radical liberalism and the
democratic socialism whose spokesman Brandes had often been.
There is the belief in the great, creative human being, which he
later developed. The works of his old age, the extensive biographies
of Shakespeare, Goethe, Voltaire, Michelangelo, and Julius Caesar,
were all written with the basic idea that everything comes from
great men. When Brandes claimed that he had become less historic,
Nietzsche's criticism of the antiquarian description of history in *Vom
Nutzen und Nachteil der Historie* (*On the Usefulness and Disadvan-
tage of History*) was in the background.

The result of Brandes' study of Nietzsche was at first a series of
lectures delivered in Copenhagen in the spring of 1888. For the first
time since his return to Copenhagen his public let him down. The
unknown German philosopher was not attractive enough to draw a
large audience, although about three hundred people came.[6] *Politiken*, the daily newspaper the Brandes brothers had helped to found,
published extensive reports from each lecture. The series came to
be especially important for August Strindberg, who was living outside Copenhagen at the time. Strindberg read the reports in *Politiken*, met Brandes at this time, and was at once seized with a passionate interest in Nietzsche. On May 17, only nine days after the
last lecture, Strindberg wrote to Heidenstam: "Buy a copy of a book
by a modern German philosopher by the name of Nietzsche. GB has
just given some lectures on him. There you have got *everything!*
Don't deny yourself that pleasure!"[7]

Via Strindberg, another Swedish writer, Ola Hansson, came in
contact with Nietzsche and later he, much to Brandes' displeasure,
published an article on the philosopher in a German publication
before Brandes' was published in the same language. Brandes became an intermediary between Nietzsche and Strindberg, and the
latter sent Nietzsche copies of *Married* and *The Father*. Two
women-haters found each other, as Nietzsche noted in a letter to his

friend Peter Gast.[8] Nietzsche became rather widely known among the writers and intellectuals in Scandinavia, and in his letters he spoke with a certain pleasure of the good nothern winds from Copenhagen. He was aware that his philosophy had begun to meet with approval.

One of the basic problems in Nietzsche's philosophy was the concept of culture, which Brandes discussed in his essay. What is culture and how should it be furthered? Like Heine, whom he admired, Nietzsche was a harsh critic of German arrogance and the pedantry that thrived in the German universities. Nietzsche hated the German nationalism that reached its high point in the war of 1870 with France. He claimed that the time of national culture was past and it was time to replace it with a European culture. Many of the educated people in different countries already felt themselves to be kindred spirits and countrymen.[9] Brandes was such a man, with contacts in both Eastern and Western Europe and in Scandinavia, and he had tackled European literature as a whole without a thought as to the different language areas. He was a pioneer in this respect. In his first letter, Nietzsche called him "ein solcher guter Europäer und Cultur-Missionär," and these words of praise, "the good European," fit few people better than Georg Brandes.

Another term the young Nietzsche coined was "educational Philistine," which Brandes also felt was a discovery. An educational Philistine is a person who thinks that his type of education is the only correct type and who reinforces this point of view by finding people of the same mind all over, people who have adopted the ideas of the great dead men and worshiped them without understanding that these seekers were not men who had found or even believed they had found truth. Nietzsche sought an education that would make people free, independent, and critical, not pious worshipers of a cultural heritage. He continued this line of thought in another of his writings from his younger days, *Schopenhauer als Erzieher (Schopenhauer as an Educator)*, in which he spoke of the good teacher as a liberator. Here Brandes could not resist a reference to Kierkegaard, who challenged his contemporaries to be "individuals." This was also what Nietzsche was striving for. But he also claimed that independent, free people had to educate themselves against the times instead of with them. This was an idea that appealed to Brandes, and he tended to move away from Taine's idea that the great man is a child, the sum of the times in which he is living: "What we call the spirit of the times, is at first only the result of a few minds."[10] This might be both correct and incorrect, since it was naturally not a question of moving in a flock and accepting everything that is new simply because it is new, as often happens. In such situations people with civil courage are needed who dare to go against "the spirit of the times" and in that way change its character.

Young Nietzsche worshiped genius, a tendency he shared with Brandes as well. He also found support for this attitude in Renan, the French philologist and religious historian whom he had always admired. Brandes quoted the following statement: "Humanity must continuously work to produce great individuals—that and only that is its task."[11] This became one of the key sentences in his essay. At times one wonders when Brandes is speaking and when it is Nietzsche's turn. The above was a quotation from Nietzsche but supported with a reference to Renan, and the quotation then became one of the points of departure in the debate that followed Brandes' essay on Nietzsche. Both Brandes and Nietzsche felt they were underrated geniuses, unappreciated by the establishment. This was one of the psychological factors behind this philosophy.

Brandes skimmed over some of Nietzsche's works such as *Menschliches, Allzumenschliches (Human, All Too Human)*, which with its aphoristic composition was difficult to understand. He also refrained from a systematic analysis of such works as *Morgenröthe (The Dawn)*, *Die fröhliche Wissenschaft (The Joyful Science)*, and *Jenseits von Gut und Böse (Beyond Good and Evil)*. He plucked small pearls here and there without any attempt at a picture of the totality, and this is an obvious weakness in his essay. On the other hand he was more interested in *Zur Genealogie der Moral*. Here is the discussion of the slave uproar in morality referred to earlier. Nietzsche claimed that the word *good* received its original meaning from the rich and the powerful, and that for them "good" meant the same thing as "powerful," "aristocratic." The lower classes were described as "common" and "low." But they, the oppressed, later changed the meaning of the word. Those who suffer, the sick, the ugly are the good, and the rich and powerful are evil. Christianity produced this morality when it directed itself to the poor and sick and to the slaves. This side of Nietzsche's philosophy is his most repellant. It is almost a question of a furious antidemocracy, the reaction of an isolated and partially unappreciated philosopher against an awakening interest in the oppressed and exploited people of the society of the nineteenth century.

One can find a similar fear of democracy in another of the German philosophers Brandes wrote about who was very popular at this time: Eduard von Hartmann.[12] Brandes protested strongly against Hartmann's claim that it was useless to wake the sleeping masses from their vegetative peace with the help of education. Both Nietzsche's and Hartmann's philosophies in part can be seen as attempts at defending a social status quo or the supremacy of their own class. And Brandes did not agree with them on this point. He had always felt himself to be something of a tribune for the people, but misanthropy and pessimism took the glow away from his progressive optimism of the early 1870s.

Nietzsche's theory on the origin of the conscience in *Zur Genealogie der Moral* was very appealing to Brandes. Nietzsche claimed that society had not come into being because of a treaty, but rather because a ruthless conquerer had subjugated the people. The oppressed, who have no outlet for their active instincts, suppress them. Their ideals become self-denial, unselfishness, and so on, instead of those previously cultivated: cunningness, rapaciousness, lust for power. A bad conscience is based on guilt feelings in relation to our ancestors and our god. The natural instincts of aggression and cruelty are directed to the individual himself and result in self-torture. Brandes obviously felt that he had found a rational explanation for the sin-guilt complex that plays such a large role in Christianity. He adopted Nietzsche's ideas on ascetic morality and ascetic priests with even greater enthusiasm. All this harmonized with Brandes' dogma of the open life-style he had been preaching since the years of the modern breakthrough.

Nietzsche's most famous book, *Also sprach Zarathustra*, received no extensive comment in Brandes' essay. In this book the dogma of the superman was preached with an almost religious pathos. From the comments he made, it is fairly clear that Brandes was skeptical of this part of Nietzsche's philosophy.

In his final evaluation, Brandes included a comparison with Eduard von Hartmann. Both were characterized as typically German, and in their praise of war Brandes found an echo of militarism on the whole. Nietzsche's great "yes" to life, his vitality, reminded him of Eugen Dühring, the blind man Brandes wrote about in a section of his book on Berlin. But with his introduction of Nietzsche, Brandes also wished to give literature and art a somewhat different direction. He felt that the Scandinavian writers had been composing their works on thoughts that had been public property for too long: "a little Darwinism, a little woman's emancipation, a little of the morality of happiness, a little free thought, a little of the popular cult, etc."[13] Other ideals were necessary to distinguish great art from average art: "Great art demands spirits which, in their singularity, independence, defiance, and noble self-will, are on a level with the most unusual personalities in contemporary thought." With his essay on Nietzsche, Brandes announced a break with many of the ideas that were the foundation of the naturalism of the 1880s. Literature had been socially oriented toward problems and dealt with the lower classes. A new individualism, a new aristocracy of the intelligentsia that would be influential in Scandinavian literature, issued from the essay on Nietzsche.

II   *The Debate on Nietzsche and Aristocratic Radicalism*

However, Brandes' presentation of Nietzsche and his reservations about Mill's and Bentham's school of philosophy were not allowed to pass without comment. Harald Høffding, the most influential university philosopher in Denmark at the time, initiated a debate, which was carried on in the magazine *Tilskueren.* He criticized Brandes on three points. He opposed the statement that it was the task of humanity to produce great men, he refuted the attack against the English welfare philosophy, and he questioned Nietzsche's version of the origin of morality. Høffding had recently published a book on ethics based on the English school and he was anxious to defend his position. He thought that if you improved the conditions of the masses then you also improved the conditions of creative people.[14] Brandes replied by referring to Goethe, Schiller, and Kierkegaard, all of whom in different situations had expressed their contempt for the masses. He said, in regard to Kierkegaard: "When Søren Kierkegaard writes: 'The masses are untruthfulness,' he means lack of regret, irresponsibility—Professor Høffding wishes to inform the glorifier of 'the individual' that the mass is made up of individuals."[15]

Later, when Brandes published his correspondence with Nietzsche, he once again clarified his point of view in relation to the German philosopher. In principle he did not want to disclaim the welfare moral in any way. One should strive for happiness and well-being for everyone. But they could not agree on the way to arrive at this society. Brandes thought that it went via the great creative person. Høffding could not understand Nietzsche because he was "a loner, unyielding, secretive, a demon, whose thoughts moved in long leaps," and Høffding was a "citoyen," *(citizen)* Brandes himself a "bohémien." Here Brandes emphasized Nietzsche's literary and artistic side, which attracted him because of his kindred temperament, but which left the academic Høffding outside, not comprehending.

Brandes' essay on Nietzsche was the beginning of his great influence on European cultural life during the next few decades. Nietzsche himself had a breakdown shortly after Brandes had delivered his series of lectures. Brandes and Strindberg each received one of the mysterious letters Nietzsche sent to the different people who had been close to him, letters that bore witness to a madness but not to a total mental darkness. Strindberg's letter was signed "Nietzsche Caesar." He became alarmed and wrote a letter to Brandes in which he wondered if that "clever Slavic was . . . playing a joke on all of us,"[16] Brandes received a letter that was signed "Antichrist." Neither Brandes nor Strindberg liked the idea of having blown their trumpets for someone who had obviously gone mad. Nietzsche's last letter to Brandes was written on a simple piece of paper without an envelope and read as follows: "Dem Freunde Georg: Nachdem Du mich entdeckt hast, war es kein Kunststück mich zu finden: die Schwierigkeit ist jetzt die, mich zu verlieren. . . . Der Gekreuzigte" ("To my friend George: Once you discovered me, it was not hard to find me: now the difficulty is in getting rid of me. . . . The Crucified").[17]

III *Zola*

An essay on Zola was included in *Essays: Foreign Personalities* that, like the essay on Nietzsche, strangely enough seemed to move away from the naturalistic viewpoint. Brandes had first come in contact with Zola's writing in the 1860s, and had followed his literary career rather closely. When naturalism had reached its culmination at the end of the 1870s, Brandes had strongly recommended that the Scandinavian writers apply Zola's working principles: to study the environment carefully, to gather material—*documents humains*— and to let the literary work grow from this material. He

wanted the Scandinavian authors to describe Nordic conditions in
the same way Zola had described the Second Empire in his series of
novels on Rougon-Macquart.[18] Brandes had also had his eyes on
Zola's programmatic writings: *Mes Haines, Le Roman experimental,
(The Experimental Novel)* and *Les Romanciers naturalistes (The
Naturalistic Novelists)*, and was greatly impressed by them. But.
when writing his essay on Zola in 1887, he concentrated primarily
on the antinaturalistic traits. To be sure, he emphasized Zola's dependence on Taine, which few could see as clearly as Brandes, who
had studied Taine so carefully. Brandes claimed that in Taine Zola
found the theory that the goal of a work of art was to reveal the
essential trait or idea of the motif more clearly and completely than
what was possible in reality. Actually, this was something German
aesthetics had already asserted. In this way Zola constructed his
familiar formula that a work of art was a piece of reality seen through
a temperament. This formula became a kind of key to the whole of
Zola's authorship. What is now dominant and what ought to dominate: reality or temperament? Zola called himself a naturalist, plac-
ing the accent on the element of reality, and not a personalist, with
the accent on temperament.

Brandes, however, found that Zola's temperament reformed the
motif to such a degree that he sometimes could be considered a
romantic, and sometimes a symbolist. Brandes listed many examples showing how Zola permitted his temperament to color the
motif in a way that almost predicted expressionism, and actually the
seed to both symbolism and expressionism could be found in
naturalism. Brandes said it had to be this way:

The answer must be that naturalism cannot avoid the recreation of reality
which is a result of the nature of art itself—the model, that is, the blood of
reality without which the imaginative creation remains lifeless.[19]

But Zola not only gave landscapes souls, as for example in the introductory section of *La Fortune des Rougon (The Rougon Fortune)*; he
also had a strong tendency to let the people and institutions he
described be symbols. The girl who wore the rebellious red flag in
La Fortune des Rougon was amazingly like the figure symbolizing
freedom in Delacroix's famous painting *Freedom on the Barricades*.
Brandes claimed that in some novels Zola could be so romantic that
he reminded one of Novalis.

Brandes' essay on Zola was important for the current away from naturalism toward the romanticism, visionary delusion, and symbolism that came into Scandinavian literature at the end of the 1880s.[20]

CHAPTER 10

Brandes and the Nineties

THE cultural climate of Europe and Scandinavia in the 1890s had a different character than that of the 1870s and 1880s. The change had already begun to take place in the middle of the eighties, but became much more pronounced during the following decade. Naturalism had brought the lower classes into literature. Writers felt a strong kinship with natural and social scientists, and often sharply attacked the established society. One could speak of a revolutionary social tendency in the wake of the Paris Commune. As a critic, Brandes had encouraged this trend and had been one of its most influential spokesmen in Scandinavia and Germany.

When the tendency to dissolution began within naturalism in the middle of the 1880's, the writers' interest shifted from man as a social being to the individual as a psychological riddle. Instead of contemporary descriptions illuminating topical social questions, there was an increase in historical narratives. Stories, legends, and myths were rewritten or paraphrased. Brandes had done his part for this changeabout with his introduction of Nietzsche. However, his position as the leader of the group of modern writers in Denmark had been weakened. Two of his closest supporters. Drachmann and Gjellerup, left him after his return from Berlin and moved away from the European radicalism he advocated toward nationalistic and antinaturalistic positions. But due to Brandes' position as critic in the newly established *Politiken* and with his access to newspapers and publications from other parts of Europe, he was still a powerful factor.

In 1889, the year of the world exhibition, Brandes traveled to Paris to feel the pulse of the literary life there. He personally met with all the leading names, both those who were beginning to fade into the background, such as Cherbuliez, Zola, Maupassant, and Edmond de Goncourt, and those who were coming more and more into the foreground, such as Bourget and Huysmans.[1] Some of the results of these meetings can be read in a collection of essays entitled *Udenlandske Egne og Personligheder (Foreign Lands and Personalities,* 1893).

This book was not one of Brandes' most important. It is characterized by a certain schism in its composition that could be interpreted as a sign of disorientation. Brandes stated in the foreword that it was tiring to speak always of books alone, and that sometimes one wanted to express oneself about the things that one has seen: "landscapes, fine and simple cities, art."[2] The first half of the book was devoted to different places he had visited in Europe. He began with an excerpt from his diary written during his long stay in Italy in 1871. Such travel impressions were beginning to be in fashion, partly because of Drachmann's and Gjellerup's books. (The diary excerpt told about a week-long hike in the Sabine Mountains with George Noufflard, the French art connoisseur.) There were a few similar sketches that mainly consisted of descriptions of nature in Switzerland and Sweden.

I *Belgium and Holland*

More important were a couple of reports from Brandes' visit to Belgium and Holland in 1871. They demonstrated his interest, which grew with time, in oppressed national minorities. At times Brandes functioned as a tribune for these minorities. He had noticed Pol de Mont and the Flemish movement as early as 1885. Brandes was at this time well known in Belgium and Pol de Mont had contacted him and had helped him with the language. In 1892 he once again wrote favorably about the leading names of the Flemish movement: Frans Gittens, Edvard Rosseels, and Emile Verhaeren. The fact that Pol de Mont had turned to Brandes and even dedicated a poem to him showed that the Danish critic was seen as a way to European renown, an opportunity to break out of national isolation.

Maeterlinck was one of the French-speaking Belgian authors who played an important role in the break with naturalistic drama. In his Belgian travel impressions Brandes spoke favorably of his two plays *Les Aveugles (The Sightless)* and *L'Intruse (The Intruder).* Later on (1902 and 1904) he wrote a couple of articles on Maeterlinck's later works. But he could never get very enthusiastic for the type of symbolism Maeterlinck represented. In his strange, static, claire-obscure dramas was a kind of belief in fate that was foreign to Brandes' rationalism. He wrote in his article from 1902:

Maurice Maeterlinck, the important Belgian writer who portended what has been called symbolism in drama, bases his older plays on a fear of the unknown which surrounds us and threatens us. The writer seems to believe in invisible and fatal powers, whose purposes are unknown, but who are hostile to anything which means happiness, joy, or even peace to us.[3]

On his Belgian expedition Brandes also came to the medieval city of Bruges, which became something of a catalyst for the increasingly aesthetic religious undercurrent that permeated the 1890s in Scandinavia. Holger Drachmann was first to make the pilgrimage to Bruges, and this resulted in his essay on Ostend-Bruges in which in long monologues he expressed his dislike of the regiment of critics led by Edvard Brandes in Copenhagen. He also aimed at Georg Brandes and the French naturalism he advocated at that time. Holger Drachmann made an extensive tour of Bruges and was clearly infatuated with the medieval milieu and with Memling, a painter from the fifteenth-century whose paintings richly decorated the city. He felt the pull of the religious atmosphere and wrote:

And what are these high, murmuring trees whispering here in the outskirts of the old medieval city where "Faith" was strong, still is strong, as strong as anywhere? Let us listen! They are whispering that in the same way that Minnewater, this lake of love, sends its water via canals wide and narrow all over the country for the transport of freight and gold, of happiness and well-being, the inexhaustible source of eternal love flows through human hearts and makes their souls fertile for the eternal concept "God"— Goodness.[4]

Drachmann used Ernest Feydeau as his guide through Bruges and quoted some of his infatuated effusions in complete agreement. Later on—in 1892 to be exact—Rodenbach, a Belgian writer, wrote the most famous tribute to the dead city of Bruges; the novel *Bruges—la morte*. Oscar Levertin, the Swedish critic, also visited Bruges in the early 1890s and was completely fascinated by its well-preserved medieval atmosphere. Like Drachmann, he fell in love with Memling's angels and mild figures of Christ. Levertin, like Brandes, was a rationalist and atheist, but nevertheless became more and more aesthetic in the cloisterlike atmosphere of Bruges. In an essay included in the collection *Diktare och drömmare* (Writ-

ers and Dreamers), an important book in Swedish literature of the 1890s, he wrote:

> Reconciliation! All at once I understand why Bruges fills my heart with such a strange uneasiness. All at once I understand what this quiet city with its talking bells wants to say to me. . . . Many of us have been troubled by a feverish dream on a winter night to flee from oneself and to haunt oneself. You persecute yourself as you would an evildoer . . .
>
> After a couple of days of wandering through Bruges in confession and conversation with oneself, a calmness descends, which the novice feels when his time of trial is at an end, a convalescence of weary melancholy and delightful well-being.[5]

It is interesting to compare these partly naïve and uncritical descriptions of Bruges with Brandes' impressions. His visit took place in 1892, after Drachmann's but before Levertin's and he did not allow himself to be enticed. On the contrary, he was upset by the fanaticism and ignorance that led parents to permit their daughters to live in lifelong imprisonment while their frivolous mothers could go to balls and with sparkling eyes tell everyone that their daughter had become a nun. Life in a cloister was strongly disciplined and often led these young women to a breakdown. He claimed that the male part of the cloister population lived an unhealthy life and that the demands for sexual abstinence often resulted in assaults on children. Such crimes were much more common in Catholic Belgium and often were not even brought to court since the church held a protective hand over her own people. Brandes said that there was a good market for French pornography with good doses of sadism, and he repeated a few incidents that revealed the depravation of the upper classes in Bruges. This was his final verdict: "Bruges is wonderful, a medieval Pompeii; but one longs to get away from there to some fresh air: all the incense and all the artificiality of clerical sexuality makes one choke."[6]

Strindberg, Jørgensen, and Levertin, all of whom began as naturalistic writers, were carried away by this religious renaissance, but Brandes maintained his sober, critical view all the while. When he fell into a trance during his journey in Belgium and Holland, it was for other reasons. During the 1890s the life and work of Rembrandt awakened a special interest, partly due to publication of Julius Langbehn's book *Rembrandt als Erzieher (Rembrandt as an Educator)* in 1890, which Brandes reviewed in *Freie Bühne.*

He expressed his veneration for Rembrandt in unusually strong
words in his Dutch travel impressions: "Actually, it is Rembrandt
who has discovered the art of painting; he is *the Painter* of all
painters. He discovered it as Pascal discovered Christianity."[7] Another one of Brandes' dead heroes was Spinoza. The reverence
he could not feel in the cloisters of Bruges he felt instead before the
statue of Spinoza in the Hague. Spinoza was named the spiritual
father of the basic philosophy behind modern science.[8]

In Holland Brandes also came in contact with a group of younger
writers who called themselves "De nieuwe Gids" *(The new leaders)*,
and who read symbolic poetry for him on one occasion in Amster-
dam. But to judge from his comments, symbolism, at least clad in
the Dutch language, did not make such a great impression on him.
In this Dutch group Verlaine and Mallarmé and their successors
were worshiped. Brandes was not especially fond of Mallarmé,
whom he found obscure and unclear. But he learned to appreciate
Verlaine for his musical poetic technique, as became clear in an
essay on French Poetry, written in 1899, in which he sketched the
line of development from Lamartine and Hugo to Mallarmé and
Verlaine.[9]

II *Suppressed Minorities*

In *Foreign Lands and Personalities* Brandes wrote a report on
another suppressed European minority—the Czechs. His visit to
Prague took place in 1892, but Czech cultural personalities had put
him in touch with Jaroslav Vrchlický, the writer, in the middle of
the 1880s. Brandes' own writings had begun to be translated into
Czech by Agnes Schulz.[10] Both Czechs and Germans wanted to
adopt Brandes during his visit to Prague in 1892. In a Czech newspaper he was presented as a German-hater and at the same time he
was delivering lectures in German clubs. Czech students invited
him to speak in their student union and asked him to deliver his
speech in French in protest against the Germanizing attempts. It
later became clear that French was not so well understood after all
and he was asked to repeat his speech in German. On this visit he
personally met with the above-mentioned grand old man in Czech
writing and wrote favorably about his postromantic authorship on
the basis of the fragmentary part of his extensive production that had
been translated. The situation in Prague reminded Brandes of his

experiences in Poland. As in Warsaw, the theater played an important role as an outlet for nationalistic feelings.

A positive reevaluation of national and regional cultural manifestations was a fairly striking trait of the 1890s in Scandinavia. Nationalism had a kind of renaissance, and a new national romanticism bloomed in art, music, and literature. Brandes' interest in suppressed minorities can be seen in this context. Later on he was to write about Armenians, Georgians, and Ruthians. In 1894 he gave a speech in the student union of the U. of Copenhagen entitled "On National Sentiments," which became a sharp squaring up of accounts with the political developments in Denmark and the demoralizing effect of the disregard of parliamentary rules. The country had not been able to hold its own culturally with the other Nordic countries. In this speech Brandes attempted to create a synthesis between his internationalism and his nationalism. To feel Scandinavian and Danish was a prerequisite for feeling European and being citizen of the world.[11] With roots and a feeling of being at home in a national sphere one could then feel like a citizen in a larger collective.

III   *"The Animal in Man"*

The most important essay in the section entitled "Personalities" of *Foreign Lands and Personalities* bore the title "The Animal in Man." Here Brandes was at the apex of his ability as a critic, and the article had everything that characterizes a good essay: it was original,, critical, and had a personal style, it brought together different literary works and discussed significant content without unnecessary discussion of details. It was based on a short story by Bourget, a novel by Tolstoy—*The Kreutzer Sonata*—, a short story by Maupassant, and a novel by Zola—*La Bête Humaine (The Monomaniac)*. Brandes claimed that all of these authors worked with the theme of the schism in man.

Bourget, who was well oriented in psychology, had a view of man that was reminiscent of the one Freud was evolving at about the same time. The human ego was divided into a conscious and an unconscious level, and here lay the explanation for many unconscious slips.[12] Bourget's view of the personality was not religiously motivated but rather based on a scientific way of looking at things.

It was a somewhat different case with Tolstoy, who set apart the sexual instinct and everything that had to do with sex and defined it as something low and dirty. The sexual life described in *The Kreutzer Sonata* Brandes felt to be negative and destructive. For Tolstoy, the animal in man made itself manifest through sexuality.

Maupassant's way of seeing sexuality as expressed in "L'inutile beauté" ("The Useless Beauty") was similar to Tolstoy's. The hero of the story saw sex life as a "humiliating and bestial state."[13] Brandes, however, directed his sharpest criticism toward Tolstoy, who otherwise argued for a new type of Rousseauianism. Brandes claimed that this was hypocrisy. In his youth Tolstoy had lived a dissipated life, but in his old age he had allowed himself to be photographed looking like a new John the Baptist with a long beard and dressed in peasant clothes. Brandes would not be fooled by this: the former bon vivant as a moralist.

In Zola's novel *La Bête humaine*, which was the title of the essay, dualism as a latent, inherited instinct for destruction, a kind of atavism that took control, manifested itself when the hero of the book, Lantier, murdered his mistress. This was a kind of badly digested Darwinism. Brandes had a healthy skepticism toward the myths of his times. He contrasted his own holistic view of man against this dualistic view, not in relation to the newest theories in psychology, but rather to the old Greeks. Body and soul were a unity for them, but here he also represented a modern, rational point of view.

There was only a glimpse of Maupassant in the above-mentioned essay, but he was the object of a longer study in *Foreign Lands and Personalities* that painted a favorable picture of him. Brandes was struck by his clear style, which dissolved all psychology into action, and by his healthy sensualism. Here was no guilty conscience or sinfulness in sexuality, none of the darkness that characterized Zola's love stories. For Zola, sexuality was often the cause of unhappiness. It was different for Maupassant, and he therefore fit in well in Brandes' program for a more open style of life.

IV   *Renan and the Poetry of the Old Testament*

Maupassant died three years after Brandes had written his study on him, and thus Brandes once more had the opportunity to write one of his many obituaries for writers. Two others, on Renan and Taine, were included in *Foreign Lands and Personalities*. These two, like Brandes, had represented a progressive, radical point of view that had developed with age into a more conservative attitude. Taine had spent his last years working on a book on French history in which he attempted to demonstrate the destructive effects of the revolution, and Renan had shown greater and greater tendencies toward skepticism and relativism. He placed his trust in scientists and philosophers as the saviors of mankind and culture, along the lines of the ideas in the work of his youth *L'Avenir de science (The Future of Science)*. This "superbelief" in scientific genius combined with contempt for the uneducated masses and for democracy became especially clear in his philosophical dialogues, which Brandes studied and wrote about extensively in his essay on Renan in *Foreign Lands and Personalities*.

While time had put distance between him and Taine, it had brought Brandes closer to Renan, the religious historian and philologist. And thus Brandes followed the general tendency in Europe of the 1890s. His essays on the Old Testament books, published in 1893–1894, were the first example of studies inspired by Renan. One after the other Brandes discussed the Book of Job, the Song of Solomon, the Book of Psalms and Ecclesiastes. Different essays by Renan had shown the way. Brandes, however, was no classical scholar, and had little or no knowledge of the original language of the texts. He treated them simply as literary texts and not as religious documents. But many felt this to be something new and fruitful. For Brandes the Book of Job was pure poetry with no historical figure in the background. Taking Renan as a model he compared Jewish poetry with the classical Greek literature. Renan implied such comparisons, but Brandes pursued them with the sure eye of the born popularizer. He began his essay with: "Open the *Odyssey* and read these lines at the end of the first song."[14] This was followed by a section from Homer that clearly and concretely described the interior of a home. Brandes claimed that the Greeks had acquired an ability for perspective and clarity in composition that was almost totally lacking in the Jewish texts. His presentation progressed in leaps and glimpses instead of on the basis of a reasonable sample of details. Brandes put the basic question in the Book of Job—the idea of justice—in relation to a fundamental thought in Jewish religion, namely, that man ought not to strive after knowledge of the innermost essence of things. This was a privilege reserved for Jahvé alone. In Brandes' opinion such a religion was inimical to culture. In such a religious climate any type of spiritual cultivation was a hostile phenomenon. Life was seen as a kind of evil drudgery, a kind of slavery. Mathematics, the basis of natural science, could not have developed in such an environment. The situation was entirely different in Greece, where Western civilization was born.

Brandes rejected all attempts to interpret the Song of Solomon allegorically.[15] It is unclear how familiar he was with German research on this work, but in any case, like Bossuet, he saw the Song of Solomon as an erotic song and dance play. He liked the healthy sensualism in this love poem and was of the opinion that it was written before pietism took over and the strict commandments of the Law of Moses stifled similar manifestations. In his study on the Psalms, which was a more obvious religious text, Brandes emphasized that its innermost core was to a great extent profane. His observations dealt primarily with composition and style, but he also touched upon religious-psychological aspects in relation to Feuerbach, whom he had so admired in his youth.

Brandes essay on Ecclesiastes or *Kohélet,* was of greater interest than this relatively brief article. The writer of this work recognized no life after death but was instead totally absorbed by this life on earth. This did not mean, however, that he agreed with the line of social reform that, according to Brandes, was so strongly rooted in Judaism. Brandes referred to such figures as Moritz Hartmann, Marx, Lassalle. Börne, and Heine. The writer of *Kohélet* did not believe in the possibility of attaining justice on earth. One had to accept the fact that life was a vale of tears, that it was brief and passing and therefore one ought to make the best of it: not deprive oneself, but rather enjoy the delicacies of earthly life. There was a pessimistic realism in *Kohélet* that appealed to the pessimism of the turn of the century and that had a certain kinship to Schopenhauer's. Brandes expressed this pessimism in a very personal way.

Brandes discussed the relation between the Old Testament and the New in a shorter essay from 1893. Here he took up the figure of Jesus and his dependence on the Old Testament, especially Isaiah. The essay foretold the older Brandes' interest in Peter and Jesus.

The essays discussed above are examples of the different manifestations of the religious renaissance of the 1890s for Brandes. It led him to take up religious texts for discussion with the same skeptical humanism that characterized Renan. The Scandinavian writers of the nineties gladly made use of the religious genres, of sagas and legends. Oscar Levertin, a Swedish Jewish critic, was a typical example of this tendency, a man who came to have the same central position in the turn-of-the-century writing in Sweden as Brandes had in Denmark. Levertin also had a lively interest in Renan and was drawn to the same sources that Brandes drew from in his essays on the Song of Solomon and *Kohélet*. Levertin combined the figure of Sulamith from the Song of Solomon, the proverbial touches from *Kohélet*, and the Eastern-tinted pessimism, in his collection of songs *King Solomon and Morolf* (1905).[16]

V *Anatole France and the Dreyfus Affair*

Levertin was representative of a tendency in the Scandinavian writing of the 1890s. He could be described as a scholarly humanist whose writing had a clear historical direction with elements of imitation and paraphrase. There was a noticeable difference between his writing and the modern writing of the 1870s and 1880s. For a long time Levertin's ideal writer was Anatole France.[17] What was Brandes' attitude toward France? The above-mentioned essay on Maupassant from 1890 was concluded with a review of the most important French writers, but France was not included in it. Until 1888 he had belonged to a politically moderate phalanx of French writers. After that he began to deal with questions of morality and upbringing in a much more radical spirit in his articles in *Le Temps*.[18] He took a clear step to the left when he supported Dreyfus in 1897. He made his definite entrance on the scene as an author with *La Rôtisserie de la reine pédauque* (*At the Sign of the Reine Pedauque* 1893), and it was only after this that Brandes began to take him seriously.

In 1897 Brandes received a letter from Daudet in which he spoke of a dinner club that had been formed in Paris with, along with the Daudet brothers, Zola, Bourget, Barrès, and Anatole France. Brandes was the only foreigner who was welcome in the group. Anyone with any knowledge of the way the Dreyfus affair developed, and the way it divided the French intellectuals into two camps, can see how impossible this dinner club was in the long run. Alphonse Daudet died the same year. Bourget, Cherbuliez, and Barrès were against Dreyfus, while Zola and Anatole France supported his cause. In 1899 Brandes wrote to Kropotkin from a spa in France saying that he had been attacked in the French right-wing newspapers and accused of being the first outside of France who supported Dreyfus. Naturally he felt honored by this.[19] He wrote several articles about the Dreyfus affair, something that surely helped to make him even better known in Paris.

In 1902 a group of French authors together with Lugné-Poe, a theater man, arranged a banquet in honor of Brandes. Anatole France was among them and it was he who made a speech to the guest of honor in which he said: "Your critical, historical and philosophical work is, along with that of Sainte-Beuve, the most eminent of our times."[20] Set on a par with Sainte-Beuve. Even considering the dining room rhetoric, this must be seen as an honorable recognition of Brandes' importance on the part of the French authors. At this time Anatole France had a central position in French and thus European literature. In Sweden he was praised by Levertin in the above-mentioned essay collection *Writers and Dreamers* (1898), and in 1921 he reached the culmination of his career when he received the Nobel Prize.

In his essay "Tanker ved Aarhundredeskiftet" ("Thoughts at the Turn of the Century"), Brandes spoke of the great French cultural personalities he had met and especially emphasized Renan. After Renan's death, Anatole France became his worthy heir. The Renan inheritance, which meant so much to Brandes, was continued in Anatole France. Brandes returned to this on several occasions in his essay on France published in 1904. He emphasized the retrospective traits in France's authorship, his love for classical culture, his extensive knowledge of the Middle Ages and of the legends of Christianity and the Orient. France often dwelled on religious phenomena and atmospheres, Brandes pointed out, but he was never so unctuous as Renan could sometimes be. Inside, France was always as sober as Voltaire. He was, however, no admirer of his own times. He was unsuitable for the times, to use Nietzsche's language. Brandes quoted a statement by France in which he frankly told a visitor that he owned no modern books and that he gave away those he received to a friend in the country. When he did choose to use material from his own times, as in *Histoire Contemporaine (Contemporary History)*, it was to make a smarting settlement of accounts with that France in which the Dreyfus affair took place. This scholarly, skeptical humanist, with touches of Voltaire and Renan, and with the ability to penetrate into the thoughts and emotional life of days gone by, rendered with ironic distance, also had

the ability to become involved in the fight against the encroach-
ments against justice of his own times. Like Brandes, he was interested in the cause of the Armenians and also stood forth as a
defender of Dreyfus. Both Anatole France and Brandes passed on
the inheritance from Voltaire, and it was completely logical that one
of Brandes' last greatest works was devoted to Voltaire.

France was also a critic. He presented a methodical explanation of
his program in the foreword of *La Vie littéraire (Literary Life)*.[21] He
claimed that the good critic reported on the adventures of his soul
among the masterpieces. There was no such thing as an objective
critic just as there was no objective art. In fact, the truth was that
one could never climb out of one's own skin. The critic could only
say, if he wished to be honest: I am going to speak of myself in
relation to Shakespeare, Racine, Pascal, or Goethe. This program
paved the way for a very subjective criticism, and even though
Brandes was influenced by this critical method, he never allowed
himself to fall into the chatty, casual style of many of the other critics
from the turn of the century.

Like France, Brandes also felt the attraction of the historic, and
proof of this is the biography of Shakespeare that occupied him
during the first half of the 1890s. Nor did he hide the fact that to a
certain extent he wrote about Shakespeare in relation to himself. As
a young man he had been attracted by the contentious, active, and
impatient Hotspur in *Henry IV*. As an older man he saw himself in
the misanthropic Timon.

VI *Shakespeare*

What was unique about Brandes' book on Shakespeare was that
he attempted to construct the inner development of the writer on
the basis of his plays and sonnets. Thus at times the biography
seems to be a novel based on the life of Shakespeare. But what
complicated the matter was that Brandes, without saying so
explicitly, brought in his own emotions, values, antipathies, and
sympathies in discussing Shakespeare's life and works. It almost
seems that he wished to write the story of his own development at
the same time he wrote Shakespeare's. This made his book something special in the literature on Shakespeare. Rubow emphasized,
supported by Brandes' own statements in *Levned (My Life)*, that
Brandes' point of departure was *Troilus and Cressida*, *Coriolanus*,
and *Timon of Athens*.[22] With these he began to read the case history

of the writer, and this was his angle of approach to the work as a whole. "On these points, English criticism has only served as a tool for him."

There was, however, one English Shakespeare researcher before Brandes who had attempted to trace Shakespeare's intellectual development with the help of his works. This was Dowden. "It is doubtful that any other exposition so brief has plagued the history of Shakespearean criticism," wrote Eastman, one of the many Shakespeare historians, in his survey.[23] Dowden noted four separate stages of development in Shakespeare. He called the first period "In the Workshop," and it was during this time that Shakespeare learned his skill as an actor and playwright. He experimented in different areas and it was a happy and carefree time of his life. The second period was called "In the World," and during this time Shakespeare developed even more, experienced more of life, and began to taste success and to lay the foundation of his fortune. During the third period, which was called "Out of the Depths," Shakespeare met with grief and trouble: his son and his father died, and his friend of the sonnets jilted him. It was at this point that he wrote *King Lear* and *Troilus and Cressida*. The fourth period, "On the Heights," was characterized by the fact that the tragic and bitter tone brightened somewhat and in the later plays one could perceive a reconciled wisdom. Dowden presented this view of Shakespeare in a larger work from 1875 entitled *Shakespeare, His Mind and Art*, and in a smaller, more schematic book entitled *Shakespeare* (1877). Swinburne, another of Brandes' authorities, followed in Dowden's footsteps in the construction of different periods in Shakespeare's development. It was to these "personalists" that Brandes turned.

Here are a few examples illustrating the way in which Brandes followed in Dowden's footsteps. The quote is taken from part one of the Danish version and deals with Shakespeare's first years in London:

It is probable that during these first years in London Shakespeare, each day enriched with new impressions, with his insatiable thirst for knowledge assimilated in his versatile activity as an often utilized actor, a man of the theater, given the task of freshening up old plays according to contemporary taste for scenic effects, and an emerging writer in whose spirit all voices found resonance, and all ideas dramatic life—had a sensibility which made him grow intellectually every day, this had been granted to him. And he felt free and light; most probably because he had freed himself from his ties to his home in Stratford.[24]

This was "In the Workshop," and here Brandes was still dealing with fairly probable hypotheses. At the end of part one when, according to Dowden, Shakespeare was thought to be in the final stage of the first period, Brandes wrote:

In case the reader would like to get an idea about Shakespeare's state of mind in this short period around the turn of the century he should try to recollect a day when he woke up feeling strong and healthy—not just free from sickness or any defined or undefined pain anywhere, but feeling that all of the organs of his body were in happy activity; his breath came easily, his head felt free and clear, his heart beat calmly, and it was a joy to be alive.[25]

Brandes continued in this way for a good while. This was not research and was hardly criticism, it was instead poetry. This was supposed to be Shakespeare at the turn of the seventeenth century. But before Brandes completed this part he predicted the change in tone that was to come:

For the time was now coming when happiness, and even the joy of living, died in his spirit. Heavy clouds were piling up on his horizon—we could only guess which—and troubling sorrows and disappointments accumulated inside him.[26]

In the second part Brandes extensively probed the reasons for the darkening of Shakespeare's horizon during the first years of the 1600s: the execution of Essex, crises with the dark lady of the sonnets and with Pembroke, the deaths of his father and his son. In his analysis of *King Lear*, Brandes once again attempted to sound the writer's private state of mind:

Of all the pain, crudeness, and baseness, of all the vice and infamy he had experienced up to now, things which embitter the lives of better men, one vice now seemed worse than all the others, more hateful and revolting, a vice he had surely been the victim of time and time again: ingratitude. He found no other meanness so exonerated, forgiven, and widespread.[27]

This is an example of how one can clearly discern Brandes' own experience. And continuing to part three of the biography, one finds the dark tone still dominant. This part begins extremely suggestively:

Out of tune—out of tune.
The instrument on which so many hundreds and hundreds of funny, pathetic, gay, loving, sorrowful, plaintive and indignant melodies were played is out of tune.[28]

In this part Brandes dealt with the three bitter and misanthropic plays that appealed to him so much, *Troilus and Cressida, Coriolanus,* and *Timon,* from the point of view that the writing of these plays was a kind of catharsis for Shakespeare. It is true that in order to fit all the puzzle pieces together Brandes was forced to move up the date of *Troilus and Cressida* a few years, but when that was done the horizon cleared as it had for Dowden: "And thus it was spoken, this last, wildest word of bitterness. The black cloud had emptied itself and slowly the sky once again became clear."[29]

What has been said here of Brandes' dependence upon Dowden is actually only valid for the idea of this type of interpretation of Shakespeare. What was original for Brandes was that his own temperament and philosophy of life emerged so strongly in a way that was greatly reminiscent of the moralizing of the German Shakespearean researchers, and for which he blamed them. The only difference was that Brandes had another view of morality that, he felt, coincided with Shakespeare's. There he found the same antipuritanic opinions he himself represented. Shakespeare had waged trench warfare against the puritans in all his plays since *Twelfth Night.* Furthermore, Shakespeare was an adherent of Brandes' own aristocratic radicalism, which, he stated, became especially clear in *Coriolanus.* Shakespeare was also a hero-worshiper like Brandes. He wrote apropos of Coriolanus: "As a result of this movement of thought Shakespeare's hero-worship had fewer demigods to worship, but at the same time became more intense. Here it appeared with heretofore unknown strength."[30] In the same context he wrote: "He had only contempt for the masses; now more than ever was he unable to dissolve them into individuals."

Thus, according to Brandes, Shakespeare created a type of

superman in Prospero, long before Nietzsche and Renan. As Rubow pointed out, *The Tempest* was read with Renan's paraphrase *Caliban* fresh in his memory. Brandes claimed that Prospero was a man of the future, a superman, and this revealed itself in his control over natural forces. Shakespeare anticipated future developments when creating a figure like Prospero.

Now it is rather easy to regard Brandes' biography of Shakespeare with a certain amount of irony and easy to focus upon its obvious faults. But one cannot deny that in its subjectivity, its bold and original evaluations, much of Shakespeare is seen in a new light. When Brandes called Shakespeare, the court dramatist of Elizabeth I and James I, an aristocrat, there was a lot of truth in the statement. When in our days *The Tempest* is played with Caliban as an exploited native and Prospero in the trappings of an English colonial, consequences are drawn that neither Shakespeare nor Brandes could have dreamed of. Brandes placed the previously neglected plays *Coriolanus* and *Timon* in the center of Shakespeare's work. Both of these have later especially interested Marxist researchers and directors, Brecht among others. As Wellek expressed it, Brandes' biography contained "some well-digested history, literary history and simple exposition and criticism."[31] Certain individual parts, such as the one dealing with *Hamlet*, still make for interesting reading. When the biography was published it stirred up a great deal of attention and had several printings in England and the United States. Echoes of it can even be discovered in Joyce, in the bizarre discussion of Shakespeare in *Ulysses*: "If you want to know what are the events which cast their shadow over the hell of time of *King Lear, Othello, Hamlet, Troilus and Cressida* look to see when and how the shadow lifts." Brandes' name appeared here together with other Shakespeare "personalists."

VII *Documents from His Youth*

In 1898 Brandes published a book about his friend Julius Lange, the art historian. Few people were so close to Brandes during his student years, in spite of the fact that their backgrounds and philosophies were very different. Lange came from one of Denmark's most well-known families. His uncle was Paludan-Müller, the writer. In his youth Lange was a believing Christian and Brandes related the story of how, on a hike through Zealand, his friend suddenly demanded that he too should become a Christian:

When we came home that night something happened which affected me so painfully that the embarrassment I felt then is still living in me, almost as intensely as when it happened. Without any introductory conversation, Julius Lange suddenly demanded that I had to become and would become a Christian, I should share his faith. His outburst moved me, and I understood that for him this was so important that it even justified all disregard of consideration.[32]

This happened in 1861 when Brandes was nineteen years old, and the pressure his friend put him under certainly was one of the reasons for his intensive studies of Kierkegaard in an attempt to understand Christianity. But the rationalist in Brandes was too strong. Long after the above episode took place the two men met on the street and Lange announced that he no longer was a believer. The book on Lange allows for many glimpses of Brandes' own development. It consists mainly of Lange's letters to Brandes and related comments. Brandes painted a picture of an unusually talented and charming human being with extensive knowledge, a bright intellect, and a brilliant conversational ability. As an art historian, Lange helped to educate· Brandes' eye for visual art during their eternal discussions and museum visits together.

The collection of youthful poetry that Brandes was bold enough to publish in 1898 under the title *Ungdomsvers (Poetry from My Youth)* was also retrospective in character. The oldest poem was from 1858, according to his own dates, and the last from 1873. A few undated poems were obviously included later. The poems reflect the private and idealistic tone of Brandes' youth, the feeling of revolt and a general militant idealism. This was true, for example, of the poem to Henrik Ibsen, written in a hospital in Rome in 1871 in reply to a letter from the Norwegian author. Here Brandes wrote: "I want to call to uproar the creative spirits," which was his answer to Ibsen's declaration that the great world dramatist needed him to play a main role and that he therefore should not die in the exposition.[33] Several of the poems seemed to be occasional verse inspired by the many women in Brandes' life. The collection hardly leaves one with the impression that Brandes would have developed into a significant poet if he had chosen that path.

VIII   *Strindberg and Lagerlöf*

Among Brandes' minor studies from the 1890s is the essay on August Strindberg from 1894, expanded in 1900.[34] Brandes followed Ibsen's development very carefully, wrote about each phase in his career, and summarized his views of the Norwegian in a book (1906). He did not devote such great attention to Strindberg. They did meet however, during Strindberg's time in Copenhagen at the end of the 1880s, and their correspondence was not insignificant, extending from 1887 to 1896. Brandes had always respected Strindberg's genius, but his essay did not reveal any deeper understanding of that which was unique and original in Strindberg's production. He was imprisoned in the image of Strindberg as a woman-hater, and his essay dealt primarily with Strindberg's view of women. The great dramas of the 1880s, *The Father* and *Miss Julie*, received fairly brief treatment. The works after the Inferno crisis, in which Strindberg aired his religious critical period, were treated very summarily, and Brandes included them in the wave of mysticism and spiritualism that came to characterize the 1890s. He pronounced a fairly harsh verdict on Strindberg's authorship:

With all of his independence Strindberg has, like few others, honored the changing literary fashions and has been almost anxiously eager always to come with the latest. Now in the nineties a fresh whirlwind of profane and sacred insanity blew across the North.[35]

Brandes is actually more positive in his extensive obituary on Strindberg in 1912, where he presents some examples of Strindberg's bizarre view of life and the ways it was expressed in the personal contacts of the Inferno period.[36]

Brandes also wrote briefly but favorably about several of the Swedish writers of the nineties: about Heidenstam, whose collection of short stories entitled *Karolinerna (the Charles Men)*, he favorably and sensitively appraised, and about Lagerlöf's *Gösta Berlings saga (The Story of Gösta Berling)*, whose original style and background material he praised, thus laying one of the cornerstones for her world reputation. Selma Lagerlöf never ceased being thankful to him for his review of *Gösta Berlings saga*.

The 1890s may be seen as an era of backlash against the wave of radicalism of the seventies and eighties, a reaction to industrialization, urbanization, and the threat of the breakthrough program against the philosophy and the religious, political, and ethical values the established society was based upon. Brandes was in the middle of this backlash and was himself divided. He stood for the breakthrough program, which the younger writers opposed. This increased his feelings of alienation. But in his Shakespeare book and in other historically oriented studies he continued his struggle against prejudice and obfuscation.

CHAPTER 11

The Good European

AT the turn of the century, with the Shakespeare book behind
him, Brandes was definitely a critic of European format. It is
no exaggeration to claim that, more than anyone either before or
after him, he regarded Europe as a cultural unit without respect to
language barriers. He kept the literature of Germany, England,
France, the Slavic countries, and Scandinavia under surveillance, at
least when it was a question of the leading figures. During the new
century he came into close contact with people like Romain Rolland,
Arthur Schnitzler, Rainer Maria Rilke, Georges Clemenceau,
Hjalmar Söderberg, and Bernard Shaw. He was acquainted with
Sigmund Freud and André Gide, Henry James, and many other
members of the European intelligentsia who are now almost or
totally forgotten. Nietzsche had called Brandes "a good European"
in one of his letters to him, and during the new century he truly
lived up to this reputation. He traveled around constantly throughout the different parts of Europe, especially in France and Germany, welcomed with greater and greater marks of respect as he
grew older. When the First World War broke out and Europe was
divided into two camps he experienced this tragedy more profoundly than many others.

I Autobiography

Brandes devoted the first decade of the new century to three
great tasks. He edited his collected works, which came to include
eighteen volumes, he published a new popular edition of *Main
Currents* (1906–1907), and he wrote his memoirs *My Life* (1905–
1908). Much of this was clearly retrospective in character. *My Life*
was comprised of three volumes, each close to four-hundred pages,
and extended up to about the middle of the 1890s. The memoirs
were based on his at times extensive diary entries written during

most of his life, and on his comprehensive correspondence, including his letters to his parents during his long journeys abroad. Therefore *My Life* is an especially important source of information; not only on Brandes' daily life and literary activity, but also on the literary history of the period in general.

The first volume describes his childhood and youth up to the journey to Italy in 1870. This is the most captivating part. Here Brandes was more personal than in the treatment of his adult life. He told about his parents, relatives, childhood and boyhood friends with great though not unreserved openness.[1] Some details of his private life are hidden in a mist, which becomes even more notable in the later parts that deal more and more with the critic as a public person, with his lecture tours and other public appearances, with his authorship and how the different books came about, and so forth. Brandes described extensively, year by year, his activity as a critic with a great assemblage of names of literary contacts in different countries, and he did not neglect to register the different signs of his growing reputation around the world. In general the autobiography has a strongly apologetic character. This is due to the fact that Brandes, during almost the whole of his lifetime, was a controversial figure in his native country and was the victim of virtual hate campaigns during the 1870s and 1880s.

II   *Armand Carrel*

Brandes began working with a smaller format, compared to the biographies of Shakespeare and Goethe, in his book on Armand Carrel, the French journalist, which was published in 1911. Armand Carrel belonged to a group of newspapermen who helped to bring about the July revolution but who, in contrast to Thiers, did not assure himself of a position in the new administration. Instead he became one of the sharpest critics of the July monarchy with his newspaper *National*. This contentious man was quite reminiscent of Lassalle in his personal attributes and, like Lassalle, he died in a duel. He had served in the Spanish war of independence against the French and was for this reason condemned to death, but was later granted a pardon. He was a hero worth imitating for many of Europe's fighting liberals. Carl Ploug, Brandes' opponent in the struggle for the modern breakthrough, had honored him in a poem in the 1830's. John Stuart Mill had met him and wrote very favorably about him in *Dissertations and Discussions*. It is probable that

Brandes was inspired by Mill to make a closer study of Carrel's life and works. Carrel's style, strict and lucid, especially appealed to Brandes. Like Brandes he was also a man of action, completely involved in doing things and in influencing people. Brandes claimed that his need for activity was so strong that he constantly rearranged the furniture in his home and constantly changed the editorial conditions at his newspaper *National*. He added that it was sad that this man of action was forced to judge what other people did and did not do as a spectator.[2] Furthermore, Armand Carrel possessed another character trait that he certainly shared with Brandes, and this was civil courage. He did not permit himself to be corrupted but struggled on with his lucid intellect, his chivalry, without becoming implacable or vulgar toward the increasingly reactionary July monarchy. Brandes' book can be read as a novel in which the dramatic culmination is the duel between Carrel and Girardin. The novel has its hero—Carrel—and its villain and man of intrigue, Girardin, who manoeuvered Carrel into a fateful duel with almost Machiavellian cunning.

III   A Bird's-Eye View

Brandes' collection of essays published in 1913 and entitled *Fugleperspektiv (A Bird's-Eye View)* gives us a good idea of his activity as a critic and lecturer during the first decade of the new century. We are able to observe the expansion of his horizons by studying the different sections. The first and most comprehensive is entitled "Danish," followed by a briefer section entitled "Stories" and then several sections entitled "Scottish," "Norwegian," "Swedish," "African," "Swiss," "Italian," "Russian," "German," and "French," respectively. One ought to note that most of the contributions included in *A Bird's-Eye View* were not long essays of the type that appeared in *The Men of the Modern Breakthrough*, but rather shorter reviews. There were, however, a few exceptions, and one of these was the extensive study of Henrik Pontoppidan. He was not included in the outline of Scandinavian authors Brandes gave with *The Men of the Modern Breakthrough* simply because at that time Pontoppidan had not yet produced very much, but he became one of the most representative figures in the breakthrough movement in Scandinavian literature. He achieved in prose what Ibsen and Strindberg achieved in drama.

Pontoppidan developed as an author under the influence of the

ideas Brandes had introduced during the 1870s.[3] Brandes' advoca-
tion in the 1870s and 1880s of a program for a socially descriptive
and analytic novel based on a careful study of reality, preferably
under the influence of French realism and naturalism, was realized,
by Pontoppidan in his great series of novels entitled *Lykke-Per*
(Lucky Peter, 1898–1904) and *De Dødes Rige (The Kingdom of the.*
Dead, 1912–1916). None of the literature from the other Scandinavian countries at this point demonstrated such a comprehensive
description of society as these novels did, and this narrative tradition was continued in Denmark in the proletarian novels of
Andersen-Nexø, especially *Pelle Erobreren (Pelle the Conqueror).*
Brandes himself pointed out the relationship between the novels of
Nexø and those of Pontoppidan in his essay on Pontoppidan.[4] It was
exactly this comprehensiveness in the description of his contemporary social and political life that Brandes noted as being especially
representative of Pontoppidan's writing:

If one asked in which Danish author one could find the most comprehensive
and true concepts of Danish ways of being, feeling, and thinking, of the
position of representative personalities in Denmark during the last generation, as far as both the urban and rural population are concerned, then there
is no doubt that the answer must be: in Pontoppidan.[5]

When Brandes stated that Pontoppidan also described "the position
of representative personalities in Denmark" it is certain that he
meant not only the lightly disguised sketches of politicians, authors,
and artists included in his authorship, but also possibly the fact that
he himself played a role in a novel that he considered to be Pontoppidan's most important work, his masterpiece: *Lucky Peter.*
    During his lifetime Brandes was the model for several figures in
contemporaneous fiction and even today he continues to fascinate
authors. Recently a play written by Lars-Olof Franzén was presented on Swedish radio with Brandes as the main character. His
portrait as Dr. Nathan in *Lucky Peter*, however, bore the closest
resemblence to him, because here he functioned as an intellectually
active force in the story of the development of a young man, placed
there by an author who himself had been strongly influenced by
Brandes and who had been close to him, not least in the fact that
they shared the same philosophy of life, during long periods of his
life.[6]

The novel's hero was torn between a philosophy that was internationally oriented, rationalistic, and antireligious and one that was nationalistically Danish, all of which was especially accented by the fact that he became engaged to Jacobe, the daughter of a Jewish wholesale dealer named Salomon. But his religious background won in the end and he instead fell in love with the daughter of a Grundtvigian minister, who came to represent the Danish *folk.* Dr. Nathan is one of the players in this polar field, and after a brief appearance in the earlier part of the book, he meets with the main character at a dinner party in Jacobe's home, where the engagement to the daughter of the house will be announced. Thus Dr. Nathan is linked to the rich Jewish internationally oriented milieu into which Per is planning to be married. The following is from the extensive sketch of Dr. Nathan:

He was little in height, and in general people did not find his face handsome. It was in any case very irregular, though I suppose it is hard to tell since his face was never in repose, but constantly changing expression and reflecting inner reactions with an uncontrolled and cramplike play of features to which years had only added a somewhat self-conscious exaggeration. He was most handsome when he listened. His expression was then enlivened by that which was most outstanding for him—his thirst for knowledge, his craving for knowledge, his insatiable desire for information. . . . However, in general company such moments did not occur frequently, he definitely preferred to speak himself. Besides his incredible receptivity—and something which counterbalanced it—he continued to possess in his old age an almost girlish need to communicate, which at times got out of hand and became gossipy and not free from malice.[7]

The picture above, though not without critical comments, was nevertheless painted by someone who himself was under Brandes' spell. When Brandes took up this sketch in his correspondence with Pontoppidan, he came with some reservations on a few points, but basically reacted favorably to it.[8]

Aside from the essay on Pontoppidan, the Danish section of *A Bird's-Eye View* has little of interest to offer. Brandes discussed a few less well-known Danish authors, and in general it was a question of short reviews or speeches on Danish subjects. To judge from these, it seemed as if Brandes had lost much of the active contact he had had with the literature of his own country during the last three decades of the 1800s. And the two "stories" included in the collection are also evidence of the fact that Brandes felt more and more alienated from the Danish cultural milieu. This became most clear in "The Story of Black Peter and Dirty Dick," which was written in 1912, the year of Brandes' seventieth birthday. Different official institutions in Denmark, the University of Copenhagen and the Writers' Association among others, wished to honor him, he who had become one of the few Danish international celebrities, with a celebration in the town hall. The magazine *Tilskueren* published a jubilee issue as a kind of Festschrift. Brandes could only have mixed feelings about this, since this recognition of his influence came at least thirty years too late, and he fretted because some of his works sold badly at home. This is what the easily penetrated symbolism of "Black Peter and Dirty Dick" deals with.

Black Peter was said to have grown up in a country where most of the people were blond and where blondness justifiably was considered to be something extremely fine. Dark people, on the other hand, were regarded with suspicion, and while it was true that Black Peter was not actually black but brown, this did not help much and after a while he got used to having people call out "Black Peter" after him. In school he shared a bench with a boy who corresponded to the national blond idea and whose name was Dirty Dick. Dirty Dick was always well dressed and polite while Black Peter always broke the rules and caused trouble. Black Peter was pretty much alone in life, but Dirty Dick's family was large and well respected in the country. Both boys became writers and one can guess how their futures took shape. Dirty Dick became a moralist and an apostle of virtue while Black Peter wrote satiric verses that no one read or appreciated. He grew old and his hair turned white and one day when he appeared bareheaded in a crowd they discovered that they no longer had any reason to call him Black Peter. They went home and paged through his books and found that his verses, which had had such a bad reputation, were now sung throughout the land. So they decided to hold a celebration in his honor, and the speaker, who himself was blond, announced that it was no longer correct to call him Black Peter and instead they had decided to call him White Peter in the future. But before this Black Peter had been to the doctor and had had removed the nerve by means of which he could sense the bad smell of the stink bombs that were thrown at him, and now he discovered that he was also unable to perceive the sweet scent of recognition.

This is the way Brandes saw his own situation, and at this same time he wrote in a letter to Pontoppidan that he had felt it necessary to "remove the nerve which permitted one to sorrow at humiliation and reproaches. I made myself very hard. But at the same time I also was forced to remove the nerve which (à la Hans Christian Andersen) allows one to feel joy in praise."[9]

The Norwegian section of *A Bird's-Eye View* contained a review of Ibsen's *When We Dead Awaken,* and the Swedish, an essay on Strindberg. The sections on Switzerland and Africa were primarily travel impressions. In the Italian section Brandes wrote about Marinetti and futurism, but was fairly negative to the worship of machines, the contempt for women, and the cult of violence expressed in Marinetti's manifesto and in the novel *Mafarka, the Futurist,* on which the essay was based. The brutal aspect of futurism, its cult of war that indicated the movement toward fascism and that partially had its roots in Nietzsche, were completely obvious to Brandes, and even if his two articles on futurism were not totally negative, they were extremely critical on these points. He noted how the futurists twisted and oversimplified Nietzsche in a way he could hardly have imagined when he was one of the first to appreciate the German philosopher.

Nietzsche was also taken up in the survey of German literature Brandes wrote in 1912. Here he made a brief character sketch on each one of the then most influential German writers: Maximilian Harden, publisher of the magazine *Die Zukunft;* Friedrich Hebbel, the dramatist; Max Reinhardt, innovator in the art of the stage; Hauptmann, the greatest writer of naturalistic drama in Germany; Sudermann; Hofmannsthal; Wassermann; and Schnitzler, of whom especially the last two were treated at length. Nor did Brandes neglect the youngest authors, such as Rilke. The survey indicates that Brandes had kept himself well oriented in German literature, and he had maintained a correspondence with several of the writers, for example Schnitzler, for many years. Brandes' own works continued to appear in German in large editions and he cannot have been an unimportant factor in German cultural life between 1870 and 1930. After the Nazi takeover in 1933 there was a distinct change in the cultural climate. Along with the works of Heine, Tucholsky, and other radical Jewish writers, Brandes' books seemed to disappear from the book market, and there has been no attempt since the war to reestablish his position.

The French section of *A Bird's-Eye View* was an account of the people Brandes had met during his many visits to Paris and his experiences from the French "salons" at the beginning of the century. Among others, he told about the sculptor Rodin, and the artist André Rouveyre, with whom he also corresponded for several years. *A Bird's-Eye View* leaves one with the impression of discord and lack of vigor. Many of the contributions are chatty in style and lack the stringency of Brandes' earlier works.

IV *Goethe*

In 1915 Brandes finally published his extensive book on Goethe on which he had been working in different periods since the end of the 1880s. His interest in Goethe, as pointed out earlier, was awakened during the first years of his studies and had remained more or less strong ever since. Goethe was one of those most often quoted and referred to in Brandes' writings. Brandes' stay in Germany during the 1870s reinforced his concept of Goethe as a central figure, and Goethe was often referred to in *Main Currents*, especially in the last volume. In his autobiography Brandes quoted a letter he had received from a reader who expressed his disappointment in the fact that the cultural revolution hailed in the first part of the book had ended up as a glorification of Goethe.[10] Actually one can understand this letter writer, since in comparison with Armand Carrel and Lassalle, for example, the *Geheimrat* (privy counsellor) from Weimar was a more conservative figure.

But Brandes' revolutionary pathos included not only political and social circumstances. Goethe represented a human and an educational ideal that never ceased to fascinate him: a great personality developed with versatility. Goethe was a man who never settled down, and the works in which this trait was best expressed were the ones Brandes liked best. Thus, not unexpectedly, he considered *Faust* to be the culmination of Goethe's authorship: "It is written for all times, will never be forgotten, as long as the German language is understood."[11] The figure of Faust is a portrait of the romantic seeker of knowledge of nature's innermost secrets. *Wilhelm Meisters Lehrjahre (Wilhelm Meister's Apprenticeship)* dealt with a more realistic search for knowledge and education. Brandes called this work a totally new type of novel. It dealt neither with love nor dramatic adventures, but with education, and the main character was a seeker. Goethe simply transferred "his own longing for a harmonious development, his own striving in the life of great values and art"[12] to the hero of the novel. But by "education" Goethe did not mean bookish knowledge; instead it was a question of a freedom from prejudice as opposed to a narrow bourgeois morality. For Goethe, it was a question of not only intellectual but also moral development. Brandes claimed that the whole of Wilhelm Meister could be summarized in the words: remember to live, *memento vivere*. It was Goethe's great "yes" to life, and Brandes concurred in spite of all the bitterness he at times felt. Thus in Goethe Brandes found both a moral openness and liberation and a kind of vitality that was in complete agreement with the central ideas of the break-through program.

One of the indications of Goethe's universality was his orientation toward the natural sciences, which Brandes took up at length in his Goethe book. Here it was not a question of an amateurish knowledge of these areas. Instead, Goethe made discoveries that pointed, for example, in the direction of Darwin. Brandes considered Goethe's paper on granite to be one of the most beautiful pieces of prose anyone could read.[13] For Brandes, Goethe was the great heathen who, free from all religious narrowness, studied nature in order to grasp the whole, the context. According to him, Goethe's view of nature was closely related to those of Spinoza and Hegel that had impressed him so deeply.

Brandes was particularly partial to Goethe's short lyrical poems, and one finds allusions to them or quotations from them throughout his writings. In general Brandes demonstrates his sure eye as a critic when it is a question of finding the genuine quality and ingenuity in otherwise rather unenjoyable and now infrequently read works by Goethe such as the musical play *Lila*. There are, Brandes claimed, a couple of clever verses that more than express the idea behind the play, and he quoted them:[14]

> Feiger Gedanken
> Bängliches Schwanken,
> Weibisches Zagen,
> Aengstliches Klagen
> Wendet kein Elend
> Macht dich nicht frei.

Allen Gewalten
Zum Trutz sich erhalten,
Nimmer sich beugen,
Kräftig sich zeigen
Rufet die Arme
Der Götter herbei.

Cowardly thinking / timid wavering / womanly flinching (despairing)
/ anxious wailing / does not change misery / does not make you free.

Despite all powers / to keep yourself, / never to yield, / showing
yourself strong / brings the arms / of the gods to you.

To Brandes, these twelve lines were worth a hundred times more
than the rest. He had used the first three lines in the second verse as
the motto of the second part of *Main Currents* in 1873. They expressed his unbending will to continue the battle he had begun.
Brandes was thus able to discover different aspects of Goethe during
different periods of his life. When he finally undertook the task of
completing the biography, much of the man and his work had become foreign to him. He nevertheless regarded himself as the first
to attempt to describe Goethe's development step by step in both
science and art.[15] Brandes concentrated more upon the man and his
work in this biography than in his others, while the social and political aspects remained in the background. The Goethe book is not as
original in its conception as the Shakespeare biography nor has it
had any long-term effects on Goethe research. The First World War
hindered its immediate translation into English. The Entente
members were negatively inclined to German culture in general.

V *Voltaire*

Brandes published the first part of his biography on Voltaire only
a year after the Goethe book had appeared. Part two then followed
in 1917, and together the two volumes comprise 973 pages. It thus
involved an enormous expenditure of energy on Brandes' part during the first years of the war. The books on Voltaire and Goethe
partly represent a new orientation in Brandes' critical monographic
technique. He had in part written his own inner history in the book
on Shakespeare, but this was hardly the case with the Goethe and
Voltaire monographs. Brandes left his own private ego and his sub-

jective experiences in the background and concentrated on the subject of his writing. Nor was it any longer a question of describing
only the man and his work. Voltaire's contemporaries were also
included in Brandes' portrait of France of the 1700s. He was especially interested in the women surrounding Voltaire. This type of
personal history had already begun to be noted in the last part of
Main Currents.

Voltaire was, of course, no new acquaintance to Brandes. He had
become absorbed in the French writer and philosopher during his
student years and had enjoyed his most famous plays, apparently
without being able to perceive their weaknesses in relation to the
plays of Racine and Corneille.[16] While studying for his doctorate
and during the preparations for *Main Currents,* Brandes had
plunged even deeper into Voltaire's writings, such as *Dictionnaire
philosophique (Philosophical Dictionary)*, *Questions sur l'Ency-
clopédie (Questions on the Encyclopedia)*, and *Micromégas.*[17] In
general, the 1700s and the Enlightenment stood out as a period
when intellects awakened and a new era was born, but this was cut
off by the reactionary parenthesis called romanticism. This picture
of the 1700s was the basis for the composition of *Main Currents.* In
Emigrant Literature Brandes wrote: "When one speaks of the spirit
of the eighteenth century, it is normally Voltaire's name which
comes to mind; it is he who compiles, summarizes, and represents
this whole era."[18]

The idea that Voltaire incarnated the eighteenth-century is one
that Brandes repeated in the composition of the long biography.
Brandes had not dealt with this century to any great extent until
1884 when he published his book on Holberg. Thus he was taking
the plunge into a new period, and, as was the case with Goethe, he
made detailed studies before tackling the final composition. In
January 1905 he wrote to Mme de Caillavet, Anatole France's inti-
mate friend with whom he had corresponded for a long time, that he
had begun to study the eighteenth century and especially Voltaire,
and later that year he reported to her that he had lectured in Berlin,
Dresden, Prague, and Düsseldorf on "Voltaire and Frederick the
Great." In 1907 Brandes announced that he was delivering new
lectures in Germany, and this time the subject was how Joan of Arc
was treated by different authors, including Voltaire in the irreverent
La Pucelle (Joan of Arc.)

One can get an idea of how Brandes composed his book on Voltaire, or abstained from composition, from the notes he wrote to his secretary, which were published in her book on Brandes: "I am working without any special plan, fairly impulsively, not even a rough draft. I do what appeals to me at the moment. Don't know whether I want to write it chronologically or use other categories."[19] This way of working has made the book seem somewhat overgrown. Large sections, such as those dealing with Louis XV's mistresses in the first part, could have been eliminated without thereby disturbing the inner context or line of thought. Brandes seems to have planned to write about "Voltaire and his times," and seen in this light, the book reveals frightening insights into the moral, intellectual, and political life of the times.

Voltaire's writings, his epics, his tragedies, and his philosophic and satirical writings, were not very profoundly analyzed. But on the other hand Brandes had a weakness for Voltaire's numerous small poems written for special occasions, whose clarity, elegance, and *esprit* appealed to him, and which he often quoted. Furthermore, Brandes was fascinated by Voltaire as an active personality. He gave a detailed description of Voltaire's struggle to get his books published, of how he was constantly battling with different authorities and rulers who wished to silence him, of his prison term, of the burning of his books on various occasions, and of the different ways Voltaire found to spread his ideas. This was Voltaire's courageous struggle for reason and humanity, which took place not only in satirical books like *Candide* and *Micromégas* but also through the fact that he actively defended the victims of religious fanaticism and inhumanity.

Brandes therefore devoted a great deal of space in the second part of the biography to the great trials, especially to that of Jean Calas, mistakenly accused of the murder of his son because he had converted to Catholicism. He was condemned to death, tortured, broken on the wheel, and executed in the cruelest way. Voltaire, by his conduct in these new trials, acted as an advocate for humanity and paved the way for increased religious tolerance in Europe. He involved the enlightened monarchs of Europe, with whom he corresponded, in his struggle, and received monetary aid from both Catherine of Russia and Christian VII of Denmark.

Voltaire, in fact, had contacts in most of the countries of Europe. He had lived in England for a long time, had spent some time with

Frederick the Great of Prussia, and then settled down in Switzerland, but retained his foothold in France. When he finally settled
down in Ferney, he received representatives from the different
corners of Europe in the manner of a prince. His activity earned him
the title of "the good European," and as the champion of religious
tolerance and reason he was a great path breaker. When Brandes
published his Voltaire book it was not strange that he was characterized as a late Voltairian. Voltaire's often expressed hatred of war
could be seen in Brandes' own articles on the First World War. Paul
Rubow, an early Brandes' scholar, said that it was possible that
Brandes had borrowed some of Voltaire's fire and passion when
writing about the First World War, but we know that Brandes had
been skilled at that before.[20]

VI *Caesar*

Brandes had hardly finished his book on Voltaire before beginning a new long biography of Julius Caesar, which he was able to
publish in two volumes as early as 1918. For someone only superficially familiar with the life and works of Brandes it may seem
surprising that he, the radical intellectual, would take on the task of
portraying the Roman military commander and politician. As was
true of so many of Brandes' preferences, his admiration for Caesar
stemmed from his youth. In 1861 when he was especially engrossed
in the classical authors, he had read Caesar's *De bello gallico (The
Gallic Wars)* and was captivated by the narration, as is clear from his
diary from that time:

Reading Caesar has been very instructive and interesting. I have received a
living picture of all those campaigns, the Gallic recklessness, lack of common sense, love of freedom, boldness. The coolness and reason of the
Romans because of their enemies' lack of culture and morality.—I have
really penetrated Caesar.

During his career as an author and critic Brandes had had periods
during which he had not hidden his admiration for strong personalities like Lassalle, Bismarck, and Disraeli. This was especially
noticeable during his exile in Germany, where he became acquainted with Mommsen, whose *Römische Geschichte (Roman History)* glorified Caesar. In his arguments with Høffding on Nietzsche
and aristocratic radicalism Brandes had opportunity to quote from

Mommsen's character sketch.[21] In his presentation of Nietzsche, who was also an admirer of Caesar, Brandes included a brief panegyric to the Roman statesman:

He, whose name even today designates the greatest power, knew and understood everything that a general and ruler of the highest rank must know. Only a few men during the Italian Renaissance were able to come up to the same level of genius.[22]

Moreover, during the 1880s, when Brandes saw himself as a victim of deceit when his previous supporters abandoned him and his ideas, he developed an unusual fixation for Caesar as a betrayed man, and consequently a true hatred for Brutus, who became in his view the prototype of the betrayer. Several of his statements indicated this. In 1888 he wrote to one of his most faithful author friends: "In politics I have one god: Caesar, and one hatred: Brutus, that idiot of a usurer, who could do nothing but stick a knife in a great man."[23] This fixation with Caesar and hatred for Brutus the betrayer was also observed by Victoria Benedictsson. She wrote in her diary on one occasion:

He began to speak of Caesar, his ideal man—and of Brutus and all who betrayed him. How he spoke! It seemed to me that he grew and became tall, his oval eyes darkened and flashed into mine, it was almost difficult for me to look at them without blinking; there was resentment, fire, force. And the low, passionate voice! And this nervous little hand which trembled around mine. He was the agitator who was carried away by his own words. Now I saw what this man could have been if he had not been abandoned by his friends. A human being, a human being! surrounded by a hundred small, crawling insects. Caesar, yes, I understand this sympathy.[24]

Sooner or later this strange admiration for Caesar would find its outlet, and this happened during the First World War. While war bulletins told of advances and strategic retreats on the western front, Brandes became frenetically engrossed in Caesar's different campaigns, which he followed with the help of a map, just as in the introductory entry from his diary. He went to the primary sources, especially the German translations, and gave detailed descriptions of Caesar's different campaigns. The first part of the biography is a kind of overture to the actual hero story, and here the military-political, economic, and social background of Caesar's appearance was painted with broad brush strokes.

Brandes had begun to realize the role of economic forces in war in relation to World War One, and his insight into the affairs of the Roman senators is one of the most readable parts of his book.[25] Brutus and Cicero were seen in an especially bad light. That Brutus would be given the role of the villain of the drama was, of course, understood even before Brandes took pen in hand. Nor were Cassius and the other conspirators given any positive appraisal. Brandes had on several occasions, including the Shakespeare book, expressed his displeasure over the fact that Caesar was not as favorably portrayed as Brutus in Shakespeare's play. In a fury he tackled the tragic final part of the book where the murder was described graphically and in detail along with the murderers, who in many cases had been the beneficiaries of the man they attacked. He dealt surprisingly little with Roman literature. However, one of his main sources was Cicero's letters, which were not treated from the literary point of view, but as sources to illustrate Cicero's own lack of character and constant opportunism in relation to Caesar. In general, all secondary characters, such as Mark Antony, Pompey, and Augustus, were cut down to allow Caesar to appear in an even more favorable light.

The biography of Caesar can be read as a documentary novel of the historical genre. There is no criticism of sources or attempt to analyze the more profound historical causal context. Nor did Brandes attempt to balance his own opinions in relation to the opinions or analyses of other scholars. Brandes was now completely supreme in his indifference to what others might have contributed to this period of Roman history. Therefore, the book on Caesar is one of the purest examples of Brandes' hero-worship. It bears his personal stamp to the greatest degree and one can only agree with one of the most well-informed reviewers, Einar Löfstedt, the Swedish classical scholar, who described the book as a "brilliant example of the intellectual energy of this prodigious accumulator of intellectual force and passion, who bears the name Georg Brandes."[26] It had taken him about a year to complete these two volumes totalling about eleven hundred pages.

VII *Michelangelo*

If one were to try to find some sort of system in Brandes' choice of subjects for his five long biographies, it might possibly look like this: Shakespeare and Goethe, and to some extent Voltaire, represent greatness in the world of writing. With Caesar he presented the

great politician, a skillful administrator and general, no tyrant, instead a man of humanity and broad perspectives. With the last book
in this series, the one on Michelangelo (1921), he described a great
man in the arts.

In his introduction to the Michelangelo book Brandes noted that
all five figures he described in the way sketched above were unique
in that they "constituted an epoch."[27] They had also meant a great
deal to him personally. The biographies of Voltaire, Caesar, and
Michelangelo were also very similar in their composition. They all
began with a general introductory character sketch of the subject,
which Brandes called "Overture." This was followed by a description of the environment and atmosphere of the times in which the
figure moved. Thus the overture in the book on Michelangelo was
followed by a description of Rome and Florence in the 1400s, with
special emphasis on the central role of the Medici family, and then a
sketch of papal history during Michelangelo's long life. In a way this
is a sociological method that is reminiscent of Hauser. Brandes emphasized the role of the church and the pope as Michelangelo's
commissioners.

Brandes wrote in the preface to the biography of Michelangelo
that in 1871, when he saw the Sistine Chapel in Saint Peter's
Church for the first time, he said to himself: "Here I stand enclosed
with that spirit which of all human spirits has most strongly struck
my soul." In 1899 he wrote: "Of all the artists, Michelangelo is the
one who has made the greatest impression on me; of all the great
spirits in the history of the world, there is hardly anyone who has
influenced my inner life as he has."[28] Such statements seem undoubtedly somewhat exaggerated, even for someone who knows
Brandes' life and works well. As a critic Brandes had the ability to
feel solidarity with the object of his interest at the moment. But
even if these were big words, something must have lain behind
them, and what was it that fascinated the apostle of the modern
breakthrough in Michelangelo, the Renaissance artist?

In his introductory character sketch of Michelangelo, Brandes
stated that Michelangelo had three traits that distinguished him.
First of all, he portrayed nakedness, not only naked faces, but naked
bodies, with all of their expressiveness and uniqueness in dynamic
movement. The second trait was his attraction to the large format,
the colossal; and third, his art bore the stamp of *pathétique*, which
was expressed in the flow of energy in bound or free passion, and all
this lyricism resulted in drama.

Brandes acquired his knowledge of sculptural art during numerous museum visits and discussions during his student years with Julius Lange, the art historian. Lange himself wrote two studies on Michelangelo, and these were included in his friend's *Udvalgte Skrifter (Selected Writings)*, edited by Brandes and Köbke. Brandes revealed in his autobiography that he had had a reproduction of the ceiling painting in the Sistine Chapel hanging in his room for ten years before he received special permission from the Vatican to visit "the goal of my pilgrimage" in 1871.[29] A few months earlier, while on a visit to London, he had taken advantage of the museums there to broaden his knowledge of Michelangelo. Thus in 1919, when he began his research on Michelangelo immediately after completing the biography of Caesar, Brandes was no newcomer to the area. He had a special preference for the Renaissance as Burchhardt and Nietzsche had imagined it. For him it was a time when people in Italy threw off the straitjacket of Christian asceticism, the Jewish-Oriental inheritance, and let the classical view of nature dominate once again.[30] To Brandes, the Renaissance was a brilliant parenthesis, preceded by the dark Middle Ages and followed by the bigotry and contempt for art of the Reformation. Michelangelo was affected by this bigotry during the latter part of his life, and Brandes described with disgust the fate of Michelangelo's fresco of the *Last Judgment* when one of his students was forced to put trousers on the master's naked bodies.[31]

Michelangelo was a sculptor, painter, drawer, architect, and poet, and thus fulfilled all the great demands on a fully developed Renaissance man. Brandes attempted to describe these different facets of his personality. For him, Michelangelo's main work was the decoration of the Sistine Chapel. He wrote about the creation of Adam:

There is music in the rhythm of this unforgettable picture, music as swellingly melodious as that which Beethoven spoke of when he wrote: "Music ought to make the human soul burn," or as that which sounds in a mass of Palestrina where the artistic weave of voices does not hide the clear melody or the easy understanding of the text.[32]

As a matter of fact, Brandes did not only once use musical analogies to graphically describe Michelangelo's art. Brandes, who liked to work with the art of comparative portraits, naturally included a discussion of the two other great Renaissance masters, Raphael and

Leonardo. In a comparison between Raphael and Michelangelo, the former was described as a Mozart type and Michelangelo once again as a Beethoven.[33] The only difference was, Brandes continued, that Michelangelo created no "An die Freude." ("Hymn to Joy"). According to Brandes, Michelangelo's later life was characterized by bitterness and misanthropy, and thus the biography had some of the self-reflective traits which were typical of the Shakespeare book.

Reading the biography of Michelangelo, one is reminded of the fact that Brandes was originally educated in aesthetics. During his student years he had hoped to win a professorship in aesthetics, and he made early attempts to understand art forms other than the literary. He wrote a significant number of art studies: on Donatello, whose statue of Saint George he especially admired because of the associations he could make to his own name; on Rubens, Rembrandt, and Max Klinger, with whom he became acquainted while in Germany. But one could hardly say that Brandes' views on art were as radical and advanced as those he held on literature.

CHAPTER 12

... and the European Tragedy

I U.S.A.

AT the time of the outbreak of World War One, Brandes' position as a critic and cultural personality was established all over Europe. His book on Shakespeare helped to make him well known in the English-speaking part of the world. In 1914, a few months before the war, Brandes traveled to the United States with an invitation to speak at Yale. In New York, where he also appeared with a speech on Shakespeare, the police were called to disperse the crowd of over a thousand people who could not get tickets to the Comedy Theater where the event was to take place.[1] In Chicago he lectured at Orchestra Hall and the Twentieth Century Club and was the guest of honor at banquets and the recipient of honorary degrees. Newspapers and magazines published extensive introductions and interviews with him. He admitted on his return home in an article in *Politiken* that his main impression of America was "80,000 idiotic reporters."[2] One of the leading American literary publications, *The Dial*, introduced its presentation of Brandes in the following way:

The present visit of Dr. Georg Brandes to the United States, although it is covering only a fortnight, is an event of the utmost importance in our cultural annals. Dr. Brandes is one of the half-dozen most famous men of letters now alive and incomparably the greatest of living Scandinavians. We doubt if this country has ever entertained a more distinguished representative of European letters. We have had of recent years, it is true, visits from M. Bergson and Lord Morley, we had about ten years ago the great Danish poet Drachmann, and thirty years ago the great Norwegian poet Bjørnson, and the visits of Matthew Arnold, Thackeray, and Dickens are marked by red letters in our calendar. The appearance of Dr. Brandes is at least as memorable as any of these, and will long be remembered by those who have come into contact with his vital and powerful personality.[3]

Brandes expressed himself in fairly sweeping terms on the subject of American literature. Thus he said in the *Independent* of June 15, 1914: "Your literature, ah, I have no hope! Your books are written by old maids for old maids." However, from his more serious comments it was clear that he admired Henry James, who had taken the initiative to a closer acquaintance during Brandes' visit to London in 1895.[4] Upton Sinclair interested him, and upon his return he wrote an introduction to *King Cole* (1917) at the request of Sinclair's American publishers.[5] Several of his statements indicated that Brandes was critical of the different ways American capitalism expressed itself. In an article on his American trip published in the collection *Napoleon og Garibaldi (Napoleon and Garibaldi,* 1917), Brandes claimed that art easily became a market product no different from any other in such a society.[6] This collection also contained a number of the speeches he gave in the United States. He claimed that American newspapers dwelled on a comment he made to journalists apropos of the Statue of Liberty on his arrival in New York: "Isn't it true that the goddess especially defends the *liberty to acquire,* that liberty which is closest to the heart of an American."[7]

II   *World at War*

Over the years Brandes had developed into a great traveler who in a very natural way felt himself at home in the capitals of Europe and wherever he had contacts: in Berlin, Vienna, Paris, Rome, and London. He was on visiting terms with Anatole France, Bernard Shaw, and H. G. Wells, to mention a few. Gertrud Rung, his secretary, presented a few glimpses from his trips around Europe before the war in her book *Georg Brandes i Samvaer og Breve* (1930). On several occasions during the decade before the war Brandes visited Karlsbad, where he used to meet with Clemenceau, the French politician and his good friend since the days of the Dreyfus affair. Brandes felt an honest admiration for the courage and strength that characterized Clemenceau's activity in French politics, such as his plea for mild treatment of the conquered Communards after the uproar in 1871. He became engrossed in the speeches and writing of Clemenceau and wrote an essay in 1903 in which he painted a detailed portrait of the author, politician, and man.[8]

Several of these friendships would, however, be broken with the outbreak of World War One, which Brandes saw as a tragedy and which set its mark on his two books concerning the war: _Verdenskrigen (World at War)_ and _Tragediens anden Del (The World Tragedy)_. These include the articles, open letters, and appeals that Brandes was led to write because of the war. _World at War_ was introduced with some articles written long before the outbreak of the war—the first one in 1881—in which he claimed that he could foresee the coming war. These presentiments were primarily based upon his experiences of the militarizing going on in Germany during his stay there. But in an article from 1913, "Frankrigs Ungdom" ("The Youth of France"), he discussed similar tendencies in France. He wrote the article because of a book by Ernest Psichari, the grandson of the much admired Ernest Renan. The book was entitled _L'Appel des Armes (The Call of Weapons)_. Brandes wrote: "No author has ever written a book with such an infatuation with the art of making weapons and with the call of war. . . ."[9] Brandes felt a certain melancholy in reading and commenting on a book like this one, since he knew that the author's famous grandfather had held a diametrically opposed view and had spoken conciliatory words during the war of 1870 with the Germans.

In another prewar article with the characteristic title "Tysk Faedrelanderi" ("German Nationalism"), Brandes claimed that if the French love of their country was infatuated, the German's was fanatic, and he gave frightening examples of how war was honored as the holiest expression of human activity. The world war was made possible, he claimed, by the fact that narrow-minded nationalism was allowed to flourish in both camps, and in an essay called "Verdenskrigens Forudsaetninger" ("Pre-conditions for a World War") written immediately after the outbreak of the war, he pointed out how people in England, for example, consistently screened off information about the new Germany, thereby paving the way for all kinds of prejudices against the Germans. The German language is unknown in every school, he wrote, and there is not one German professorship in all of Scotland and only one in the German language and literature in England. All of the warring countries call upon God to forward their just cause. In Germany God was also called "the old ally from Rossbach," and he protected the kaiser, who was his representative on earth.[10]

Brandes thus had difficulties in feeling solidarity with either of the warring parties. His five-year stay in Berlin had left its mark on him, and his familiarity with the German cultural inheritance from the

romantics to the expressionists made it difficult for him to turn
against the Germans. In the same way he felt deeply in debt to
France and England. The fact that Brandes' son-in-law, Reinhold
Philipp, married to Brandes' only daughter, was a German citizen
and served on the front as an artillery officer must also have been of
great importance for Brandes' position.

In a series of articles Brandes took up the arguments of the warring powers to justify their participation in the war. He noted, with
a certain amount of irony, that both camps saw themselves struggling for Western culture. Thus Brandes cited a statement of Bergson
made to the French Academy: "The struggle against Germany is
civilization's struggle against barbarity."[11] And further on in his
book, when he outlined the German point of view, he quoted a few
words from Harnack, the theologian: "If we should fall, God and our
strong arms forbid, then all of the higher culture of our part of the
world goes into the grave with us."[12]

What especially irritated Brandes in the constellation of great
powers that were at war with each other was that England and
France, which to a great extent were democracies, had allied themselves with a reactionary tyranny like czarist Russia. He sym-
pathized with the social reformative and revolutionary currents in
Russia, and he was upset by the anti-Semitic tendencies that were
so strongly felt, not least in Poland. In his article "Tilstande in
russisk Polen" ("The Situation in Russian Poland"), Brandes was
forced to note that some of his former writer friends from the 1880s
had   become   ardent   anti-Semites.   Regarding   Alexander
Świętochowski he stated that there was a time when he would have
sworn that he would never live to see the day when Świętochowski
would become a nationalist and head of the anti-Semites.[13] It was
feared that the Jewish minorities would not be true to their country
in its moment of danger. The result was pogroms both in Poland and
in Russia.

Thus the people of Europe fell into ranks under their respective
European flags and the time of the great mass murders began, the
time of nationalistic insanity. And the intellectuals of Europe also
joined in the slogan shouting. Romain Rolland wrote to Brandes in
September 1914 and asked him to join in an appeal against the
German bombing of Louvain and Reims, where valuable cultural
monuments had been destroyed: "A great European like you ought
to march in the front ranks of the defenders of European civiliza-

tion."[14] But Brandes defended himself by claiming that Denmark was neutral and that he did not publically wish to take sides for either of the warring parties, especially since his younger brother Edvard was a member of the government. Brandes' refusal did not lead to a break in his relations with Romain Rolland, and their correspondence also continued after the war. It was different with his relations with Clemenceau and William Archer, the English critic with whom he became involved in a public dialogue.

The temperamental Clemenceau felt a great deal of aversion to the neutrality of the Nordic countries, and was of the opinion that, keeping in mind that Denmark had lost a good deal of its territory in 1864, it would have been only natural for Denmark to join in on the side of the Entente. He criticized the position of the Nordic countries in sarcastic terms in his newspaper *L'Homme Enchainé*. In February he learned of a statement Brandes was said to have made regarding the German violation of neutrality in marching into Belgium. Brandes was not very indignant but according to Clemenceau was said to have remarked: "Germany, whatever anyone says, is a civilized power, a great civilized power."[15] Clemenceau did not mention Brandes by name in this article but referred to him as "one of the most famous thinkers of a Scandinavian country" and it was obvious whom he meant.

Brandes, who attempted to keep up with what was being written in the more important European newspapers, replied with an open letter to Clemenceau that was published in *Politiken* and *L'Homme Enchainé*. Brandes had been especially upset because Clemenceau had called Denmark "a people without pride." And even if the Germans had been hard on the German minority in Schleswig, he thought it would be completely insane for Denmark to declare war against Germany. He also wrote that he had felt a personal reproach in Clemenceau's articles on Denmark, and referred to the above-quoted passage. At the same time he wrote in this way in his open letter to Clemenceau, he wrote to him privately and informed him that he was not able to choose his viewpoints freely in matters of foreign affairs since his brother was a member of the government. Clemenceau, the polemic, did not hesitate to make use of this in his public reply in *L'Homme Enchainé*:

You said you were restrained because your brother was a minister: Oh really! I do not know what a minister is worth in Denmark, but I can assure you that in France we do not make such a big issue out of them.

. . . Louvain, Dinant, Reims, these are not less interesting for the future of civilization than the portfolio of Georg Brandes' brother.[16]

It was thus a case of fairly blunt polemics and an almost insulting insinuation on the part of Clemenceau. In his reply Brandes refuted with good conscience the accusation that he had any economic advantages because of his brother's ministerial post. He furthermore claimed that he had never publically retracted anything they had agreed upon during the times they spent together in Karlsbad over the years. Brandes wrote that while he thought that the German invasion of Belgium was a glaring injustice, it was nevertheless predicted and discussed in the military publications of several countries so one was less surprised that it happened than at the fact that France was so ill prepared. And while he wished France success, at the same time he pointed out that a victory for the allied forces would be a great misfortune if it also led to success for Russia, which would result in a reinforcement of the European reaction.

Clemenceau's reply was published in *L'Homme Enchainé* on March 29, and in *Politiken* on March 30, and began with the words: "Adieu, Brandes. If the conversation is to be something more than a simple chitchat then we must have some fundamental ideas about feelings or thoughts in common. I find nothing like this between us."[17] Clemenceau explained that he was forced to find words that did not yet exist to express how totally irreconcilable their points of view were regarding the war, and he concluded his long letter with the words: "You see that henceforth there is no point to a conversation between us. Adieu, Brandes."

Brandes was sad about the rift with Clemenceau, but this did not prevent him from returning to Clemenceau's personality and writings in a couple of articles after the war, which were included in a collection of essays entitled *Liv og Kunst (Life and Art)* published posthumously in 1929. The continued development of the war and Clemenceau's activity at the peace conference demonstrated the fact that the two were bound to separate sooner or later. Clemenceau was the politician who was most ruthless in humiliating Germany, thus paving the way for the Second World War, which was just what Brandes had feared. He expressed these thoughts in an appeal for peace publicized in May 1916, in which he urged the warring parties to begin negotiations since they would be forced to in any case sooner or later. What was the moving of a few border posts in one direction or another in relation to the waste of young men's lives on the battlefield? The further development of the war was, in his opinion, to a great extent dependent on the United States. Would this country prefer to profit by the war or to use its influence to further peace? For Brandes, the world war was more barbaric than the wars of religion of earlier times. He was one of the first to realize that the most profound causes of the war were economic.

Brandes' appeal was answered by William Archer, among others, the well-known English critic and Ibsen translator, who published a brochure against Brandes entitled *Colourblind Neutrality* (1916); translated into both Danish and Swedish. This could be seen as a phase in the Entente's propaganda war in Scandinavia. Archer took up the problem of who had the blame for the war and placed it all on Germany. England had tried to avoid the war as long as possible. Brandes inspected Archer's arguments closely in a series of articles in *Politiken*, later included in *World at War*. He analyzed English colonial policy and compared England's annexation of Persia to the German aggression against Belgium. He claimed that in Persia, England had quietly taken over all the natural resources of the country, especially oil, without any thought to world opinion, and had sent in troops along with Russia and Turkey in spite of the fact that the country had declared itself neutral. Brandes devoted several articles to the Persian question and showed that Russia and England had begun a systematic colonial exploitation of the country even before the war.

III   *The Russian Revolution and Postwar Europe*

Thus the war policy of the Entente was partly based on imperialistic grounds and the war had further accentuated the antagonism between classes. Brandes guessed, therefore, that the war would result in a new revolution, just as the war of 1870 had resulted in the Paris Commune.[18] He wrote in his reply to Archer:

The poor slaves who worked for minimal daily wages in peacetime and who are, like slaves, dressed in uniform and sent into the fire in time of war in the name of that beautiful and glorious good, universal military service, will at one point be driven to such despair that the social revolution, fancied for so long but suppressed, as long as humanity retained the slightest bit of common sense, will break out with the same ferocity as the war has now.[19]

Brandes had closely followed the inner developments in Eastern Europe ever since his visits to Poland and Russia in the 1880s and had been upset by the unsatisfactory social conditions there. In 1895 he had met two of the leading men of the revolutionary movement, Peter Kropotkin and Serge Stepniak, in London, where they were living in exile. In 1897 he wrote an article about Stepniak that was later used as an introduction to the first Russian publication of his novel *The Career of a Nihilist*. Brandes corresponded frequently with Kropotkin until a short time before the latter's death. Brandes had written favorably about Kropotkin's educational work among the workers of Saint Petersburg in *Impressions of Russia*, and he later attempted to become familiar with the writings of both Stepniak and Kropotkin.[20] When Kropotkin was going to publish his autobiography, his English publisher requested a foreword and he asked Brandes to write one, which he did. In this way he tried to support Kropotkin, whose *Memoirs of a Revolutionist* came out in England and America at the same time in 1900. Kropotkin envisioned a type of socialism based on voluntarily created production units rather freely tied to each other, somewhat reminiscent of the guilds of the Middle Ages. Brandes was rather skeptical about this grassroots democracy with no true leader, but he seems to have been more attracted to this type of socialism than to that of the totalitarian state that Lenin represented. Therefore, when the Russian Revolution broke out in March 1917, Brandes saw it as something positive and he hoped that all the exiled Russian revolutionaries he had met during his life would now be able to return. His thoughts went especially to Kropotkin, whose human socialism he found appealing, and who as a thinker he found "more profound and fruitful than Marx, from whom Europe has learned everything he had to teach."[21]

When the more hardhanded Bolsheviks took over Russia Brandes saw it as a degeneration of the revolution, but he nevertheless regarded Lenin as a fairly sympathetic figure:

Personally, Lenin inspires only conditional sympathy: the cruelty of his way of acting inspires almost none. But he obviously believes in his cause and in his right. His way of feeling has, not without reason, been likened to the Great Inquisitor's. Like Torquemada he is an honest believer, and like him he conducts his regime of terror with torture, burnings at the stake, and bonfires, convinced that he is serving a good cause and bringing the kingdom of God down to earth.[22]

In Brandes' eyes Lenin, as autocratic ruler, had quite simply taken over after the incompetent czar and governed by force of his superior will and intelligence.[23] First and last it depends on the man in question, and then what do the concepts of socialism, communism, parliamentarianism, and republicanism matter? In some strange way, almost against his will, history had proven Brandes right when he stressed the necessity of discerning leadership in his discussions with Kropotkin. The Russian Revolution was, in any case, a necessary historic fact, and Brandes therefore fought against the intervention policy the allies initiated after the war to set back the clock of history. He claimed that the Western powers had a moralizing, almost theological concept of the Bolsheviks.[24]

In general Brandes regarded the play performed on the European stage after the war with skepticism and bitterness. During the war he had become more and more critical toward the allied forces, in spite of the fact that his sympathies were to a great extent with France and England. On the one side—the German—he saw brutality, and on the other—that of England, France, and America— hypocrisy. The allies went into the war with beautiful mottos about freedom and democracy, but the underlying forces were the struggle for natural resources and for markets for industrial products, and it was only a few influential capitalists who directed the political game.[25]

Added to this was the accelerated exploitation of the colonies, practiced by England especially, that was given even more possibilities thanks to the results of the Peace of Versailles. One hundred fifty years of English rule in India had transformed that country from its position of cultural leader in Asia to an area of material and cultural poverty, while independent Japan had joined in the competition with Europe in most fields. The peace conference was a tragic farce for Brandes, and he went through Wilson's famous fourteen points that were the basis for the cease-fire, and showed how practically every one was ignored in the peace settlement. For Brandes the European, Europe at the end of the war was one large bankrupt's estate, and Clemenceau, his old friend from Karlsbad, completely controlled the Congress of Versailles by his will and his language ability, forcing the passage of his policy of revenge at the cost of the conquered Germany.

When the borders opened again after the war, Brandes could once again take up his travels, and he visited Italy and Greece, but the world had changed and he was beginning to feel his years. He turned to the oldest myths and writings of humanity in his last books, to come to terms with the origins and foundations of Western culture. He took up these questions in *Hellas* (1925), *Sagnet om Jesus (Jesus: A Myth*, 1925), *Petrus* (1926), and *Urkristendom (Original Christianity*, 1927).

IV *Hellas*

Hellas is comprised of essays on Homer and Xenophone, and travel impressions from a visit to Greece in 1922. The classical period of antiquity, Athenian culture in the fourth century B.C., represented an ideal stage in the history of humanity during all of Brandes' active life. He primarily emphasized the feeling for moderation and balance, which he felt was characteristic of this time in his picture of Greece. While Christianity dealt continuously with death, the "other side" was only a pale land of shadows for the Greeks. He sang the praises of Pallas Athena. She was the personification of thought and reason and she discovered art. The Greeks accepted nature as something good and positive. It was different in the north, which received its religion from a German monk who believed he had re-created the original Christianity. There people believed in original sin and the cursedness of nature. To Brandes this was barbaric. He honored the classical Greeks as the most richly gifted people of ancient times, and ever since the Renaissance there have been people around the world who have been imbued by their spirit and sought clarity and flexibility and felt aversion to obfuscation, illogicality, and formlessness, who have valued joy and beautiful dreams and who have not prized asceticism for its own sake but only as a means.[26] Brandes thought of himself as an heir and champion of the Greek inheritance. When he wrote about the *Iliad* and the *Odyssey* at the age of almost eighty, it was with a surprising freshness and verve. He did not get tangled up in scholarly discussion of the Homeric question or in disputes with everyone who had analyzed the Homeric poems. He approached the works like the alert and receptive reader he always was, and therefore the *Iliad* and the *Odyssey* become fantastically vivid in his interpretation.

In 1922 Brandes made the trip to Greece, a last pilgrimage, and he climbed the Acropolis with the same reverence that Renan expressed in his famous "Prière sur Acropole" *(Prayer on the Acropolis).* "I have longed for this moment all of my life," Brandes said to his traveling companions, but he was eighty years old before his dream came true.[27] At last he was granted the possibility of seeing the originals behind all the antique imitations he had run into:

At last! At last no more of Thorvaldsen's Danish-Greek neo-classicism, no more Greek Glyptoteque-architecture in Munich, no more French La Madeleine-style, no more Greek statues coarsened in Roman technique, no more Sicilian landscapes and coasts as surrogates for Greek, at last no more of the imitative Dutch which was called the Athens of the North, which triumphantly competed with Aarhus, but the real Athens, the only, eternal, true![28]

In the concluding essays of *Hellas* Brandes contrasted ancient Greece with the Greece of modern times, which had been hard hit by World War One. He claimed to be completely aware of the fact that ancient Greece was by no means an ideal state, and left a long list of practically all the famous men and women of ancient Greece showing how they, in one way or another, were persecuted, exiled, or executed. The list of injustices against modern Greece would be at least as long, Brandes said, primarily because Europe was now governed by men with little wisdom.

V *Endgame*

Brandes was a freethinker and very tolerant in his views, and he didn't seek out unnecessary polemic controversies in religious questions, even if his basic philosophy often shone through his writing. The foundations of the Christian religion became very topical questions in different periods of his life. He became acquainted with the ideas of Friedrich Strauss, the most famous German Bible critic, during his years of study. In his book *Das Leben Jesu (The Life of Jesus,* 1835), Strauss did not question the historical existence of the prophet, nor did Renan in his sentimental biography of Jesus, which Brandes often mentioned. When Brandes once again began to study the life of Jesus and the activity of the apostles in the last years of his life, it was under the influence of the findings that had been made in anthropological and mythological research. Thus he had been influenced by Frazer's well-known work *The Golden Bough* (1890) and by Robertson's *Christianity and Mythology* (1900). And he did not forget the Germans, especially Arthur Drew's *Die Christusmythe (The Myth of Christ)* (1909–1911), in which the historical existence of Jesus was completely denied, and which seem to have been of great importance for Brandes' three books of religious criticism: *The Story of Jesus, Peter,* and *Original Christianity.* It is possible that Bengt Lidforss's book *Kristendomen förr och nu (Christianity Then and Now)* stimulated him into taking up these questions. Both Robertson and Drews had influenced Lidforss.

The pervading theme in the three books is that the leading figures of Christianity have mythical character. This is primarily true of Jesus. There are no sure historical documents that prove that he ever lived. He himself wrote nothing that has been preserved. None of the evangelists had ever seen him, and their stories were written long afterward. Paul, who was the true disseminator of Christian teachings, had never seen his master in life. There is nothing in Roman documents about the life and work of Jesus. The passion story of a god who dies and arises again has striking similarities with other myths in Asia Minor, especially the story of Osiris. Many of the parables and winged words Jesus was supposed to have said may be traced to the Old Testament. Brandes felt he had found almost all of the Sermon on the Mount in the Book of Jesus Syrach.[29] Not even the Lord's Prayer was a product of the New Testament, but rather a compilation with a prototype from the Old Testament.

The same was true of the figure of Peter. Brandes was struck by the fact that he had several names: Simon led to associations with the heathen god Semo, and Brandes related Peter to the at times so triumphant god of the cliffs, Mithra, whose influence culminated with Julian the Apostate. Brandes linked the powers the Roman church later granted Peter, such as the keys of heaven and the guarding of the gates of heaven, with Janus, the two-headed Roman god of all entrances and exits, who in Roman mythology closed the gates of heaven in the evening.[30] Brandes claimed that the Bible's Peter was a purely fictional figure who dissolved into a blue mist when one tried to grasp him.

It follows that the figure of Judas was also an unhistoric figure created as a personification of the Jewish people who were said to have crucified Jesus. Judas's contribution as the betrayer of the master at his arrest was completely superfluous.

In *Original Christianity* Brandes emphasized that the first Christian congregations were definitely communistic in character, and they thus constituted a continuation of groups that had been formed during Jewish times. These groups of landless or poor created a front against the capitalistic estate owners in the Roman Empire. Early Christianity was a socialistic movement among slaves and the landless, directed toward the owners of capital. According to Brandes, modern technology had demonstrated a certain fear for this communism, which originally was a revolt against the dominating Roman cult of riches.

With the appearance of Paul in the first century came the great change in the situation of the Jewish sects. Actually, Christianity is Paul's creation, even if the letters attributed to him seem to have other authors. The central aspect of his Christian message was the mystical aspect of Jesus's life on earth, his death and resurrection, but this aspect could also be applied to Dionysus, Attis, Adonis, Mithras, or Osiris. This mystical aspect introduced by Paul was foreign to ancient Jewry. The core of Christianity is a strongly developed awareness of the value of each individual. Brandes' historical religious authorship was greatly dependent upon English, German, and French research, but it was also a continuation of the impulses he had received at an early age from the German leftist Hegelians, Feuerbach, Strauss, and Bruno Bauer. All of these walked against the crowd and spread annoyance in their questioning of theological Bible research. Nor had Christian dogmatism mellowed very much when Brandes published these three books in the 1920s. In *Original Christianity* Brandes claimed that in comparison to Holland, Denmark was not very tolerant in religious questions.[31] Even in the twentieth-century it was still the stronghold of orthodoxy. Thus Brandes was still able to challenge and stir up debate with his books in the autumn of his years.

During the 1920s Brandes worked almost exclusively with a smaller format, with the exception of his biography of Michelangelo. An example is *Hertuginden af Dino og Fyrsten af Talleyrand (The Duchess of Dino and the Prince of Talleyrand, 1923)*, a microbiography of a woman's fate in the shadow of the Napoleonic wars and the Vienna Congress. As in *Uimodstaaelige (Irresistibles, 1924)*, it permits insight into a private life on the basis of letters, memoirs, and diary entries. The irresistible is primarily the Duke of Biron, military commander, diplomat, and above all *charmeur* in Casanova's class, a typical product of prerevolutionary France. Both books are entertaining and may be read as a kind of documentary novel, which, even with its piquant sexual content, still gives perspective on the incredibly miserable social and economic conditions that paved the way for the great revolution.

Brandes' last years were darkened by sickness, which nevertheless did not totally prevent him from traveling. In 1925 he visited Berlin and gave a lecture there in spite of the fact that his voice could hardly be heard in the large hall. He then went on to Vienna, where he met von Hofmannsthal, Max Reinhardt, and Schnitzler, with whom he was especially close. He was also visited by Freud, whom he liked very much and definitely believed to be a great man.

Brandes felt more and more isolated during the last years of his life: "My line of the species has died out; I have never had a disciple nor have I ever wished for one," he wrote in 1926, and the next year, shortly before he died, he wrote: "I am through with the world. I do not think, do not read, do not write."[32] When he was taken to the hospital he was aware that he would not get well again. He who in his youth had said to his friend and benefactor Brøchner, the professor of philosophy, that he could not reconcile himself with the thought of death, he who up to the last moment possessed such intellectual vitality and who had always worshiped life, had finally accepted the relentlessness of death. One of his last statements was, "It has lasted long enough."

CONCLUSION

The Critic as an Outsider

BRANDES' path was that of an outsider. Because of his Jewish origins, he regarded much in Danish and European cultural life from an early age from the point of view of an outsider. His family had relatives in different parts of Europe, and it was a natural thing for him to move about outside the Danish cultural environment. He assimilated the new philosophy that came forth under the influence of the progress made in the natural sciences during the middle of the 1800s with surprising promptness. He became the spokesman for a radical new philosophy that demanded that literature illuminate social problems and become a progressive force both inside and outside Scandinavia.

As a critic Brandes passed through different stages. Before 1870 he adopted a critical approach that can be traced to Hegel and his followers. As a spokesman for French naturalism he borrowed a number of terms from the natural sciences, with environment and heritage as the cornerstones. He saw a work of art in relation to the society in which it was created, and thus he can be considered an early representative of the sociological approach to literature. All the time, however, Brandes was a *comparatiste,* and that is perhaps his most distinguishing feature. He wished to use literature as an instrument for breaking through provincial isolation. From the middle of the 1870s, when writing his biographies of Kierkegaard, Lassalle, Tegnér, and Disraeli, he may be regarded as a personalist, a technique that culminated with his extensive biographies of Shakespeare, Goethe, Voltaire, Caesar, and Michelangelo.

One of the striking traits of Brandes' life and work was his tendency to go outside national boundaries. Besides his native tongue, Swedish, Norwegian, and the classical languages, he also knew

185

German, French, English, and Italian, and he was proud of being able to keep up with literary developments in the most important language areas in Europe. He spread his influence primarily as a lecturer, and one of the reasons for his great influence may be found in the magnetism of his personal approach in dealings with people and on the podium. In general he preferred personal contacts and became friends with many of the leading authors of Europe. His essays were based not only on reading but also on a personal impression of the writer in question. His correspondence was extremely extensive and included such contemporary authors as Henrik Ibsen, Bjørnstjerne Bjørnson, Alexander Kielland, Henrik Pontoppidan, August Strindberg, Verner von Heidenstam, Gustaf Fröding, Hjalmar Söderberg, Anatole France, Emile Zola, Romain Rolland, Paul Heyse, Friedrich Nietzsche, and Peter Kropotkin.

Another remarkable trait was Brandes' versatility. His authorship included fiction, philosophy, religion, history, art history, and other closely related areas. His versatility did not always have a corresponding depth and originality. Actually, he was the great assimilator. He could have made Molière's saying "je reprend mon bien partout où je le trouve" (*I take up what is good for me wherever I can find it*) his own. In many cases he functioned as a popularizer of others' ideas. This did not mean that he was lacking a conscious and well-thought-out philosophy. It was characterized by rationalism, passion for freedom, and a strong social commitment. His political views were rooted in the liberalism of the 1800s with John Stuart Mill as an important stimulus, but all political doctrines were too narrow for him. He had an avid interest in different varieties of socialism and was profoundly impressed by such different socialistic philosophers as Proudhon, Lassalle, Marx, and Kropotkin. His political profile is marked by a certain dualism. He did not succeed in bridging the gap between the democratic radicalism of Mill and the left-wing Hegelians, especially Lassalle, and the aristocratic radicalism developed from his studies of Nietzsche.

All of Brandes' activity was characterized by a tendency to take active part in the social, political and cultural debate. One of the mottos he adopted was "To me, a book is an action." He was also attracted to definite men of action and will like Lassalle and Clemenceau. But this did not prevent him from appreciating writers who represented a versatile and often pronounced aesthetic educational ideal, such as Goethe. Brandes also spread his influence to a great extent as a critic in newspapers and magazines and through his essays. He continued the tradition of essay writing in European literature in the line of Sainte-Beuve, Taine, Renan, and Bourget. Brandes was almost exclusively interested in contemporary literature during the first decades of his work. His great book *Main Currents* is a survey of European literature up to the middle of the 1800s. As he grew older he came to deal with earlier periods, especially the Renaissance and the 1700s.

Brandes' style was characterized by clarity and lucidity and reflected his feeling for rationality and tangibility. His point of departure was often an illustrative anecdote or quotation. The scope of his reading was impressive, and his memory held an inexhaustible supply of thoughts and expressions he could mobilize quickly. His critical technique demonstrated great flexibility and ability to adapt to the theme he was treating. He was a critic of ideas who searched for the author's ethical and social philosophy. Involvement, vitality, and passion distinguish his way of writing. He was a perceptive critic who was primarily interested in originality, utility, and uniqueness. For this reason he was able to appreciate writers who did not share his philosophy, such as Hans Christian Andersen, Søren Kierkegaard, Selma Lagerlöf, Honoré de Balzac, and Feodor Dostoevsky.

As an outsider, Brandes chose to question the attitudes and values that were the foundations of the society in which he worked, and he was therefore seen by many as an amoral rebel. But a society that forces critical voices into silence finally turns into a petrified organism. In his lectures from 1871, Brandes launched the nineteenth-century radical vision of a different kind of society with no class differences, no double morality, no oppression of women, a society in which individuals could develop freely without regard to prejudices and social and economic handicaps. Brandes did not see his dream come true, but achieved at least partly the goal he had set himself as a young disciple of Hegel: to work as a soldier in the service of progressive thought. He experienced the fate of many social critics: both spiteful persecution and exaggerated adoration.

Notes and References

Chapter One

1. Brandes, *Søren Kierkegaard*, pp. 2–3. All quotations from Brandes are translated from the Danish original by Mrs. Katy Lissbrant and the author.
2. Brandes, *Levned*, I, p. 20.
3. Fenger, *Georg Brandes' læreår*, p. 1.
4. Fenger, *Den unge Brandes*, pp. 59–69.
5. Nolin, *Den gode europén*, pp. 140–41.
6. Brandes, *Æsthetiske Studier*, pp. 284–285.
7. Fenger, *Georg Brandes' læreår*, p. 81.
8. Nolin, pp. 311–13.
9. Letter to his mother, Emilie Brandes, January 15, 1867. In the Brandes Archive, Det Kongelige Bibliotek, Copenhagen.
10. Brandes, *Den franske Æsthetik i vore Dage*, pp. 29–30.
11. Ibid., p. 171.
12. Ibid., p. 183.
13. Fenger, *Georg Brandes' læreår*, pp. 37–56; Rubow, P. V., *Georg Brandes' briller*, pp. 237–58.
14. Brandes, *Den franske Æsthetik i vore Dage*, pp. 127–132.
15. H. Taine, *Philosophie de l'art*, II (G. Baillière, Paris: 1893), p. 273.
16. Letter to Paul Heyse, December 23, 1872. *Correspondance de Georg Brandes*, III, p. 13.
17. H. Taine, *Histoire de la littérature anglaise*, (Hachette, Paris: I, 1863), p. xxiii.
18. Brandes, *Kritiker og Portraiter*, p. 423.
19. Brandes, *Hovedstrømninger i det nittende Aarhundredes Litteratur*, I, p. 8.
20. Brandes, *Kritiker og Portraiter*, p. 324.
21. Ibid., p. 483.
22. S. Linnér. "Komparativ litteraturforskning," in *Forskningsfält och metoder inom litteraturvetenskapen*, ed. L. Gustafsson (Wahlström & Widstrand, Stockholm, 1970), pp. 78–80.

189

Chapter Two

1. Brandes, *Mennesker og Værker*, pp. 375–415.
2. Ibid., p. 338.
3. Fenger, *Georg Brandes' læreår*, pp. 372–81.
4. Letter to his parents, May 14, 1871. In the Brandes Archive.
5. Letter to his parents, May 20, 1871. In the Brandes Archive
6. Letter from Emil Petersen, December 7, 1871. In the Brandes Archive.
7. Brandes, *Hovedstrømninger*, I, p. 15.
8. Fenger, *Georg Brandes' læreår*, p. 361.
9. Letter to his parents, July 9, 1871. In the Brandes Archive.
10. *Hovedstrømninger*, I, p. 20.
11. Ibid., p. 21.
12. Fenger, *Den unge Brandes*, p. 227.

Chapter Three

1. B. Juncker, "Debatten omkring 'Emigrantlitteraturen,'" in *Den politiske Georg Brandes*, ed. H. Hertel and S. Møller Kristensen (Copenhagen: Hans Reitzel 1973), pp. 27–66.
2. Fenger, *Den unge Brandes*, p. 241.
3. Ibid., p. 245.
4. Brandes, *Forklaring og Forsvar*, pp. 45–46.
5. J. Paludan, *Laerefriheden og Demokratiet* (Copenhagen: Wilhelm Prior 1880).
6. *Naer og Fjaern*, 1877. 14/10–4/11.
7. Brandes' letters to Ibsen are lost but Ibsen's to Brandes are published in *Georg og Edvard Brandes' Brevveksling med nordiske Forfattere og Videnskabsmænd*, IV (1939).
8. Letter to his parents, October 12, 1872. In the Brandes Archive.
9. Fenger, *Den unge Brandes*, pp. 121–29. In the Brandes Archive.
10. Letter to Henriette Strodtmann, probably October 2, 1873. In the Brandes Archive.
11. Gerda Brandes, "Lyse Minder," *Politikens Magasin*, October 13, 1935.

Chapter Four

1. R. Wellek, *Concepts of Criticism.* (New Haven: Yale University Press, 1963), pp. 242–43.
2. Brandes, *Hovedstrømninger*, I, p. 91.
3. Ibid., pp. 54–55.
4. Ibid., p. 69.
5. Ibid., p. 64.
6. Ibid., p. 125.
7. Ibid., p. 151.

8. Ibid., p. 188.

9. Puls, "Wie Georg Brandes deutsche Litteraturgeschichte schreibt," *Archiv für das Studium der neueren Sprachen und Litteraturen,* XLII (1888).

10. A more extensive survey of Brandes' relationship to German literature appears in my book *Den gode európén,* pp. 13–150.

11. Brandes, *Hovedstrømninger,* II, p. 21.

12. Ibid., p. 14.

13. Ibid., p. 66.

14. Ibid., p. 119.

15. Ibid., pp. 121–23.

16. A. Ruge, *Sämtliche Werke* (Mannheim: Grohe 1847), pp. 360–61.

17. Brandes, *Hovedstrømninger,* II, p. 142.

18. Ibid., p. 162.

19. Ibid., p. 219.

20. Ibid., p. 233.

21. A. Jung, "Das Literaturwerk von G. Brandes," *Blätter für literarische Unterhaltung,* 1877. No. 22, May 31.

22. Brandes, *Levned,* II, p. 143.

23. Brandes, *Hovedstrømninger,* III, p. 47.

24. Ibid., p. 56.

25. Ibid., pp. 62–63.

26. Ibid., p. 80.

27. Ibid., p. 151.

28. Brandes, *Levned,* II, p. 154.

29. R. Haym, *Die romantische Schule* (Berlin: Weidmannsche Buchhandlung 1870), pp. 14–15.

30. Brandes, *Hovedstrømninger,* IV, p. 39.

31. Taine, *Histoire de la littérature anglaise,* III, p. 486.

32. Aa. Kabell, "Shelley og Georg Brandes," *Orbis Litterarum,* vol. 2, 1944. pp. 188–215.

33. Nolin, *Den gode európén,* p. 25.

34. Letter from Edmund W. Gosse to Brandes, January 6, 1874. *Correspondance de Georg Brandes,* II, p. 24.

35. Brandes, *Hovedstrømninger,* IV, p. 331.

36. Letter from Brandes to Arthur Fitger, December 23, 1883. *Correspondance de Georg Brandes,* III, p. 362.

37. Nolin, pp. 194–99.

38. Ahlström, *Georg Brandes' Hovedstrømninger,* p. 51.

39. Brandes, *Hovedstrømninger,* III, p. 348.

40. Taine, III, p. 561.

41. Brandes, *Hovedstrømninger,* IV, p. 513.

42. Brandes, *Hovedstrømninger,* V, p. 33.

43. Nolin, p. 277.

44. Brandes, *Hovedstrømninger*, V, p. 37.
45. Fenger, *Georg Brandes' læreår*, p. 295.
46. Brandes, *Hovedstrømninger*, V, pp. 190–91.
47. E. Zola, *Documents littéraires* (Paris: G. Charpentier 1881), pp. 236–37.
48. F. Brunetière, *Le roman naturaliste* (Paris: C. Lévy 1896), p. 62:
49. Fenger, *Georg Brandes' læreår*, p. 304.
50. Brandes, *Hovedstrømninger*, V, p. 274.
51. H. Taine, *Essais de critique et d'histoire* (Paris: Hachette 1866).
52. P. Bourget, *Essais de psychologie contemporaine* (Paris: A. Lemerre 1901)
53. C.-A. Sainte-Beuve, *Causeries du lundi*, IX (Paris: Garnier frères s.d.) p. 304.
54. Brandes, *Hovedstrømninger*, V, p. 311.
55. Ibid., p. 440.
56. Letter to Henriette Strodtmann, April 1874. In the Brandes Archive.
57. B. Weinberg, *French Realism: The Critical Reaction, 1830–1870* (New York MLA & London: Oxford University Press 1937), p. 29.
58. Brandes, *Hovedstrømninger*, V, p. 416.
59. Brandes, *Levned*, III, p. 273.
60. Fenger, *Georg Brandes' læreår*, p. 8.
61. P. Kieft, *Heinrich Heine in westeuropäischer Beurteilung: Seine Kritiker in Frankreich, England und Holland* (Zutphen: W. Y. Thieme 1938)
62. Brandes, *Hovedstrømninger*, VI, p. 163.
63. Ibid., pp. 382–83.
64. P. Kogan, "Brandes," in *Russkaja mysl'* 1903, book 7, pp. 90–107.
65. W. Bölsche, "Heinrich Heine bei Georg Brandes," *Freie Bühne*, December 10, 1890, pp. 1177–1181.
66. *Preussische Jahrbücher*, January–June 1891, p. 712–14.

Chapter Five

1. Letter to Georges Noufflard from Brandes, June 5, 1877. *Correspondance de Georg Brandes*, I, p. 82.
2. Brandes, *Levned*, II, p. 120.
3. Brandes, *Ferdinand Lassalle*, pp. 10–11.
4. See note 1.
5. *Forklaring og Forsvar*, pp. 52–53.
6. Brandes, *Ferdinand Lassalle*, pp. 261–80.
7. Ibid., p. 278. See also Hans Hertel's informative paper in *Den politiske Brandes*, pp. 192–307; and H. Fenger, *The Heibergs*, Twayne's World Authors Series, no. 105 (New York: Twayne, 1971).
8. Letter to Brandes from V. Pingel, May 5, 1883. *Georg og Edvard Brandes Brevveksling*, III, p. 369.

9. Letter to Edvard Brandes from A. Strindberg, July 29, 1880. *Georg og Edvard Brandes' Brevveksling*, VI, p. 7.

10. Fenger, *Georg Brandes' læreår*, pp. 131–38.

11. Brandes, *Levned*, II, pp. 202–04.

12. Brandes, *Hovedstrømninger* I, pp. 69–70.

13. Ibid., p. 250.

14. Ibid., II, pp. 51, 67–68, 79–80.

15. Brandes' diary, November 18, 1861. In the Brandes Archive. Brandes, *Søren Kierkegaard*, p. 35.

16. Brandes, *Levned*, I, pp. 83–84.

17. Brandes, *Søren Kierkegaard*, p. 120.

18. Ibid., p. 174.

19. Ibid., p. 108.

20. Ibid., p. 246.

21. Ibid., p. 259.

22. Letter to F. Levison, June 7, 1878. In the Brandes Archive.

23. Brandes, *Esaias Tegnér*, p. 192.

24. Ahlenius, *Georg Brandes i svensk litteratur*, p. 22.

25. Letter to Emilie Brandes, July 3, 1878. In the Brandes Archive.

26. The letters to Gosse are published in *Correspondance de Georg Brandes*, II.

27. Brandes, *Benjamin Disraeli*, p. 315.

Chapter Six

1. Brandes, *Levned*, II, p. 248.

2. Letter to Emilie Brandes, February 24, 1880. In the Brandes Archive.

3. Brandes, *Levned*, III, pp. 28–29.

4. Bredsdorff, *Henrik Pontoppidan og Georg Brandes. En redegørelse for brevvekslingen.*

5. The relationship between Bjørnson and Brandes has been analyzed by H. Fenger in *Edda*, 1964. vol. 64, pp. 81–116.

6. See note 7, chapter 3.

7. *Georg og Edvard Brandes Brevveksling*, IV, p. 204; Brandes, *Levned*; I, pp. 378–79.

8. Fenger, "Ibsen og Georg Brandes indtil 1872," *Edda*, vol. 64, pp. 166–208, 1964.

9. Letter to his parents, September 19, 1872. In the Brandes Archive.

10. Brandes, *Det moderne Gjennembruds Mænd*, p. 167.

11. Fenger, *Georg Brandes' læreår*, p. 120.

12. *Correspondance de Georg Brandes*, III, p. 5.

13. Ibid., p. 362.

14. Brandes, *Mennesker og Værker*, p. 436.

15. Brandes, *Samlede Skrifter*, XVI, p. 65.

16. *Georg Brandes' Breve til Hjemmet 1870–71*, pp. 61–62.
17. *Georg og Edvard Brandes Brevveksling*, IV, p. 14.
18. *Ibid.*, p. 43.
19. *Correspondance de Georg Brandes*, I, p. 160; Brandes, *Mennesker og Værker*, p. 501.
20. Brandes, *Mennesker og Værker*, p. 509.

Chapter Seven

1. Nolin, *Den gode europén*, pp. 205–50.
2. *Prawda*, 1885, p. 75.
3. St. M. Rz., "Jerzy Brandes," in *Tygodnik Illustrowany*, 1885, vol. 5, p. 103.
4. Letter to Emilie Brandes, February 1885. In the Brandes Archive.
5. S. Krzemiński, "Jerzy Brandes w Warszawie," *Bluszcz*, 1885, p. 62, "Brandes w Warszawie," *Prawda*, 1885, p. 76.
6. Letter to Emilie Brandes, February 15, 1885. In the Brandes Archive.
7. Brandes, *Levned*, III, p. 160.
8. Brandes, *Indtryk fra Polen*, pp. 118, 356; Brandes, *Samlede Skrifter*, X, pp. 112, 139–40.
9. Brandes, *Levned*, II, p. 372.
10. *Delo*, no. 8, 1881, p. 98.
11. *Correspondance de Georg Brandes*, I, pp. 159–60; Brandes, *Levned*, III, pp. 196–97.
12. Letter to S. Schandorph, January 16, 1883. In the Brandes Archive.
13. *Georg og Edvard Brandes Brevveksling*, III, p. 224.
14. Brandes, *Indtryk fra Rusland*, p. 407.
15. *Ibid.*, p. 470.
16. Brandes, *Udenlandske Egne og Personligheder*, pp. 288–98.

Chapter Eight

1. Brandes, *Ludvig Holberg*, p. 14.
2. *Ibid.*, pp. 136–39.
3. *Ibid.*, p. 289.
4. P. V. Rubow, *Litterære Studier* (Copenhagen: Levin & Munksgaard 1928), p. 145.
5. Brandes, *Essays: Danske Personligheder*, p. 2.
6. Brandes, *Levned*, III, p. 151.
7. Fenger, *Georg Brandes' læreår*, p. 43.
8. Brandes, *Essays: Danske Personligheder*, pp. 138–39.
9. Brandes, *Samlede Skrifter*, XII, p. 51.
10. See E. Bredsdorff, *Den store nordiske krig om seksualmoralen: En dokumentarisk fremstilling af sædelighedsdebatten i nordisk litteratur i 1880' erne* (Copenhagen: Gyldendal 1973).

11. Brandes, *Essays, Fremmede Personligheder*, pp. 97–98.
12. *Georg og Edvard Brandes Brevveksling*, IV, pp. 183–86.
13. Brandes, *Essays. Fremmede Personligheder*, p. 119.
14. Brandes, *Samlede Skrifter*, XIII, p. 528.
15. Bredsdorff, *Den store nordiske krig om seksualmoralen*, pp. 247–250.
16. Brandes, *Samlede Skrifter*, XIII, p. 452.
17. Ibid., p. 464.
18. Ibid., p. 468.
19. Ibid., p. 489.
20. *Correspondance de Georg Brandes*, III, p. 293.
21. Böök, *Victoria Benedictsson och Georg Brandes*.

Chapter Nine

1. F. Nietzsche, *Gesammelte Briefe*, III, (Leipzig: Insel-Verlag 1900–1909), p. 269.
2. Brandes, *Levned*, III, p. 229.
3. *Correspondance de Georg Brandes*, III, pp. 439–441.
4. Ibid., p. 297.
5. *Georg og Edvard Brandes Brevveksling*, III, p. 234.
6. Brandes, *Levned*, III, p. 230.
7. H. H. Borland, *Nietzsche's Influence On Swedish Literature* (Gothenburg: Wettergren & Kerber 1945), p. 17.
8. Nietzsche, *Gesammelte Briefe*, IV, p. 346.
9. Brandes, *Essays: Fremmede Personligheder*, pp. 160–161.
10. Ibid., p. 167.
11. Ibid., p. 169.
12. *Berlin som tysk Rigshovedstad*, pp. 193–208.
13. Brandes, *Essays: Fremmede Personligheder*, pp. 242–44.
14. *Tilskueren*, November-December 1889, p. 854.
15. Ibid., January 1890, p. 19.
16. *George og Edvard Brandes Brevveksling*, VI, p. 296.
17. *Correspondance de Georg Brandes*, III, p. 479.
18. Nolin, *Den gode europén*, pp. 362–64.
19. Brandes, *Essays: Fremmede Personligheder*, p. 328.
20. Ahlenius, *Georg Brandes i svensk litteratur*, pp. 372–78.

Chapter Ten

1. Letters to Gerda Brandes, October 26, 1889, and to Emilie Brandes, October 19, 1889. In the Brandes Archive.
2. Brandes, *Udenlandske Egne og Personligheder*, "Forord."
3. Brandes, *Samlede Skrifter*, XVI, p. 87.
4. H. Drachmann, *Skyggebilleder* (Copenhagen: Gyldendal 1883), pp. 266–67.

5. O. Levertin, *Diktare och drömmare* (Stockholm: Bonniers 1898), pp. 68–69.

6. Brandes, *Udenlandske Egne og Personligheder*, p. 121.

7. Ibid., p. 146.

8. Ibid., p. 142.

9. Brandes, *Samlede Skrifter*, VII, p. 247.

10. Brandes, *Levned*, III, p. 175.

11. Brandes, *Samlede Skrifter*, XII, p. 199.

12. Brandes, *Udenlandske Egne og Personligheder*, p. 284.

13. Ibid., p. 301.

14. Brandes, *Samlede Skrifter*, XI, p. 337.

15. Ibid., pp. 374–84.

16. C. Fehrman, *Levertins lyrik* (Lund: Gleerups 1945), p. 338.

17. F. Böök, *Oscar Levertin* (Stockholm: Bonniers 1944), p. 258.

18. C. Jefferson, *Anatole France: The Politics of Skepticism* (Rutgers University Press, New Brunswick, New Jersey: 1965), pp. 43–48.

19. *Correspondance de Georg Brandes*, II, p. 155.

20. A. France, *Vers les temps meilleurs: Trente ans de vie sociale*, I (Paris: Emile-Paul 1949), p. 87.

21. A. France, *La vie littéraire*, I (Paris: C. Lévy 1888), pp. iii–ix.

22. Rubow, *Georg Brandes' briller*, p. 212–13.

23. A. M. Eastman, *A Short History of Shakespearean Criticism* (New York: Random House 1968), p. 139.

24. Brandes, *William Shakespeare*, I, pp. 65–66.

25. Ibid., p. 454.

26. Ibid., p. 471.

27. Ibid., II, p. 423.

28. Ibid., III, p. 1.

29. Ibid., p. 210.

30. Ibid., pp. 156–57.

31. Wellek, *A History of Modern Criticism*, IV, p. 366.

32. Brandes, *Samlede Skrifter*, XIV, pp. 433–34.

33. Ibid., XII, p. 367, *Georg og Edvard Brandes Brevveksling*, IV, p. 207.

34. Brandes, *Samlede Skrifter*, III, pp. 633–661.

35. Ibid., p. 658.

36. Brandes, *Fugleperspektiv*, pp. 269–80.

Chapter Eleven

1. Fenger, *Den unge Brandes*, pp. 28–29.

2. Brandes, *Armand Carrel*, p. 73.

3. Pontoppidan's relationship to Brandes has been analyzed by Elias Bredsdorff in *Henrik Pontoppidan og Georg Brandes: En kritisk undersøgelse*.

4. Brandes, *Fugleperspektiv*, p. 21.

5. Ibid., pp. 2–3.

6. Both Knut Ahnlund and, later, Elias Bredsdorff have pointed out that Brandes and Pontoppidan periodically were very close to each other. K. Ahnlund, *Henrik Pontoppidan: Fem huvudlinjer i författarskapet* (Stockholm: Norstedt 1956).

7. Quoted from Bredsdorff, *Henrik Pontoppidan og Georg Brandes*, En kritisk undersøgelse, p. 145.

8. Ibid., pp. 159–60.

9. Bredsdorff, *Henrik Pontoppidan og Georg Brandes. En redegørelse for brevvekslingen* pp. 32–33.

10. Brandes, *Levned*, III, p. 384.

11. Brandes, *Wolfgang Goethe*, I, p. 201.

12. Ibid., II, p. 37.

13. Ibid., I, p. 301.

14. Ibid., p. 252.

15. Bredsdorff, Henrik Pontoppidan og Georg Brandes. En redegørelse for brevocholingen, p. 129.

16. Fenger, *Georg Brandes' læreår*, p. 27.

17. Ibid., p. 219.

18. Brandes, *Hovedstrømninger*, I, p. 35.

19. G. Rung, *Georg Brandes i Samvaer og Breve* (Copenhagen: Gyldendal 1930), p. 67.

20. P. Rubow, *Georg Brandes' briller*, p. 35.

21. Brandes, *Samlede Skrifter*, XII, p. 6.

22. Brandes, *Essays: Fremmede Personligheder*, p. 213.

23. *Georg og Edvard Brandes' Brevveksling*, III, p. 233.

24. Böök. *Victoria Benedictsson och Georg Brandes*, p. 45.

25. See Th. Nordby, "Georg Brandes og imperialismen," in *Den politiske Brandes*, ed. Hertel and Møller Kristensen, pp. 145–147.

26. E. Löfstedt, "Georg Brandes om Caesar," *Svenska Dagbladet*, January 1, 1919.

27. Brandes, *Michelangelo Buonarroti*, "Forord."

28. Ibid.

29. Brandes, *Levned*, I, p. 402.

30. Brandes, *Hovedstrømninger*, I, p. 217.

31. Brandes, *Michelangelo Buonarroti*, p. 388.

32. Ibid., p. 250.

33. Ibid., p. 290.

Chapter Twelve

1. *George Brandes und Arthur Schnitzler. Ein Briefwechsel* herausgegeben von Kurt Bergel (Bern: Francke 1956), p. 204.

2. S. A. Larsen, "Georg Brandes' Views on American Literature," *Scandinavian Studies*, vol. 22, 1950, pp. 161–165.

3. *The Dial*, vol. 61, June 1, 1914, pp. 447–448.

4. "Henry James, the American writer you know, has come here for my sake to see me at Andrew Long's dinner tomorrow." Letter to Emilie Brandes, November 11, 1895.

5. Bredsdorff, *Henrik Pontoppidan og Georg Brandes, En redegørelse for brevvekslingen*, pp. 149, 156.

6. Brandes, *Napoleon og Garibaldi*, p. 271.

7. Ibid., p. 268.

8. Brandes, *Samlede Skrifter*, XVI, pp. 110–32.

9. Brandes, *Verdenskrigen*, p. 21.

10. Ibid., p. 63.

11. Ibid., p. 94.

12. Ibid., p. 111.

13. Ibid., p. 131.

14. *Correspondance de Georg Brandes*, I, p. 421.

15. *Correspondance de Georg Brandes*, I. Notes et références, p. 105.

16. Ibid., p. 112.

17. Ibid., p. 120.

18. Nordby, "Georg Brandes og imperialismen." in *Den politiske Georg Brandes*, p. 149.

19. Brandes, *Verdenskrigen*, p. 278.

20. *Correspondance de Georg Brandes*, II, p. 115.

21. Brandes, *Verdenskrigen*, p. 403.

22. Brandes, *Tragediens anden Del*, p. 50.

23. Ibid., p. 183.

24. Ibid., p. 90.

25. Brandes, *Verdenskrigen*, pp. 308–18.

26. Brandes, *Hellas*, p. 44.

27. G. Rung, *Georg Brandes i Samvaer og Breve* (Copenhagen: Gyldendal 1930), p. 136.

28. Brandes, *Hellas*, pp. 106–107.

29. Brandes, *Sagnet om Jesus*, pp. 67–69.

30. Brandes, *Petrus*, p. 56.

31. Brandes, *Urkristendom*, p. 31.

32. Rung, *Georg Brandes i Samvæer og Breve*, pp. 226 and 232.

Selected Bibliography

PRIMARY SOURCES

1. In Danish

Dualismen i vor nyeste Philosophie. Copenhagen: Gyldendal, 1866.
Æsthetiske Studier. Copenhagen: Gyldendal, 1868.
Den franske Æsthetik i vore Dage. Copenhagen: Gyldendal, 1870.
Kritiker og Portraiter. Copenhagen: Gyldendal, 1870.
Forklaring og Forsvar. Copenhagen: Gyldendal, 1872.
Hovedstrømninger i det nittende Aarhundredes Litteratur. 6 vols. Copenhagen: Gyldendal.
    I. *Emigrantlitteraturen.* 1872.
    II. *Den romantiske Skole i Tydskland.* 1873.
    III. *Reactionen i Frankrig.* 1874.
    IV. *Naturalismen i England.* 1875.
    V. *Den romantiske Skole i Frankrig.* 1882.
    VI. *Det unge Tyskland.* 1890.
Danske Digtere. Copenhagen: Gyldendal, 1877.
Søren Kierkegaard. Copenhagen: Gyldendal, 1877.
Esaias Tegnér. Copenhagen: Gyldendal, 1878.
Benjamin Disraeli. Copenhagen: Gyldendal, 1878.
Ferdinand Lassalle. Copenhagen: Gyldendal, 1881.
Mennesker og Værker. Copenhagen: Gyldendal, 1883.
Det moderne Gjennembruds Mænd. Copenhagen: Gyldendal, 1883.
Ludvig Holberg: Et Festskrift. Copenhagen: Gyldendal, 1884.
Berlin som tysk Rigshovedstad. Copenhagen: P. G. Philipsens Forlag, 1885.
Indtryk fra Polen. Copenhagen: Gyldendal, 1888.
Indtryk fra Rusland. Copenhagen: Gyldendal, 1888.
Essays: Danske Personligheder. Copenhagen: Gyldendal, 1889.
Essays: Fremmede Personligheder. Copenhagen: Gyldendal, 1889.
Udenlandske Egne og Personligheder. Copenhagen: Gyldendal, 1893.
William Shakespeare. Copenhagen: Gyldendal, 1895–96.
Julius Lange: Breve fra hans Ungdom. Copenhagen: Gyldendal, 1898.
Ungdomsvers. Copenhagen: Gyldendal, 1898.
Henrik Ibsen. Copenhagen: Gyldendal, 1898.

Samlede Skrifter. 18 vols. Copenhagen: Gyldendal, 1899–1910.
Levned. 3 vols. Copenhagen: Gyldendal, 1905–08.
Armand Carrel. Copenhagen: Gyldendal, 1911.
Fugleperspektiv. Copenhagen: Gyldendal, 1913.
Wolfgang Goethe. 2 vols. Copenhagen: Gyldendal, 1915.
Verdenskrigen. Copenhagen: Gyldendal, 1916.
François de Voltaire. 2 vols. Copenhagen: Gyldendal, 1916–17.
Napoleon og Garibaldi. Copenhagen: Gyldendal, 1917.
Cajus Julius Caesar. 2 vols. Copenhagen: Gyldendal, 1918.
Tragediens anden Del. Copenhagen: Gyldendal, 1919.
Taler. Copenhagen: Gyldendal, 1920.
Michelangelo Buonarroti. 2 vols. Copenhagen: Gyldendal, 1921.
Hertuginden af Dino og Fyrsten af Talleyrand. Copenhagen: Gyldendal, 1923.
Uimodstaaelige. Copenhagen: Gyldendal, 1924.
Sagnet om Jesus. Copenhagen: Gyldendal, 1925.
Hellas. Copenhagen: Gyldendal, 1925.
Petrus. Copenhagen: Gyldendal, 1926.
Urkristendom. Copenhagen: Gyldendal, 1927.
Liv og Kunst. Copenhagen: Hage & Clausens Forlag, 1929.
Store Personligheder. Copenhagen: Hage & Clausens Forlag, 1930.
Kulturbilleder. Copenhagen: Hage & Clausens Forlag, 1932.
Georg Brandes' Breve til Hjemmet 1870–1871. Udgivet af Alf Hjorth-Moritzen. Copenhagen: H. Hirschsprungs Forlag, 1938.
Georg og Edvard Brandes Brevveksling med nordiske Forfattere og Videnskabsmænd. 8 vols. Udgivet af Morten Borup, Francis Bull og John Landquist. Copenhagen: Gyldendal, 1939–42.
Correspondance de Georg Brandes. Letters selected and annotated by Paul Krüger. 3 vols. Copenhagen: Rosenkilde og Bagger, 1952–1966.
2. In English Translation
Anatole France. London: W. Heinemann, 1908; New York: McClure Co., 1908.
Creative Spirits of the Nineteenth Century. New York: Crowell, 1923. Reprinted New York: Books for Libraries, 1967.
Eminent Authors of the Nineteenth Century. New York: Crowell, 1886.
An Essay on the Aristocratic Radicalism of Friedrich Nietzsche. 1909.
Ferdinand Lassalle. London: W. Heinemann; New York, Macmillan, 1911. Reprinted New York: Bernard G. Richards, 1925; Bergman, 1968.
Friedrich Nietzsche. New York: Macmillan, 1909; London: Heinemann, 1914.
Hellas: Travels in Greece. New York: Adelphi, 1926. Reprinted New York: Books for Libraries, 1969.
Henrik Ibsen. Björnstjerne Björnson. London: Heinemann, 1899; New York: Macmillan, 1899. Reprinted New York: Blom, 1964.

Impressions of Russia. London: Scott, 1889; New York: Crowell, 1889. Reprinted New York: Crowell, 1966; Apollo, 1968.

Jesus: A Myth. London: Brentano's, n.d.; New York: A. & C. Boni, 1926.

Lord Beaconsfield: A Study. New York: Harper, 1878. London: R. Bentley, 1880. Reprinted New York: Scribner's, 1880; Harper & Brothers, 1881; Crowell, 1966; Apollo, 1968.

Main Currents in Nineteenth Century Literature. 6 vols. London: Heinemann, and New York: Macmillan, 1901–05. Reprinted New York: Boni & Liveright, and London: Heinemann, 1923.

Michelangelo: His Life, His Times, His Era. New York: Ungar, 1963.

Naturalism in Nineteenth Century English Literature. New York: Russell & Russell, 1957 and 1960.

On Reading. New York: Duffield, 1906 and 1923.

Poland: A Study of the Land, People, and Literature. London: Heinemann, 1903; New York: Macmillan, 1903.

Recollections of My Childhood and Youth. London: Heinemann, 1906.

Reminiscences of My Childhood and Youth. New York: Duffield, 1906.

Revolution and Reaction in Nineteenth Century French Literature. New York: Russell and Russell, 1960.

Voltaire. New York: A. & C. Boni, 1930; Tudor Publishing Company, 1930 and 1934. Reprinted New York: Ungar, 1964.

William Shakespeare. London: Heinemann 1898, 1899, 1902, 1905, 1909, 1914, 1917, 1920, and 1926. New York: Macmillan, 1898, 1899, 1909, 1920, 1924, 1927, 1931, 1935, and 1936. Reprinted New York: Ungar, 1963.

Wolfgang Goethe. New York: N. L. Brown, 1924; Frank Maurice, 1925. Reprinted New York: Crown Publishers, 1936.

The World at War. New York: Macmillan, 1917.

SECONDARY SOURCES

AHLENIUS, H. *Georg Brandes i svensk litteratur till och med 1890*. Stockholm: Bonniers, 1932.

AHLSTRÖM, G. *Georg Brandes' Hovedstrømninger: En ideologisk undersökning*. Lund: Gleerup, and Copenhagen: Munksgaard, 1937.

————. *Det moderna genombrottet i Nordens litteratur*. Stockholm: Rabén & Sjögren, 1973.

ANDERSEN, J. K., and C. Jackson. "Georg Brandes: Emigrantlitteraturen."*Danske studier*, vol. 66. 1971, pp. 58–80.

BREDSDORFF, E. *Henrik Pontoppidan og Georg Brandes*. 2 vols. Copenhagen: Gyldendal, 1964.

————. "Georg Brandes og de politiske ideologier." *Tidskrift för litteraturvetenskap*, no. 3–4, 1971–1972.

————. "Georg Brandes as a Fictional Character in Some Danish Novels and Plays." *Scandinavian Studies*, 45, 1973, pp. 1–26.

BÖÖK, F. *Victoria Benedictsson och Georg Brandes.* Stockholm: Bonniers, 1949.

FENGER, H. *Georg Brandes' læreår: Læsning ideer smag kritik 1857–1872.* Copenhagen: Gyldendal, 1955.

———. *Den unge Brandes: Miljø venner rejser kriser.* Copenhagen: Gyldendal, 1957.

———. "Ibsen og Georg Brandes indtil 1872." *Edda,* vol. 64. 1964, pp. 166–208.

———. "Bjørnson og Georg Brandes før det moderne gennembrud." *Edda,* vol. 64, 1964, pp. 81–116.

———. *Georg Brandes et la France: La formation de ses goûts littéraires 1842–1872.* Paris: Presses universitaires de France, 1963.

FRANZÉN, L.-O. "Frihetens dialektik: Skisser till en utredning om Georg Brandes och kulturradikalismen." *Ord & Bild,* 82, no. 8 (1973), pp. 467–486.

HAUGEN, E. "Georg Brandes and his American Translators." *Journal of English and Germanic Philology,* 37, 1938, pp. 462–487.

HERTEL, H. and S. Møller Kristensen, eds. *Den politiske Georg Brandes.* Med bidrag av Carl Erik Bay, Elias Bredsdorff, Olav Harsløf, Hans Hertel, Beth Juncker, Sven Møller Kristensen, Thomas Nordby, Bent Søndergaard. Copenhagen: Hans Reitzel, 1973.

HOUMAN, B. *Havørn og proletar: Martin Andersen Nexøs forhold til Georg Brandes.* Copenhagen: Sirius, 1972.

KRISTENSEN, S. Møller. "Georg Brandes Research: A Survey." *Scandinavica* 3, no. 2 (1964), pp. 121–132.

———. *Digteren og Samfundet,* II. Copenhagen: Munksgaard, 1970.

MORITZEN, J. *Georg Brandes in Life and Letters.* Newark: D. S. Colyer, 1922.

NATHANSEN, H. *Georg Brandes: Et portraet.* Copenhagen: Gyldendal, 1950.

NOLIN, B. *Den gode europén: Studier i Georg Brandes' idéutveckling 1871–1893.* Stockholm: Svenska Bokförlaget/Norstedts, 1965.

RUBOW, P. V. *Georg Brandes' briller.* Copenhagen: Levin & Munksgaards Forlag, 1932.

SEIDLIN, O. "Georg Brandes." In his *Essays in German and Comparative Literature.* Chapel Hill: University of North Carolina Press, 1961.

STANGERUP, H. *Kulturkampen.* 2 vols. Copenhagen: Gyldendal, 1946.

SÖRENSEN, B. A. "Uber die Schönheitsauffassung von Georg Brandes." *Jahrbuch für Æsthetik und allgemeine Kunstwissenschaft,* ed. H. Lützeler. No. 3, 1958.

WELLEK, R. "The Lonely Dane." In his *A History of Modern Criticism,* IV. New Haven: Yale University Press, 1965.

Index